MW01441022

Copyright © 2023 David D. Sullivan

All rights reserved

The characters and events portrayed in this book are fictitious. Any similarity to real persons, living or dead, is coincidental and not intended by the author.

No part of this book may be reproduced, or stored in a retrieval system, or transmitted in any form or by any means, electronic, mechanical, photocopying, recording, or otherwise, without express written permission of the publisher.

ISBN-13: 9798218343521

Cover design by: Canva & KDP
Library of Congress Control Number: 2023924733
Printed in the United States of America

CONTENTS

Copyright	
Know Thyself	2
Welcome to Wellness	11
Three Little Cousins, Part 1	27
Three Little Cousins, Part 2	53
Rabbit Power	78
Three Little Cousins, Part 3	85
As a Person Thinketh…	98
The Power of Reframing	115
Career Considerations	130
Embrace the Process	145
Throw a Rock in a Lake	157
OCD, Pesky Tics, Skin-Picking, Hoarding and Cutting	167
Turning the Page	188
Assertive Communication and Boundaries	200
For Couples	213
Substances Impact Mental Health	256
Beyond Tentativeness	276
About The Author	310

FORWARD

The book you are about to read has the potential to jumpstart your life, and give you much-needed solutions to some of the concerns you may have at the moment. This book is the result of several decades of learning, applying, experiencing, simplifying, and solidifying. That about sums it up. I have been a student of life and of human behavior my entire life, unfortunately. I say unfortunately because I was kind of forced into this endeavor as a young boy and onward. But we all are products of our past in some ways, and recipients of much learning and applying as we move along.

I truly and sincerely hope that you will be blessed, equipped, prepared, and helped to move forward in life, as a result of your reading. This is my goal. I simply want to give back to others what I have received and organized. I am at once humbled by this prospect, and gladdened by the potential good that can come from our time together in this book. I write just like I talk. So, this should be a relatively easy and down-to-earth read.

Enjoy the journey!

David D. Sullivan

KNOW THYSELF

In this opening chapter, we will initially discuss a few of the major mental health diagnoses. We will also explore three ways that we can know ourselves a little better. This is important, because it's much easier to move forward in life when we first know who we are in the first place. So, it might be helpful to view this book as a nice, delicious, full-course meal that, when internalized and implemented, can lead to a very satisfying and meaningful life. This is my hope anyway. So you can think of these first two chapters as "setting the table."

The DSM-V criteria used to diagnose a major depressive episode indicate that the individual must either have a depressed mood or a loss of interest or pleasure in daily activities consistently, for at least a two-week period. This mood must represent a change from the person's normal mood. Social, occupational, educational, or other important functions must also be negatively impaired by the change in mood.

A major depressive episode is also characterized by the presence of five or more of these nine symptoms:

- Depressed mood most of the day, nearly every day, as indicated by either subjective report or outside observation.
- Markedly diminished interest or pleasure in all, or

almost all, activities most of the day, nearly every day.
- Significant weight loss or weight gain or decrease or increase in appetite nearly every day.
- Insomnia or hypersomnia nearly every day.
- Psychomotor agitation or retardation nearly every day.
- Fatigue or loss of energy nearly every day.
- Feelings of worthlessness, or excessive or inappropriate guilt nearly every day.
- Diminished ability to think or concentrate, or indecisiveness nearly every day.
- Recurrent thoughts of death, recurrent suicidal ideation without a specific plan, or a suicide attempt or a specific plan for committing suicide.

Persistent Depressive Disorder (Dysthymia) is characterized by low-level depression that is not as severe as Major Depressive Disorder, but may be longer lasting. Any way you slice it, depression is horrible and debilitating.

According to the American Psychiatric Association, anxiety is an emotion characterized by feelings of tension, worried thoughts, and physical changes like increased blood pressure. People with anxiety disorders usually have recurring intrusive thoughts or concerns. They may avoid certain situations out of worry. They may also have physical symptoms such as sweating, trembling, dizziness, or a rapid heartbeat.

Anxiety, or anxious thoughts, tend to build on themselves in a cumulative fashion. I know this from working with many clients for over two decades, and I also know this from personal experience, having experienced in the past severe anxiety and panic attacks. We can literally think and talk ourselves right into a full-blown panic attack, if we are not careful with our focus and our self-talk.

According to the Mayo Clinic, mania and hypomania are two distinct types of episodes, but they have the same symptoms. Mania is more severe than hypomania and causes more noticeable problems at work, school, and social activities, as well as relationship difficulties. Mania may also trigger a break from reality (psychosis) and require hospitalization. Two diagnoses which involve, at times, periods of mania, are Bipolar I and Bipolar II.

Both a manic and a hypomanic episode include three or more of these symptoms:

- Abnormally upbeat, jumpy or wired
- Increased activity, energy or agitation
- Exaggerated sense of well-being and self-confidence (euphoria)
- Decreased need for sleep
- Unusual talkativeness
- Racing thoughts
- Distractibility
- Poor decision making— for example, going on buying sprees, taking sexual risks or making foolish investments.

Patients suffering from psychosis have impaired reality testing; that is, they are unable to distinguish personal subjective experience from the reality of the external world. They experience hallucinations and/or delusions that they believe are real, and may behave and communicate in an inappropriate and incoherent fashion. Psychosis may appear as a symptom of a number of mental disorders, including mood and personality disorders. It is also the defining feature of schizophrenia, schizophreniform disorder, schizoaffective disorder, delusional disorder, and the psychotic disorders (i.e. brief psychotic disorder, shared psychotic disorder, psychotic disorder due to a general medical condition, and substance-induced psychotic disorder).

I frequently tell individuals and couples that it is difficult to ascertain where we are going in life, if we do not truly know ourselves first. There are many ways one can know oneself. I recommend three basic but foundational ways to know ourselves better: values, temperaments, and Love Languages. These are each a part of our basic wiring, come into play often, and are three different angles on knowing yourself a lot better.

The Three Ways

Values

A value is something that you can't imagine living without. Think of values as your "non-negotiables." Our values are the aspects of life that are most important to us. Whether we have explored them or not, there is no doubt that our values still impact us often. We tend to notice when one or more of our values is being compromised or is being trampled on. It definitely gets our attention. We want to stand up and say, "Now just a minute here. No, I don't think so. No, no. This isn't right. Not on my watch." Our values are actually one of the main sources of anger and frustration, not because they are bad (they are not bad, but actually a part of us, and important), but because sometimes something that happens, or something somebody says, *impacts us deeply on the level of values, and it definitely gets our attention.*

So we might as well know what they are. Because if we can allow our values to inform and impact our daily living and decision-making, life is more peaceful; we are more in sync with who we are.

In addition, if you feel uneasy when interacting with a certain person, or feel uneasy in a particular situation, you might want to take a step back, and ask yourself if any of your values are on the line in this interaction, or this situation. In this case, this would definitely be a red flag, and should get our attention. In other words, our values can help us and serve as a basic guide to us, if we are open to it.

No one can choose your values for you, and the only things that can remove or nullify your values is either your own decision to go in a direction away from your values (not advisable, usually leads to chaos), or substance dependence, in which case that substance of choice has replaced or supplanted your values, and has become the overwhelming "value" that everything else in life revolves around. In recovery, a person is able to be reunited with his or her values, and have a meaningful life.

It is important to have a good understanding of at least your top ten values in life. Just do an Internet search, and type "values clarification worksheet printable." Pick a couple of websites, and try to isolate three big lists of values. They look like a big list of words on a page. Then print three of these worksheets or lists, lay them side-by-side on a table or desk, and just circle that ones that really resonate with you—the ones that are truly important to you. Beyond important —*vital, necessary—can't imagine living without them*—those are the ones you circle.

I say three worksheets or lists, because this broadens the field from which to choose. You might circle three on this sheet, maybe five on this one, and maybe four on the third sheet. Your top ten or so values, or what's most important to you in life. And by the way, try to write down these "Three Ways" in your phone notes, for easy access.

Temperaments

The second way, or angle, for knowing yourself better, is *Temperaments*. According to Farlex Partner Medical Dictionary, a temperament is the psychological and biological organization peculiar to the individual, specifically, an individual's pervasive and characteristic manner of perceiving, thinking, and acting. It represents one component of personality, the other is character. A synonym would be disposition. You can think of your temperament as basically *the way you come at life, or at your world—the way you function in your world.* This will help you understand why you do things a certain way.

I am referring to the four original temperaments, that go way back to the early centuries.

The idea of the four temperaments traces back to the ancient Greek medical theory of the four humours, which held that there were four fundamental bodily humours (blood, yellow bile, black bile, and phlegm) and that illness was caused by an imbalance in these. The terms *sanguine, choleric, melancholic and phlegmatic* were coined by the Greek physician Aelius Galenus to describe the effect of the humours on personality. The four temperaments have not been a part of medicine or psychology for over 100 years, but remain popular in the writings of several prominent self-help and spirituality authors, and the idea remains relatively well-known.

Although the history is a bit vague and even strange, I have come to understand just how foundational the four temperaments are, in terms of how we operate in our world. Having an understanding of our highest scoring temperament, and second highest scoring temperament, which has a modifying effect on the top temperament, can help us understand certain patterns and characteristics and even preferences in our lives.

There is a website for this one, to make it easy. Just go to openpsychometrics.org, and scroll down until you see "Four Temperaments Test." That's the one you click on. Don't click on the "Fisher" inventory—that is not the one I'm referring to. Click on "Four Temperaments Test." Then take the little online test, answering the questions honestly, how you *actually are, not how you want to be.* It will be a lot more accurate of a tool if you do it this way.

Just keep track of your top 2-3 temperaments—most of us are a *cluster* at the top, and the others drop down. Whatever that cluster is, the top two or three. There are numbers, and you can write down the numbers. The secondary temperaments will have a modifying effect on the top temperament. Most of us a are a mix of two or three.

Writer these down in your phone notes, for easy access. This is how you *roll,* or function.

Love Languages

The Love Languages were formulated by Dr. Gary Chapman. What I often tell individuals and couples is that just like it's possible for two people to *talk right past each other* at times, it is also possible for two people to *love right past each other,* if they are not loving each other in a manner that is *meaningful* to that person.

So, for instance, knowing your partner's top Love Languages helps you to love your partner "more on target" or more intelligently. And vice versa.

The five Love Languages are Words of Affirmation, Quality Time, Receiving Gifts, Acts of Service, and Physical Touch. Again, you want to know your highest scoring Love Language, and your secondary Love Languages. Again, it is also very helpful to know these about your partner. Knowing these about your partner can help you love that person in a manner that is truly meaningful to that person. A knowledge of Love Languages can save a couple from undue and unnecessary confusion and heartache.

For this one, you go to the website 5lovelanguages.com. Then you choose "5 Love Languages" from the options. Then you answer a couple questions—adult or adolescent, and relationship or no relationship. Then you take the little online test, and answer the questions honestly, how you *actually are, not how you want to be.* It will be a lot more accurate of a tool if you do it this way.

Just keep track of your 2-3 highest scoring Love Languages, whatever that cluster is. You can write down the numbers also. Again, the secondary Love Languages will have a modifying effect on the top one.

The above are three easy but meaningful ways to know yourself better. It is actually a lot of fun. This exploration will help to ground you in the present, which is very healthy, and will help you to be a little more comfortable in your own shoes.

If you have a partner or are in a relationship, it is very helpful (and wise) to know your partner's three ways also.

Application

So, let's say your top temperament is Melancholic, and your top Love Language is "Words of Affirmation." Both of these aspects of your basic "wiring" can predispose you to being more sensitive and creative in general, and also placing a huge emphasis on your words and others' words, in general. Let's also say that that these aspects are coupled with possible anxiety, and a possible compromise in your personal values.

This combination of factors can all combine in such a way to culminate in much confusion and consternation.

What I am saying is, it is useful to know these three aspects of who you are, because it will help you understand situations and interactions with others a little better. It will make more sense.

For instance, let's say a wife's top Love Language is "Acts of Service" and her top temperaments are "Melancholic" and "Choleric." This wife will most likely be quick to notice when her husband follows through with something important, and when he does not. This wife will also likely have the tendency to *speak up* about it (Choleric) and to read into it and be oversensitive about it (Melancholic). She will need to be careful *not* to read into anything or to make assumptions, or to believe that she can read her husband's mind, or thoughts. This will be very important for this wife to remember, because the above will be the tendency. And the husband in this situation will be wise to be diligent about following through with what he says he will do, thereby loving and caring for his wife intelligently.

So, these "Three Ways" are very practical and useful. Keep all three in your phone notes, for easy access. Keep your partner's there as well, as this will *improve the dance.*

So remember that life is a journey, and enjoy the journey.

WELCOME TO WELLNESS

Dr. Neil Nedley examined ten cause categories as predictors of depression:1 (1) Genetic, (2) Developmental, (3) Lifestyle, (4) Circadian Rhythm, (5) Addiction, (6) Nutrition, (7) Toxic, (8) Social/Complicated Grief, (9) Medical Condition, and (10) Frontal Lobe.

Genetic hit category: Family history of depression or suicide in a first-degree relative.[2]

Developmental hit category: Early puberty in girls (beginning menstruation by age 11 years or younger)[3], history of depression in adolescence,[4] not being raised by both biological parents,[5] sexual abuse,[6] and being raised or living with someone who is an alcoholic or drug addict.[7]

Nutrition hit category: Low dietary tryptophan[8]; low omega-3 fat intake[9,10]; low folic acid[11] intake; low vitamin B intake[12]; diet high in cholesterol[13], saturated fat[14], and sugar[15]; and marked anorexia and weight loss.[16]

Social hit category: Absence of social support[17-19], negative or stressful life events[20,21], low social class[22,23], being raised by grandparents[24], an immediate family member being an alcoholic or drug addict[25,26].

Toxic hit category: High lead levels[27,28]; high mercury levels[29]; high arsenic, bismuth, or other toxin levels[30]; or high risk of exposure to these toxins.

Circadian rhythm hit category[31]: Regular insomnia, routinely sleeping more than 9 hours per day or less than 6 hours per day, and not having regular hours for sleeping and eating.

Addiction hit category: Use of alcohol[32,33], cigarette or tobacco use[34,35], heavy caffeine use[36], recreational drug use (including marijuana),[37] daily use of benzodiazepines, or chronic narcotic use for more than 30 consecutive days.

Lifestyle hit category: Not on a regular aerobic exercise program,[38] not regularly exposed to daylight or a medical-grade light box for at least 30 minutes a day,[39] and rarely breathing fresh air.[40]

Medical condition hit category: Hepatitis C,[41] recent head injury,[42,43] stroke,[44] heart disease,[45] terminal cancer,[46] Parkinson's disease,[47] uncontrolled diabetes,[48] severe postpartum stress,[49] premenstrual tension syndrome,[50] inadequately treated thyroid disease,[51] lupus,[52] inadequately treated adrenal gland disease.[53]

Frontal lobe hit category: On low carbohydrate diet,[54,55] on high meat or high cheese diet or eating lots of rich food,[56,57] entertainment TV or movie addiction,[58-60] entertainment Internet or chat Internet addiction,[61,62] frequent sexual stimulation that activates right frontal lobe,[63,64] regular exposure to syncopated rhythm music and/or videos,[65-67] conscious suppression of frontal lobe activity,[68-74] lack of regular abstract thinking,[75] acting against one's conscience or known value system.[76]

Of these 10 hits, only the genetic and the developmental are not reversible.

Having five of these hits means that a person will more than likely have symptoms of depression.

THE EIGHT LAWS OF HEALTH

(From avirtuouswoman.com)

1. Nutrition – Eating plenty of fruits and vegetables, or even cutting out meat completely, will promote good health, more energy, and a longer life.

2. Exercise – It is so important to get up and get moving! Exercise for 15–20 minutes at least four times a week to lose weight, strengthen your heart and have more energy!

3. Water – Your body is made up mostly of water. When you do not take in enough water, your body dries up and cells begin to die. A healthy body is a hydrated body. Water cleanses the body by helping to eliminate waste and toxins. Drink one ounce per two pounds of body weight, every day.

4. Sunshine – Spend time outside in the sunshine every day. The morning hours or the late afternoon hours are ideal. The sunshine provides needed vitamins and elevates your mood.

5. Temperance – Self-control is so important in every area of life. Temperance means having a healthy balance between working, resting, faith, eating and drinking. It also means using self-control to choose not to do things that are harmful, such as drinking alcohol, using drugs, or having promiscuous sex.

6. Air – Breathing fresh air is essential to good health. Breathing deeply fills the body with oxygen and can help to relax you when you are tense.

7. Rest – First, sleep is very important to maintain a healthy body. When you are exhausted and run down, you are more likely to get sick. Ideally, adults should get 6–8 hours of sleep every night (8 is optimal). The hours before midnight are the most beneficial.

8. Trust in God/Higher Power (according to your understanding) – People of Faith and people for whom spirituality is important are calmer, happier, and live longer that those who do not have trust in this area.

What We Eat

For 12 years, researchers tracked the diet habits and health outcomes of more than 43,000 women—none of whom had depression at the start of the study period. Here's what they found: women who sipped soft drinks, ate fatty red meat, or consumed refined grains (like pasta, white bread, crackers, or chips) daily were 29 to 41% more likely to be diagnosed or treated for depression than those who stuck to a healthier diet. Blood tests revealed that women who ate the above foods also tested significantly higher for three biomarkers of inflammation.[77]

Although healthy amounts of inflammation are necessary to help your body fight off disease and bounce back from injury, dozens of recent studies have linked out-of-control inflammation to ailments ranging from heart disease and stroke to diabetes and cancer. This new study isn't the first to link certain diet choices to inflammation and depression, but it is one of the most complete to date.

It's not clear exactly how inflammation and depression are linked, says study co-author Michael Lucas, PhD, of the Harvard School of Public Health. He says the physiological and cognitive underpinnings of the mood disorder remain elusive. But evidence is mounting that certain foods increase both inflammation and depression risk, while others appear to have the opposite effect.

There appears to be a link between inflammation and

depression. Processed foods, like potato chips, cookies, boxed meals, canned meats, and soft drinks can increase inflammation in the body. It is best to eat foods as natural and as fresh as possible, and to prepare your own meals if you can.

For example, Dr. Lucas' research found foods like olive oil and vegetables including carrots, sweet potatoes, and leafy greens—if consumed daily—can help reduce inflammation and depression. A Mediterranean-style diet heavy in olive oil as well as fish and vegetables has also been linked to lower rates of the mood disorder.

Now here's where *epigenetics* comes in—certain foods, such as broccoli and other cruciferous vegetables, garlic, and onions contain substances that act as *histone inhibitors,* which essentially block the histone, allowing your tumor suppressor genes to activate and fight cancer. By regularly consuming these foods, you are naturally supporting your body's ability to fight tumors. (Cellular biologist Bruce Lipton, PhD, is one of the leading authorities on how emotions can regulate genetic expression, which are explained in-depth in his excellent books *The Biology of Belief* and *Spontaneous Evolution*).

Importance Of Activity

Regular exercise may help ease depression and anxiety by:

Releasing feel-good endorphins, natural brain chemicals (endogenous) and other natural brain chemicals that can enhance your sense of well-being.

Taking your mind off worries so that you can get away from the cycle of negative thoughts that feed depression and anxiety (Mayo Clinic).

Your lymph nodes are partially responsible for keeping everything circulating. It's your body's defense against disease and infection, as the lymph nodes produce the immune cells that fight invading pathogens, germs, and microbes. If you are noticing swelling in your neck lymph nodes, it's often the result of a strong infection your body is trying to eliminate. Your body has no way to reduce the swelling in those nodes, as there is no heart to pump the blood. Instead, it's up to you to drain your neck lymph nodes (imagine that!).

The more exercise you do, the more blood and lymph fluid your body can move. It will encourage the drainage of the lymph nodes, leading to better overall lymph function. The best type of exercise to drain your lymph nodes is cardiovascular exercise, including running, jogging, cycling, and rebounding (jumping on a trampoline). Do 10 to 30 minutes of this type of exercise for optimum results. Make sure you consult with your physician before beginning any exercise program.

Importance Of Sleep

We basically need eight hours of sleep ongoing. When we sleep, our body—including our brain—heals. When we sleep, we work through our fears, our fantasies, our what-ifs, and we try out various options and strategies and see where they might lead. In short, we deal with issues during sleep that are not wise or safe to deal with during our awake hours. If we are sleep-deprived, our brain is not able to work through all these issues subconsciously (where it's safer to do so). Instead, we start working through complex fears and such while we are awake (which is not good).

Chronic sleep problems are associated with an increased risk of anxiety, depression and reduced quality of life. Sleep disorders such as restless leg syndrome, sleep apnea, and narcolepsy interfere with your sleep and contribute to anxiety sleep disorder.

Lack of sleep creates anxiety disorder and can cause insomnia. Inadequate sleep can cause tiredness. If you do not sleep for the required amount your body needs, it leads to poor work performance, poor school performance, poor health, increased risks and wrong judgment.

Self-Care

• To control anxiety disorder, make sleep a priority for you and your family.
• Take 7 to 9 hours of time for uninterrupted sleep.
• Establish a regular bedtime of going to bed and getting up at the same time.
• You should not engage in stimulating activities right before going to sleep.
• Your bedroom should be quiet, calm and dark. Go to bed when you are sleepy. Keep in mind that your body will get used to the routine that you set for it, so for the first week or two you will have to probably go to sleep even if you are not sleepy.
• Do not watch television or work on the computer before going to bed. Try to have a winding down or calming down time before bed.
• Try to use the bedroom only for sleep and calmness and intimacy. Try to have discussions and strategizing and arguments outside of the bedroom, prior to going to sleep.
• You should do the "Personal Inventory" prior to going to sleep, and take no unfinished business with you to bed (more on this later). When laying in bed, you should not think about problems and worries. Do not think about what to do the next day. Hopefully you have already planned for this and dealt with this prior to going to bed.
• Try not to drink any liquids the last hour you are up before going to bed. Two hours is even better. You can drink a tall glass of water one our prior to bedtime, so that you can

eliminate it before going to bed. This will get rid of at least one reason to wake up in the night.
• Do not exercise before going to bed. Exercise 3-4 hours before bedtime.
• Do not consume caffeine, alcohol, and chocolate in the evening and before going to bed.

I think it is clear to see, with just a surface treatment, that the physical health impacts the mental and emotional health. It is all connected.

It is all about balance and wellness. If we are endeavoring to do our best with diet, exercise, sleep, water intake, sunlight etc., this will help us to be happier and more productive.

Be well....

---

1. Neil Nedley, MD and Francisco E. Ramirez, MD. Nedley depression hit hypothesis: identifying depression and Its causes. Am J Lifestyle Med. 2016 Nov-Dec; 10(6): 422-428.

2. Smith JP, Smith GC. Long-term economic costs of psychological problems during childhood. Soc Sci Med. 2010;71:110-115. [PMC free article] [PubMed] [Google Scholar]

3. Hayward C, Killen JD, Wilson DM, et al. Psychiatric risk associated with early puberty in adolescent girls. J Am Acad Child Adolesc Psychiatry. 1997;36:255-262. [PubMed] [Google Scholar]

4. Weissman MM, Wolk S, Goldstein RB, et al. Depressed adolescents grown up. JAMA. 1999;281:1707-1713. [PubMed] [Google Scholar]

5. Kendler KS, Kessler RC, Neale MC, Heath AC, Eaves

LJ. The prediction of major depression in women: toward an integrated etiologic model. Am J Psychiatry. 1993;150:1139-1139. [PubMed] [Google Scholar]

6. Arnow BA. Relationships between childhood maltreatment, adult health and psychiatric outcomes, and medical utilization. J Clin Psychiatry. 2004;65:10-15. [PubMed] [Google Scholar]

7. Anda RF, Whitfield CL, Felitti VJ, et al. Adverse childhood experiences, alcoholic parents, and later risk of alcoholism and depression. Psychiatr Serv. 2002;53:1001-1009. [PubMed] [Google Scholar]

8. Smith KA, Fairburn CG, Cowen PJ. Relapse of depression after rapid depletion of tryptophan. Lancet. 1997;349:915-919.

9. Hibbeln JR. Fish consumption and major depression. Lancet. 1998;351:1213.

10. Hibbeln JR, Umhau JC, George DT, Salem N., Jr. Do plasma polyunsaturates predict hostility and depression? World Rev Nutr Diet. 1997;82:175-186.

11. Fava M, Borus JS, Alpert JE, Nierenberg AA, Rosenbaum JF, Bottiglieri T. Folate, vitamin B_{12}, and homocysteine in major depressive disorder. Am J Psychiatry. 1997;154:426-428.

12. Penninx BW, Guralnik JM, Ferrucci L, Fried LP, Allen RH, Stabler SP. Vitamin B12 deficiency and depression in physically disabled older women: epidemiologic evidence from the Women's Health and Aging Study. Am J Psychiatry. 2000;157:715-721.

13. Modai I, Valevski A, Dror S, Weizman A. Serum cholesterol levels and suicidal tendencies in psychiatric inpatients. J Clin Psychiatry. 1994;55:252-254.

14. Beezhold BL, Johnston CS. Restriction of meat, fish, and poultry in omnivores improves mood: a pilot randomized

controlled trial. Nutr J. 2012;11:9.

15. Westover AN, Marangell LB. A cross-national relationship between sugar consumption and major depression? Depress Anxiety. 2002;16:118-120.

16. Smith KA, Fairburn CG, Cowen PJ. Relapse of depression after rapid depletion of tryptophan. Lancet. 1997;349:915-919.

17. Sullivan HS, ed. The Interpersonal Theory of Psychiatry. Boston, MA: Routledge; 2013.

18. Friedman RJ, Katz MM, eds. The Psychology of Depression: Contemporary Theory and Research. New York, NY: Halsted; 1974.

19. Klerman GL, Weissman MM. Interpersonal Psychotherapy of Depression: A Brief, Focused, Specific Strategy. New York, NY: Jason Aronson; 1994.

20. Post RM. Transduction of psychosocial stress into the neurobiology. Am J Psychiatry. 1992;149:999-1010.

21. Kendler KS, Kessler RC, Neale MC, Heath AC, Eaves LJ. The prediction of major depression in women: toward an integrated etiologic model. Am J Psychiatry. 1993;150:1139-1139.

22. Rodríguez Espínola S. Relación entre nivel socioeconómico, apoyo social percibido, género y depresión en niños; Relation between socioeconomic level, perceived social support, gender and depression in children. Interdisciplinaria. 2010;27:261-276.

23. Tomita A, Burns JK. A multilevel analysis of association between neighborhood social capital and depression: evidence from the first South African National Income Dynamics Study. J Affect Disord. 2013;144:101-105.

24. Minkler M, Fuller-Thomson E. The health of grandparents raising grandchildren: results of a national study. Am J Public Health. 1999;89:1384-1389.

25. Hammen C, Henry R, Daley SE. Depression and sensitization to stressors among young women as a function of childhood adversity. J Consult Clin Psychol. 2000;68:782.

26. Daley SE, Hammen C, Rao U. Predictors of first onset and recurrence of major depression in young women during the 5 years following high school graduation. J Abnorm Psychol. 2000;109:525.

27. Baker EL, Feldman RG, White RA, et al. Occupational lead neurotoxicity: a behavioural and electrophysiological evaluation. Study design and year one results. Br J Ind Med. 1984;41:352-361.

28. Baker EL, White RF, Pothier LJ, et al. Occupational lead neurotoxicity: improvement in behavioural effects after reduction of exposure. Br J Ind Med. 1985;42:507-516.

29. Lishman WA. Organic Psychiatry: The Psychological Consequences of Cerebral Disorder. London, UK: Blackwell Scientific; 1987.

30. Trimble MR, Krishnamoorthy ES. The role of toxins in disorders of mood and affect. Neurol Clin. 2000;18:649-664.

31. Ford DE, Kamerow DB. Epidemiologic study of sleep disturbances and psychiatric disorders: an opportunity for prevention? JAMA. 1989;262:1479-1484.

32. Peirce RS, Frone MR, Russell M, Cooper ML, Mudar P. A longitudinal model of social contact, social support, depression, and alcohol use. Health Psychol. 2000;19:28-38.

33. Boden JM, Fergusson DM. Alcohol and depression. Addiction. 2011;106:906-914.

34. Breslau N, Peterson EL, Schultz LR, Chilcoat HD, Andreski P. Major depression and stages of smoking: a longitudinal investigation. Arch Gen Psychiatry. 1998;55:161-166.

35. Brown RA, Lewinsohn PM, Seeley JR, Wagner EF. Cigarette smoking, major depression, and other psychiatric disorders among adolescents. J Am Acad Child Adolesc Psychiatry. 1996;35:1602-1610.

36. Jacobsen BK, Hansen V. Caffeine and health. Br Med J (Clin Res Ed). 1988;296:291.

37. Tasman A. Psychiatry. Vol 1 Milton, QLD, Australia: John Wiley; 2003.

38. Farmer ME, Locke BZ, Mościcki EK, Dannenberg AL, Larson DB, Radloff LS. Physical activity and depressive symptoms: the NHANES I Epidemiologic Follow-up Study. Am J Epidemiol. 1988;128:1340-1351.

39. Kryger M. Principles and Practice of Sleep Medicine. 2nd ed. Philadelphia, PA: Saunders; 1994.

40. Munger MA, Stanek EJ, Nara AR, Strohl KP, Decker MJ, Nair RN. Arterial oxygen saturation in chronic congestive heart failure. Am J Cardiol. 1994;73:180-185.

41. Yates WR, Gleason O. Hepatitis C and depression. Depress Anxiety. 1998;7:188-193.

42. Binder LM. Persisting symptoms after mild head injury: a review of the postconcussive syndrome. J Clin Exp Neuropsychol. 1986;8:323-346.

43. Evans RW. The postconcussion syndrome and the sequelae of mild head injury. Neurol Clin. 1992;10:815-847.

44. Pohjasvaara T, Leppävuori A, Siira I, Vataja R, Kaste M, Erkinjuntti T. Frequency and clinical determinants of poststroke depression. Stroke. 1998;29:2311-2317.

45. Gonzalez MB, Snyderman TB, Colket JT. Depression in patients with coronary artery disease. Depression. 1996;4:57-62.

46. Hyman SE. Depressive and bipolar mood disorders: depression in the medically ill. Sci Am. 2000;3:1.

47. Cummings JL. Depression and Parkinson's disease: a review. Am J Psychiatry. 1992;149:443-454.

48. Robertson SM, Amspoker AB, Cully JA, Ross EL, Naik AD. Affective symptoms and change in diabetes self-efficacy and glycaemic control. Diabet Med. 2013;30:e189-e196.

49. Stern G, Kruckman L. Multi-disciplinary perspectives on post-partum depression: an anthropological critique. Soc Sci Med. 1983;17:1027-1041.

50. Forrester-Knauss C, Zemp Stutz E, Weiss C, Tschudin S. The interrelation between premenstrual syndrome and major depression: results from a population-based sample. BMC Public Health. 2011;11:795.

51. Leigh H, Kramer SI. The psychiatric manifestations of endocrine disease. Adv Intern Med. 1984;29:413-445.

52. Carr FN, Nicassio PM, Ishimori ML, et al. Depression predicts self-reported disease activity in systemic lupus erythematosus. Lupus. 2011;20:80-84.

53. Pariante CM. Risk factors for development of depression and psychosis. Ann N Y Acad Sci. 2009;1179:144-152.

54. Markus CR, Panhuysen G, Tuiten A, Koppeschaar H, Fekkes D, Peters ML. Does carbohydrate-rich, protein-poor food prevent a deterioration of mood and cognitive performance of stress-prone subjects when subjected to a stressful task? Appetite. 1998;31:49-65.

55. Markus R, Panhuysen G, Tuiten A, Koppeschaar H. Effects of food on cortisol and mood in vulnerable subjects under controllable and uncontrollable stress. Physiol Behav. 2000;70:333-342.

56. Crichton GE, Murphy KJ, Bryan J. Dairy intake and cognitive health in middle-aged South Australians. Asia Pac J Clin Nutr. 2010;19:161.

57. Westover AN, Marangell LB. A cross-national relationship between sugar consumption and major depression? Depress Anxiety. 2002;16:118-120.

58. Lucas M, Mekary R, Pan A, et al. Relation between clinical depression risk and physical activity and time spent watching television in older women: a 10-year prospective follow-up study. Am J Epidemiol. 2011;174:1017-1027.

59. Young men who watch a lot of television are prone to depression. Nurs Stand. 2009;23:17.

60. Korkeila J, Markkula J, Korhonen P. High level of TV viewing is associated with silent inflammation. Eur Psychiatry. 2010;25:814.

61. Stojakovic M. Depression and internet addiction: correlation and treatment approaches. Eur Psychiatry. 2011;26:2195.

62. Cheung LM, Wong WS. The effects of insomnia and internet addiction on depression in Hong Kong Chinese adolescents: an exploratory cross-sectional analysis. J Sleep Res. 2011;20:311-317.

63. Tucker DM, Dawson SL. Asymmetric EEG changes as method actors generated emotions. Biol Psychol. 1984;19:63-75.

64. Stoleru S, Grégoire MC, Gérard D, et al. Neuroanatomical

correlates of visually evoked sexual arousal in human males. Arch Sex Behav. 1999;28:1-21.

65. Schreckenberg GM, Bird HH. Neural plasticity of Mus musculus in response to disharmonic sound. Bull N J Acad Sci. 1987;32:77-86.

66. Kalof L. The effects of gender and music video imagery on sexual attitudes. J Soc Psychol. 1999;139:378-385.

67. Rustad RA, Small JE, Jobes DA, Safer MA, Peterson RJ. The impact of rock videos and music with suicidal content on thoughts and attitudes about suicide. Suicide Life Threat Behav. 2003;33:120-131.

68. Freedman AM, Kaplan HI, Sadock BJ. From Synopsis of Psychiatry. Williams & Wilkins; Philadelphia, PA: 1980. Comprehensive Textbook of Psychiatry; vol 3.

69. Gruzelier JH. Frontal functions, connectivity and neural efficiency underpinning hypnosis and hypnotic susceptibility. Contemp Hypnosis. 2006;23:15-32.

70. Garden M. Can meditation be bad for you? Humanist. http://thehumanist.com/magazine/september-october-2007/features/can-meditation-be-bad-for-you. Accessed September 1, 2014.

71. Mander J. Four Arguments for Eliminating Television. New York, NY: HarperCollins; 1978.

72. Guyton AC, Hall JE. Textbook of Medical Physiology. 8th ed. Philadelphia, PA: Saunders; 1991.

73. Halsband U, Mueller S, Hinterberger T, Strickner S. Plasticity changes in the brain in hypnosis and meditation. Contemp Hypnosis. 2009;26:194-215.

74. Wang DJ, Rao H, Korczykowski M, et al. Cerebral blood flow changes associated with different 7 meditation

practices and perceived depth of meditation. Psychiatry Res. 2011;191:60-67.

75. Watkins ED, Teasdale JD. Rumination and overgeneral memory in depression: effects of self-focus and analytic thinking. J Abnorm Psychol. 2001;110:353-357.

76. Prosen M, Clark DC, Harrow M, Fawcett J. Guilt and conscience in major depressive disorders. Am J Psychiatry. 1983;140:839-844.

77. Michael Lucas, PhD, et al. Inflammatory dietary pattern linked to depression among women. Brain, Behavior, and Immunity, October 1, 2013.

THREE LITTLE COUSINS, PART 1
MY STUFF/THEIR STUFF & SELF-TALK

There are three coping strategies that I like to call the Three Little Cousins, that work together to help us greatly decrease both anxiety and depression. The first of these three little cousins I like to call "My Stuff/Their Stuff & Self-Talk." This chapter is basically the foundation of everything that follows, and as such is very important.

First, we must understand that there are several sources of anxiety, and that one of the main causes of anxiety is spending time and energy on matters that are completely out of our control. It is futile. Not a thing we can do about it. It's like a hamster running in a wheel, going nowhere. This is what can *fuel* anxiety—spending time and energy on matters that, though important, are completely and utterly out of our control. It is borrowing trouble.

So to begin, envision or better yet write on a blank piece of paper two large circles on top of each other, like a giant eight, leaving about a half-inch of space between them. In the left margins, you can write "My Stuff" for the top circle, and "Their Stuff" for the bottom circle.

"My Stuff" is anything that is indeed under our control. "Their

THROW A ROCK IN A LAKE

Stuff" is everything else that is not at all under our control, even though it may be something of importance.

Now, you can apply these two circles to any situation, to any role that you have in life, to any circumstance, or to any relationship that you have in life. There are aspects in each of these that are indeed under your control, and there are aspects in each of these that are not at all under your control. And it's good to know the difference.

And it's not a bad idea, if you have a concern about a certain situation, to write two circles vertically on a page, and just apply them to that particular situation. Just ask yourself, "What's on me in this situation, and what's not under my control?" Just start writing. And then you can ascertain where you are spending the lion's share of your time and energy. It's actually an eye-opening experience, and helpful. Not only eye-opening, but it can make the difference between being able to go on with your day, and anxiety messing up your day. You can do this any time, very useful.

But that's not what we're going to do right now.

Right now I am just going to give you some aspects that you can write in your top circle—aspects that are under our control *in general.* I'm not going to apply them to a specific situation.

So start writing *small* in your top circle, these aspects:

For the most part, we are in control of our *thoughts,* our *emotions* (we'll come back to both of these—they both have to qualified), our *priorities,* our *time management* (how we spend our time—even if our direct supervisor lays it all out for us, it's still on us to organize and get things done in a timely manner. That supervisor can't do this for us). Also, write our communication style (speaking of *verbal communication,* the three main aspects thereof being our *choice of words,* our *tone of voice,* and our *volume*—just do a few small bullet points under *verbal*). These are on us.

Also write our *non-verbal communication,* which is often more telling, even louder, than our verbal communication. Do a few small bullet points under this also. Included in non-verbal communication are aspects such as our *body language* (that's an old expression), our *facial expressions* (yeah, that's communicating, and our facial expressions sometimes betray us. It's healthier if we can just act the way we feel. But often we have to maintain a professional air, and keep our composure. But if someone asks how you are doing, and it's not just small talk, you can be honest with that person).

Write also our *hand gestures* (yeah, these are communicating. I use a lot of hand gestures—people think I'm from New York —I guess New Yorkers are famous for being quite expressive. Hand gestures just help me to emphasize a particular point I'm trying to make). Write also our *eye contact* (or lack thereof —yeah, this is always communicating. And it's not very nice when the person we are talking to is looking all over the place. We can tell the person just isn't in the moment. They are elsewhere). Also write our *posture* (whether we stand up straight or we slump—even this is in our top circle, and is communicating). And even the *attitude* with which we carry out a task. Yes, people can sense that.

We are always communicating, and impacting others, whether we know it or not.
We are always setting the tone for everyone around us.
It's good to be mindful of our impact,
and aware of our influence.
Because it is always happening.
And it's for the most part happening *silently.*

Let's continue. Also in our top circle is *how we respond to others* (and it's always wise to *think* about what we're gonna say before we utter it, or post it, before we hit *send*. And I can think of several prominent politicians, professional athletes, movie stars and musicians who could really benefit from *pausing* before they speak or post something. They should at least hire a filter gal or filter dude to *run it past first, and to polish it up and make it more palatable* before getting it out there in the cyber universe. They can save themselves millions of dollars if they would just pause. And I wouldn't mind being in that role as someone's filter guy, if it paid enough. I would enjoy that.

Also in our top circle is "who we hang with." I suppose the proper way to say this is the *people with whom we associate.* But either way will get you there. Yeah, this is an important one, because these people—these associates—*are going to impact us greatly.* So we need to pick them wisely.

Also in our top circle is *what we focus on.* I suppose the king's way of saying this is *the aspects on which we focus.* But either way will get you there, and I like the first way better. It's actually a lyric line in one of the songs I wrote.

But this is really what these two circles are all about. They have a lot to do with what we are focusing on, and spending our time on. And this is HUGE because….

**The body and and the brain
will always travel in the direction
in which we are focusing.**
Always.
So, be careful what you focus on.

For instance, if I am always focusing on my failures and mistakes and lack of follow-throughs, my whole mind will be caught up in *Failureville.* I'll be digging this pit of depression for myself. And after a while my *body* will go there as well, and

I'll start having *physical manifestations* associated with this now *valley* of depression I'm digging for myself. Now I got the big ole' Tonka toys out there moving dirt around—it's serious business. And over time I will become *a severely depressed person*—all because of my focus.

And by the way, that's the name of the album I'm currently working on—*Valley*.

It's a lot healthier for us to *catch ourselves doing something right*. This sets the tone for ourselves, and momentum starts setting in after a while. It's good to catch others doing something right also—just to give someone an affirmation of some kind—"Hey, I like how you took care of that situation. I don't think I could have done it like that. Pretty cool. You rock." It feels good for you, and it feels good for that person. And you never know, but that one validation may be just the thing that person needs to be ignited, and to move forward in life. You never know what you are *setting in motion* by one single instance of catching someone doing something right.

And it's more in line with reality also. Most of us are doing more correctly than we are doing incorrectly. Most of us are following through with more than we're not following through with. So, focus on what you are actually doing, and what you are actually following through with. Thankfully, this ability—our focus—is in our top circle.

Also in our top circle are our *values* (or our non-negotiables—what we consider to most important to us in life. Nobody has a right to choose our values for us. Parents can and should guide their little ones along these lines, but it is still on us, as we come into our teens and young adulthood, to choose or solidify our values, and make them our own).

Also in our top circle are our *hopes,* our *dreams,* our *passions* (we need to be about these, in some way), our *personal goals* including our career goals, our *romantic pursuits* and the people we date, and even daily aspects such as the *clothes we put on*, the *food we eat,* the *music we listen to,* the *shows and movies we may watch,* the extent to which we immerse ourselves in *video games* or any other *entertainment* aspects, our *recreational pursuits, whether or not we abuse substances,* and anything related to *lifestyle* in general. Also our *preferences.* It's all on us.

Also in our top circle is *whether or not we hold on to grudges and resentments.* Ooooh, that's a tough one. But resentment only hurts us; it doesn't hurt the other person who wronged us. They are impervious to it. But it sure hurts us. *Resentment is toxic. It usually gets internalized and turns into depression or anger,* or both. It eats us up on the inside. So we need to let it go. I am not suggesting that this is easy. It takes time, and it takes healing. But in time we can learn to release that person. We can even learn to forgive that person for what they have done or said to us that is hurtful and damaging. *We can release that person, and release the emotional pain connected with that maltreatment. But in doing so we are not in any way condoning what that person has done or said; not in the slightest. It is still wrong, and it will always be wrong. It's not about that. It's about getting past it. Getting past the emotional pain that is connected with it.*

Thankfully, this is in our top circle.

And one more thing you can write in your top circle. *I can learn from the past.* That is all we can do with the past—we can't go back in time. Time is a dynamic, and is always moving. No, we can't go back. *But we can sure learn from it.* There are *takeaways.* We learn that some aspects of our past hurt us and damage us, and other aspects of our past enhance us and sharpen us. But *there is important learning going on in both areas. And the net result of that learning can actually help us to have some boundaries in our lives. That learning can help us to have some self-respect in life. That learning can help us to have a voice in life.*

That learning can even help us to move forward in our lives. That is very important learning.

And this is often what songwriters such as myself write about. I've often written songs about what I am learning, what I'm applying. This is very common in music, and in all the arts. People who sculpt often sculpt about what they are learning, what they are applying. People who are freelance painters often paint about what they are learning and applying. People who journal often write or type about what they are learning, and what they are applying. They are *connecting the dots, and collecting their thoughts.*

This is important learning. And thankfully, this is in our top circle.

I am just scratching the surface. There is actually quite a bit that is under our control, if truth be told. And all of these aspects are quite important—they are pretty much the stuff of everyday living.

Now I will give you something that you can write in your bottom circle, and it won't take much time at all. I will save us two weeks of straight time right here. All you need to write at the top of your bottom circle is: **"Everything in top circle, as related to other people, from their perspective."** Write small.

In other words, we can't do a thing about anyone else's thought process, or emotional state (we'll come back to both of these), or their time management, communication style, what their priorities are, what they focus on, how they respond, what attitude they have, etc. *It's all completely and utterly out of our control—not a thing we can do about it.*

Even the people closest to you that you care about the most—who have your back—even these people—you can't do a thing about they feel about you, what they think about you, what their priorities are, what they focus on, how they respond, etc.

These are out of our reach entirely.

Now, I said we'd come back to our thoughts and emotions, because these need to be qualified. Yes, we can *contribute* to other peoples' thoughts and emotions, and they can *contribute* to our's as well. Sure, it happens all the time, all around the world. We can definitely be touched with other people's situations. No doubt.

But this is merely a *contributory impact, not a causal relationship.*

Let me explain. Let's say your friend calls you up and he is all down and sad because he just lost a loved one. In between his tears he explains that even though he sort of expected it, this has still hit him like a ton of bricks. I am sure that you will probably try to support that friend, be in the moment with that friend, and try to help that friend as best you can. You might even have some sadness for your friend, by way of empathy. Possibly even a couple of tears. Because the two of you go way back. Certainly. We can be touched with other people's situations.

I hope this doesn't happen, but life can throw curve balls at us sometimes. Let's say 15 minutes later another friend calls you up, and she is jumping for joy and all excited. She can hardly contain herself. In between her gasps for air she explains that she just won the lottery! And she's an instant millionaire. Talk about an emotional rollercoaster—to go from the above to this. But I imagine you will try to be glad for your friend, and will try your best to rejoice with her (and hopefully she will be generous, that would be nice).

Yes, we can be touched with other people's situations, and they can be touched with our's. It's the same for our thought process. We can share information, we can provide guidance, sure, teachers teach, trainers train, professors share formulas and history and principles, counselors share coping strategies, etc. Most of us have provided guidance to someone at one point or another, or have trained someone, or have given directions to someone. There's a constant dissemination of information going on all around us all the time. Certainly, we can contribute to other people's thought processes and understanding, and that they can also contribute to our's.

You can do a lot, actually. You can come alongside someone. You can support someone. You can provide active listening for someone and give them the gift of hearing. You can even challenge someone, and try to motivate someone. Sure, you can at least try.

You can even *carefully, delicately, humbly* point out a blindspot in someone's life whom you care about, because they just don't see it (hence, a blindspot). We all have those. When we're learning how to drive, they teach us to look over our shoulder and to check our blindspot. Well, we have those in our personal lives as well. And you can tell that this is clearly hurting that person. And maybe no one else in that person's life has the courage to talk to them about it. But if you are careful, and delicate, and humble, you can point out that blind spot for that person. But because you care, you can be care*ful* in what you say.

And here's the thing—most people can sense we we actually care about them. Unless they are under the influence of some substance. But most people can tell when we are being careful with our words, and our tone of voice, and our volume. So you have that going for you. Most likely that other person will see this for what it is, and will instantly know that you are not insulting them, or speaking down to them in a condescending way, or pointing the finger at them. So, it is at least likely or possible that this person will not bite your head off in their response.

So, that person can be thankful (even if they may not agree

with you). He/she might say, "Hey, thanks. Wow. Thanks for having my back. Thanks for caring. I know it took a lot of guts for you to talk to me about this. Thanks for caring. Uh, I don't see it exactly like this—I'm just being honest. But I tell you what—I'm gonna be thinking about this. I'm gonna reflect on it. And I'll get back to you. I'll let you know what's going on with it. Yeah, I know you have my back. We're good."

Oh, that would be wonderful! You have just elevated that friendship to a whole new level of trust and integrity. Kudos.

But you know and I know that *there is no guarantee at all.* That same person can become IRATE and light you up one side and down the other. That same person can be *defensive* and *enraged*—he can talk about your mama and say "She's so low she's gotta play handball with the curb." He can talk about your aunt, and say "She's so ugly she's gotta sneak up on glass of water!" (borrowed that from Steve Martin). Just *mean!* That person can be vengeful, passive-aggressive, mean-spirited, inflammatory, or he can give you the silent treatment and go off and pout (which is not very nice). That person's response *is completely and utterly out of your control. Not a thing you can do about it.*

You can be decent and courteous with someone, and that person *can still get all bent out of shape.*

> **We cannot make a decision for anyone else**
> **(unless they are a child of ours),**
> **and we cannot control the attitude, response,**
> **lifestyle or words of anyone else.**
> **We cannot implement anything for anyone,**
> **and we cannot interpret anything for**
> **anyone (we can only suggest).**

In other words, *we cannot process anything for anyone else.* We cannot be on the receiving end for that person. We cannot do that for them—that is on *them.*

The problem is, most people do not have basic ownership for much. They blame everyone and their grandma instead of having a little bit of of accountability.

And secondly, most people *do not process anything. They REACT. They just go with whatever thought that is going through their heads, and they are all over the map, and in Chaosville.*

No, we cannot process anything for anyone else.

And that is why I place our thoughts and emotions in our top circles, and other people's thoughts and emotions in our bottom circles. Because when it comes to thoughts and emotions, it is *contributory* rather than *causal*. And one more thing:

> **Nor should we make ourselves responsible**
> **for anyone else's attitude**
> **or response or words or actions.**
>
> **This is *false guilt*.**
>
> **Be careful. These are completely out of our control.**
> **We do this a lot.**
> **We kick ourselves and shame ourselves**
> **for other people's *stuff*.**
> **And when we do this, we are living in our *bottom***
> ***circle*, taking on other people's responsibilities**
> **and *stuff*, just spinning our wheels.**
>
> **This will always lead to anxiety.**

Now, if the top circle existed in real life, it would be about the size of a basketball. If you had some time, you could probably fit in that space everything you can think of in your life that is indeed under your control. You might have to write small.

If the *bottom* circle existed in real life, it would be huge. It would be about the size of Iowa, or at least New Hampshire. It would be absolutely gigantic, because, as you can imagine, *everything in your top circle multiplied by 8.whatever billion people there are in the world* (and it's always growing)—and India just overtook China as the most populous nation—that's a lot of people, and a lot of *stuff* in that bottom circle.

Oh, and not just people. Businesses, corporations, banks, universities, colleges, hospitals, clinics—their policies, protocols, hiring practices, vision statements—it is all in your bottom circle, and completely and utterly out of your control (unless you happen to sit on the board of a particular entity, then you might have a say with that one entity). But otherwise, it's all down there in your bottom circle. Not a thing you can do about any of it.

Also in the bottom circle are government offices, and the speed with which they work (notoriously slow—remember *Zootopia* and the DMV experience). Ha!

There is *peace* in your top circle; there is *utter chaos* in your bottom circle.

That bottom circle is one vast ocean of chaos. Better said, it is one giant *cesspool* of chaos. Very toxic.

Unfortunately, we all live in the bottom circle much too often, to our detriment.

There is peace in your top circle.
There is utter chaos in your bottom circle.

But here's the problem. We all spend a lot of time in our bottom circles. We borrow trouble. We swim around down there at times. So, the next time your mind is wandering to the *what if's,* or *what could be's,* or "What is she thinking right now," or

"*What is he doing right now,*" or "*What's going to happen next week,*" or any other bottom-circle consideration, quickly bring your thoughts back to….

**Right here, right now,
and ask yourself "What can I do right here, right now
that is clearly under my control and doable?"**

**Then pour yourself into that next right thing.
Do it with all of your might.
And enjoy yourself.**

And what you are doing here is quite simple. You are reorienting yourself back—pointing yourself back to your top circle, where there is *peace and productivity.*

But yes, this takes practice. We are dealing with neural pathways in the brain, and it takes time for us to get used to actually choosing our focus points. It takes time, but this becomes easier and easier. And remember, you don't have to constantly do this, just at times. This is a PRN, as-needed coping strategy that you use only when your mind is wandering.

We can do this. This is something that sets us apart from the animal kingdom. Now, I love doggies and kitty cats and birdies (I am very fond of birds actually, and I'm always watching them and feeding them. I even had a Macaw at one point). No, this is no knock on animals. I love critters.

But if one dog walks up to another dog and starts growling, pretty soon that other dog will be growling right back. And sometimes the little Pomeranians or Chihuahuas are more ferocious than the big dogs! And they might get into a tangle—you might have to step in and separate them (carefully). That's because dogs are guided by *reactions and instincts.*

WE are different.

        We can actually take a step back
(and take some deep breaths, as this always helps)

We can actually think about what we think.
(Imagine that, in other words, we can *process* something. And I don't know of any other species that can do that the way we can do it.)

And we can actually *choose* what we focus on.

And that is huge! Because, remember, our body and our brain will always move in the direction in which we are focusing. Always.

Try to get into the practice of being mindful of how you are using your time and energy. You will be training yourself to live in your top circle, where there is peace, and productivity.

Our Self-Talk

So, literally you can turn your page over, because this second aspect of the First Little Cousin is actually the flip-side of the two circles. As important as these two circles are, this second aspect is even more important, when it comes to anxiety, and wellbeing in general. And that is our self-talk, or thought process:

What we *tell ourselves* about a situation.
What we *believe* about that situation.
What we tell ourselves about somebody's words.

What we believe about those words.

Our self-talk. How we *relate* to that situation. Our thoughts are traveling at the speed of electricity. Very fast. We don't just experience anxiety, or intrusive, debilitating depressive thoughts, in a *vacuum, for no reason at all.* It is our self-talk—how we are relating to the situation—it is our thought process that results in, culminates in both our emotions, and our behaviors. That is the flow. It all starts with our thought process. But it's happening extremely fast.

Now, your anxiety may seem to be almost automatic, and that it happens quickly for no apparent reason. But if that is the case, it is only because those neural pathways in the brain involved with *reacting* and just *going with whatever thought we are having*—those neural pathways have become so prominent, like an expressway. And so your brain is used to reacting, and that can explain why it sometimes seems like you automatically become anxious. We will talk more about automatic, intrusive thoughts a little later in this chapter, because this requires a slightly different approach.

But usually it all starts with what you tell yourself about the situation; how you relate to it. Our self-talk is so powerful, we can literally *talk and think ourselves right into a full-blown panic attack, if we're not careful.* And unfortunately this is happening all around the world at any given time. If you've ever had a panic attack, you know how horrible it is. You basically feel like you're gonna die. Indeed, people end up in the hospital because of this. It happened to me over twenty years ago. I was in the hospital for two days because of good ole' anxiety. Fun, fun.

The reason that a panic attack can happen so easily, so readily, is because....

Anxiety is *cumulative* in nature.
It builds on itself.

It is cumulative in a *macro* sort of way, when something happens or someone says something that is *remotely similar* to something traumatic or emotionally painful that happened in the past, it can *bring it all back.* And all these painful memories come flooding in on the person, negatively impacting sleep, work, and basic functioning. And we usually call this PTSD, and much healing and closure is needed in these cases, and it takes time. More on this later.

Anxiety is also cumulative in a *micro* sort of way, in the here-and-now, in the moment, regarding a panic attack, and this is what we are talking about right now. It is cumulative in nature. It builds on itself. And it's happening very fast. So, I'm going to slow this down for a moment, so we can see what is actually going on. In this illustration I will be listing some of the more prominent cognitive distortions that we all engage in at times. You may want to write these down.

It is one *assumption* placed on another assumption, piled on with yet another assumption. Piled on with another *overgeneralization* (blowing something up way out of proportion—fairly common). Piled on with yet another *mind-reading,* piled on with yet another *fortune-telling,* piled on with yet another *comparing yourself to someone else,* piled on with another *self-sabotage,* piled on with yet another *assumption,* just as icing on this proverbial anxiety cake.

And by this time you are not doing well at all. Your heart is pounding so hard you feel it might pound right up out of your chest, and you might have to go chasing it down the sidewalk. You might feel dizzy and disoriented, like you're going to pass out at any time, and you're looking for a place to land. You might be hunched over with chest pains, or chest tightness, or numbness in parts of your body. It's horrible! You feel like you're gonna die! People end up in the hospital because of this! And you heart is thinking while all this is going on, "I don't know what's going on here, but I better get busy. I don't know why, but I better get busy." It takes a big toll on the heart. It doesn't know the difference. It's very real for the heart.

All of that, because of a *faulty thought process.*

So, the next time you start to feel anxious or tense (you can usually tell, because you f*eel different).* Take a step back, take some deep breaths as you take that step back, and *try to capture that self-talk,* write it down in your phone notes, or a little pad of paper you have with you, or grab a paper towel—one of the truisms of life—"Paper towels are everywhere." It's good to have a *visual* on this initially. You can learn to do this on the fly, but at first you need to SEE what you are telling yourself about the situation, and see what you are dealing with. So write it down. Ask yourself, "What am I telling myself about this situation? What am I believing about it? How am I relating to it?"

Then start writing, and you will see, it's a bunch of cognitive distortions. You're getting in the weeds with your thinking. It might be an assumption or two, which is extremely common. What I tell people about assumptions is that they are distorted and not very reliable. They are mainly useful in emergency situations, and crisis situations, like bank robberies, war zones, natural disasters, etc. when you have to think really fast. But they are *not* very helpful in every-day living and productivity. They are at best half-truths. Not very useful. So try to *avoid* them.

Or you might be blowing something up way out of proportion —an overgeneralization. Very common. Or you might be *sure* that you *know* what someone is thinking about you. You just

just *know.* You can tell. That's mind-reading. But you really don't know. Here's the truth—most people are so caught up in their own personal lives and preoccupied with their own stuff, *they do not have time to think about us.* That's the truth. Now, as soon as I say that, I have to qualify it. There is a small group of people scattered all around the world apparently who are busybodies. They seem to love drama. They like to get into other people's business, and gossip, and spend their time in Dramaville. I usually distance myself from such people, and I imagine you do as well.

But think about it. Does it really matter what anyone else thinks about you? What is far more important is what YOU think about *yourself.* Your self-appraisal is what truly matters. So be reasonable with it. Ask yourself, "Am I living consistently with my values, and personal goals, and convictions, and passions in life?" These are better better questions. Not "What does so-and-so think?"

Or you might be sure that you know what is *right around the bend,* but it's just speculation. That's fortune-telling. Or you might be *comparing yourself to someone else,* which is not very useful or healthful. You don't need to be anyone else; just be the best YOU that you can be. This is actually a distortion of something healthy, which is basically admiring someone or acknowledging their particular skills or talents. Nothing wrong with that—you're just telling the truth. But when we start comparing ourselves to that person, and kicking ourselves, and shaming ourselves—now we're getting in the weeds with our thinking, and this is distorted and will only lead to anxiety.

But you will see as you engage in this initial visual—it's all distorted. And then, do some returns in your phone notes, or on your paper start a new section, or even turn the paper over, which is helpful. And then *change your self-talk and correct it.* Do it right away. And here is what we need to correct our self-talk to—something....

True,
Valid,
and Reasonable.

Because a lot of what we tell ourselves is not very true, and it's not very reasonable.

That is what need at a time like this, when we are starting to feel anxious and tense. It's not so much pie-in-the-sky positive thinking that we need right now (although this is very helpful in general, certainly). What we need right now in the midst of anxiety is the *simple truth.* The simple truth clears away the fog. It simplifies. It clarifies. So ask yourself, "What's the **truth** in this situation?" Then start writing, "Well, I guess *this* is the truth, and I suppose this is also true in this situation. And what is *valid* here? What is real, legitimate, and actually applicable to my life? How can I remain in ____ville (insert your name) on this, and **have a voice in this situation, and be authentic?** And what does it look like to have a voice in this situation?" (That's what I mean my *valid*). "And I guess the reasonable thing is this…"

And then let this become the NEW WAY you are now relating to the situation. And this will have a *calming effect* on you, because that which is "true, valid, and reasonable" will not get you in the weeds, and will not result in anxiety. Our organic super computer brain can make sense of it. The brain understands it.

**The brain has a difficult time with distortion,
and chaos, and borrowing trouble.
But it absolutely loves the simple truth,
and authenticity, and reason.**

Yes, what I am suggesting is that we *can indeed back ourselves right up out of our anxiety or intrusive depressing thoughts* by telling ourselves the truth, having a voice in the situation, and being reasonable. It doesn't have to get any worse, and it certainly need not culminate in a panic attack.

We can back right up out of it. And then go on with our day.

This takes time, and it takes practice. But we can do this. You can even in time correct your self-talk while driving or working, on the fly, and just ask yourself "What's the truth here? How can I have a voice in this situation? What's the reasonable thing here?" And this will have a calming effect, and will get you out of the weeds.

Think of your self-talk as the rudder on a boat. The rudder is sometimes attached to the outboard motor of a boat, and it determines the entire direction in which that boat travels. And that is what our self-talk is to our lives. It determines the entire direction our lives go. It *becomes* our focus.

You can also apply this filter of "true, valid, and reasonable" to *people's words.* You probably have figured out that most people are not very careful with their words, but rather are quite haphazard with them. They just throw their words around. We have to be careful with how we *receive* those words.

> **Do not believe those words,**
> **don't embrace them,**
> **don't internalize them,**
> **and certainly don't have ownership for them,**
> **unless it's *true, valid, and reasonable.***
>
> **Let this be your filter for the incoming words of people,**
> **and you will save yourself from much**
> **anxiety and misunderstanding.**

And sometimes we have to pick the little kernel truth out of somebody's words that is actually helpful and applicable to our lives, and *discard the rest.* It's basically rubbish, *so let it go,* and hang on to the little kernel of truth that you plucked from their words. This can still enhance you in some way, but you can choose that which is helpful to you.

It is *especially* important for us to utilize this filter if *Words of Affirmation* is one our top Love Languages, or *Melancholic* is one of our top temperaments.

Please remember that the moment you START to sense that you are becoming anxious or tense—THIS is the time to take a step back, and correct your self-talk (or the way you are relating to the situation) to something *true, valid, and reasonable.* Do it right away. Don't wait until you are extremely anxious or having physical manifestations. In that case, you have waited too long.

There are two more applications of "true, valid, and reasonable." This is *a good way to prepare for anything that is upcoming.* It may be an upcoming interview, or upcoming presentation, or upcoming date, or upcoming family get-together, etc. Beforehand, ask yourself, "What is the *truth* about this upcoming thing? How can I *have a voice* in this situation, and what does that look like? And what is *reasonable* about this upcoming situation?" Then go with that, and prepare for that upcoming event in this way. This will help you to have a peaceful segue and preparation for that upcoming event, and it will keep you out of the weeds as you prepare.

And lastly, "true, valid, and reasonable" is *a good way to actually live.* It is a good approach to living, in general. Try to be "truthful" in general, "reasonable" in general, and try to remain in ____ville and to have a voice *in general, as a way of life.*

Then you will see those weeds coming before they get to you. You will be better able to navigate safely through situations, because your eyes are open, you are more aware, and you are remaining in ____ville.

Indeed, there are other sources of anxiety, such as **having too full of a plate** (or as my mother used to say, "Too many arns in the far." She had a Southern accent). Sometimes we pile too much on ourselves, or too much on a particular day, in which case we need to *simplify,* and *spread things out,* and possibly recalibrate and let a couple non-essential aspects go. We need to *embrace the process.* More on this later.

Also, **transitional time** and general **uncertainty** in life can result in anxiety for a person. No doubt about it. More on this later, as well.

Also, **traumatic, painful memories** regarding the past can result in anxiety. This is often what happens with PTSD. A closure experience is needed in these cases, and much healing.

But the two main causes or sources of anxiety are spending our time and energy on matters that are completely out of our control, and having distorted, untruthful self-talk. Fortunately, both of the coping strategies above, regarding these two sides of the same coin, are PRN or as-needed in nature. We only have to correct our self-talk at times, when we are starting to feel anxious or tense. We can usually tell, because we feel *different.* And we only have to point ourselves back to our top circle when our mind is wandering, which can be occasionally for most folks, or often for those with ADHD in the mix.

Again, you can think of self-talk as the rudder on a boat. That little rudder stays in the water, and determines the whole direction that boat travels. That is how our self-talk works for us. *It basically determines the direction our lives go,* and as such, is very important.

Intrusive And Automatic Distressing Thoughts

First of all, there are three main parts of the brain:

1. The Forebrain, or Cortex. This is our "thinking" brain, and is logical. This is where our verbal processing is located.

2. The Midbrain, or Limbic System or Amygdala. This is our anxiety center. This is where our flight/fight/freeze impulses are. This midbrain is also sometimes called the "OCD brain" and we will discuss OCD later.

3. The Hindbrain, or "Old Brain." This is the lower part of the brain stem, and it includes the Cerebellum. Our hindbrain coordinates functions that are vital to survival, such as breathing, motor activity, sleep, and wakefulness.

OCD and intrusive anxiety are more associated with our emotional brain, or midbrain, and not so much with our thinking brain or cortex. Anxiety can sometimes be at work without the thinking brain, and be more or less automatic. This can be important, and can actually help us to stay alive in some extreme instances. But because our emotional brain can sometimes *misjudge* danger, our brains can sometimes feel emotionally hijacked, when very anxious. In this case, anxiety is basically a *survival mechanism that is misfiring.*

So, for this type of intrusive/automatic anxiety, I utilize components of *ERP* (Exposure Response Prevention) to bring about a reduction in anxiety.

>**Functional Assessment**

• **Fear Cues**: External triggers: Identification of stimuli that evoke distress. Ask yourself: "What specific things an I afraid of? What situations do I fear or avoid? In what situations do I have safety behaviors?" Internal triggers: What bodily sensations concern me? What happens in my body that makes me feel afraid? What symptoms set off health-related concerns?" Intrusive mental content: "What upsetting thoughts or memories trigger my anxiety? What thoughts do I try to avoid or get rid of? What is it that triggers the thoughts or memories?"

• **Fear Expectancies**: Your goal here is to understand the core concerns or consequences associated with your fear cues. Ask yourself: "What do I fear will happen if I __(encounter fear cue)__? What do I tell myself when I __(encounter fear cue)__?" Try to identify your core feared concern. Try to come up with a "feared hypothesis" that you can *test via exposure*.

• **Safety Behaviors**: These are efforts you make to *avoid* or *prevent* anticipated consequences. Check for passive avoidance: avoiding low-risk activities associated with a fear cue (for instance, not eating in public, not entering a cancer clinic, etc.). Check for checking and reassurance-seeking that is aimed at verifying what is actually known (for instance, checking locks, researching symptoms online). Check for compulsive rituals—repetitive acts to "undo" or remove a perceived danger (for instance, handwashing, rehearsing before speaking). Check also for safety signals—stimuli associated with absence or prevention of feared outcomes (for instance, a cell phone, a "safe" person, or even a particular food item).

When you go through the above process, you are enabled to better understand *the flow.* You begin to get an idea about your actual fears and triggers, your feared outcomes, *and the efforts and rituals you are using to alleviate your fears and distresses, and to feel safe.*

This is an important process. You are learning a lot about yourself, your symptoms, and your maladaptive efforts to help yourself that *only serve to perpetuate the entire process of intrusive anxiety.*

It becomes a vicious cycle. Your thinking style leads to feeling fearful when fear cues are encountered, and feeling fearful in turn leads to urges to reduce fear via safety behaviors. *But this only results in short-term relief, and the cycle begins again.*

When we *confront* our fears and stop safety behaviors, our anxiety will *actually start to decrease the longer we are facing our fears.* Our feared outcomes are actually less likely to happen, and the situation becomes more bearable than we thought. We learn that we can *tolerate the distress, coexist with it, and actually move on with what's important to us.*

You can now creatively plan some *exposures* that will help you to *live alongside the distress,* and survive it just fine. This is very important. Start with a challenging, yet manageable task that you can do. Try to adopt the strategy of "lifestyle exposure," being opportunistic about seeking occasions to practice exposure on a regular basis.

We purposely *place ourselves in direct contact* with the discomfort-inducing stimuli (germs, public places, elevators, etc.) that typically trigger obsessive thoughts, or ritualized compulsive behaviors, fear, or anxiety.

This methodology helps us to get used to distressing thoughts, and to not engage in compulsive behaviors when exposed to the stimuli. It also helps you to let go of intrusive thoughts after being triggered by exposure.

Think of exposures as ways to practice *being in the midst of stress, fear,* and *discomfort.*

>Exposure Hierarchy

In ERP therapy, we try to design an *Exposure Hierarchy,* which is a simple list of potentially fear or anxiety-causing tasks or experiences. This list starts out with several easier, more manageable tasks that expose you gradually to distress and discomfort. As you have some successes with several easier exposures, you can then try an exposure that is a bit more distress-causing. The "toughest" tasks would be towards the top of this Exposure Hierarchy. You are working your way up the hierarchy, little by little. Think of it as a fear ladder.

ERP is a proven methodology that is consistent with best practices. It is highly successful and frequently recommended as the treatment of choice for OCD, eating disorders, intrusive and automatic anxious thoughts, and social anxiety. We will talk more about this later in this book.

But for now, I just want you to understand that anxiety that involves intrusive and automatic thoughts can effectively be treated with ERP techniques. I have summarized some of the basics for you, above. But you can also seek the guidance of a clinician who is trained in ERP, if you have a mind to. There are also some very useful websites that can give you more details regarding ERP strategies related to severe anxiety.

THREE LITTLE COUSINS, PART 2
AN INTENTIONAL SET ROUTINE

The second of the Three Little Cousins is what I would call basically the oldest of the three. This is the main component and main vehicle of this threefold strategy to beat anxiety and depression. It is what I call an Intentional Set Routine. There are three main aspects of the Intentional Set Routine.

This happens to be the single most powerful coping strategy I am aware of to beat both depression and anxiety. If you implement this strategy, I can pretty much guarantee you that you will experience a great decrease in both depression and anxiety. But like any coping strategy, it does not work unless you actually work it. It must be implemented in order to work for you.

The Foundation

There are three aspects to an Intentional Set Routine. The

first aspect is the foundation. Here is what I mean by an Intentional Set Routine: The same basic time every night for going to sleep, preferably before midnight. Pick a span, like 10-11, or 9-10, etc. It's easier to hit a span than a punctiliar point. The medical community has long been aware of the importance of going to sleep prior to midnight. Previous studies have indicated higher rates of metabolic dysfunction and cardiovascular disease associated with being a night owl. Now research involving nearly a half-a-million participants is indicating that people who stay up late have a 10% greater chance of dying prematurely[78].

Now back to defining an Intentional Set Routine. The same time every morning for waking up, 8-9 hours later, and the same time for breakfast, which actually is the most important meal of the day. And here is why. You probably already know this, but this meal is actually a "break" from the "fast" of sleep. In sleep we are dealing with and processing our fears, our fantasies, our what-if's, our what-could-be's, and our strategies. These are the five main processing categories of sleep. A lot of healing takes place in sleep, and it's much safer for the brain to process all of this in the subconscious sleep, rather than in the waking hours. And it takes about eight hours for the brain to actually optimally process all it has to process.

Now, when a person is sleep-deprived, which is getting under eight hours of sleep for a considerable time, it's almost like the brain and body get into a huddle of sorts, and they say, "You, know, it doesn't appear like this person is going to get proper sleep any time soon. We might have to start processing all of this right in the middle of his/her day." And that is exactly what happens. The person is zoning big time, and barely there. The person can't concentrate, is confused, paranoid, possibly seeing things and hearing things, with exaggerated startle reflex, and not able to get much done at all. And everyone around them knows that this person needs to go home, and get some rest.

In sleep, all of our systems are calmer, and slower. Even our involuntary systems are slower. Our breathing is slower. Our heart rate is slower. And even our blood pressure is calmer. And during sleep our digestive system is getting a much-needed break, because it's been working hard all day.

So, if you eat your last meal of the day, say, early evening, 4-5 hours after that the first phases of processing are done, and from that point all the way through the rest of the evening, and throughout the sleeping hours, your digestive system is getting a much-needed break. Now, if you eat into the late evening, you are overtaxing your digestive system, causing it to work overtime, into the sleeping hours. And it doesn't get overtime pay either. Now and then is probably not too big of a deal. But doing this frequently can have a detrimental impact on mental health, physical health, not to mention messing up one's sleep.

So, if you're going to have a third meal, it should be lighter than the typical third meal most people have (we'll come back to this in a bit). And, it should be as early as possible. This way the first phases of the digestive process will be accomplished, and your brain can focus on those very important areas mentioned above.

So, by the time we come around to morning and breakfast time, our body and our brain have been fasting for 10-12 hours. They are incredibly hungry, and in dire need of fuel! The body actually starts utilizing stored fat for fuel even after eight hours. Half of what we need for the day, in terms of phyto nutrients, complex carbs, proteins, aminos—all the good stuff —half of what we need is based on that one meal. This first meal is a very strategic meal of importance, and it sets the tone for the entire day. So I think it is safe to say that breakfast is probably not the meal to skip, if you are planning to skip a meal. The third meal would be a better candidate for that. A healthy breakfast contributes to proper immune function, lowers your cholesterol, reduces the risk of heart disease and diabetes[79], and breakfast is linked to improved cognitive function, including concentration[80].

So, the same time for sleep, wake, breakfast, lunch, and optional third meal. There should be four, preferably five hours between each meal, and try to avoid snacking or grazing between meals, as this can slightly interfere with the digestive process. And you won't be very hungry between meals if you are eating a robust and satisfying breakfast and lunch. It will carry you through to the next meal just fine.

As for the third meal, I say "optional" because we just don't need that much for the evening hours. We are starting to wind down. Now, this is for a person with a daytime work/school/operating schedule. If a person works third shift, their sleep/wake cycle is upside down (not the best), in which case the third meal becomes their first meal. But a third-shift person can also have a lighter third meal, no problem. But for the rest of us, we should go lighter on the third meal (it can still be yummy), or we can even skip it altogether, if we are trying to lose weight (or we can have a fruit smoothie for the third meal). It can still be delicious, and even your favorite food. It just doesn't have to be huge.

Having the third meal as the largest meal of the day is one of several reasons why we have in America some of the highest rates of heart disease, Type II Diabetes, obesity, inflammation, and some forms of cancer. And we are not the only ones that have a huge third meal. Unfortunately, we have shared our bad eating habits with the rest of the world. Many countries struggle with this same problems. These illnesses are mostly lifestyle-related; they are preventable in the first place, and often they are reversible, with healthy lifestyle changes.

So, an Intentional Set Routine involves the same basic time for sleep, wake, meals, and exercise. By exercise I mean at least three times per week getting your heart rate up to about 75% of it's max, for at least 15-20 minutes. And please be sure to check with your primary care physician and make sure it is advisable for you to engage in aerobic, cardiovascular exercise. This IT (Intermittent Training) methodology is actually better for us, and more productive, in terms of muscle toning and weight loss, than pouring it on for a whole hour for five days a week. That's overkill. We need to give our bodies a chance to heal, in between our workouts. Those muscles get torn, and they have to heal. Having a day of cushion between your workouts is a good idea.

There are so many benefits associated with regular exercise. It does wonders for your heart.

Regular exercise has wonderful effects on overall heart health. For instance, a regular exercise regime can help:

- Lowering blood pressure

- Lower risk of developing diabetes

- Maintaining healthy body weight

- Reducing overall inflammation throughout the body

There are additional benefits of exercise:

- Regular exercise improves our muscles' ability to pull oxygen out of the blood to the muscles

- Regular exercise reduces stress hormones in the body that put an extra burden on the heart

- Regular exercise works like a beta blocker to slow the heart rate and lower blood pressure

- Regular exercise increases high-density lipoprotein (HDL, "good" cholesterol) and helps control triglycerides

In addition, several studies have shown that people who exercise regularly are less likely to have a sudden heart attack or other life-threatening cardiac event[81].

Exercise also helps the lymphatic system (lymph nodes) to empty out and move lymphatic fluid around the body. This is our frontline defense to fight off intruders. The lymphatic system does not have the ability to pump out fluid by itself. We need to move it, move it so that our muscles can act as a pump for our lymph nodes to move out waste, like bacteria, viruses, toxins and abnormal cells that can lead to cancer[82].

Most people know that we feel better after we exercise. You have probably heard of endorphins. There are more than 20 types of endorphins in the body. Endorphins are released when we experience pain or stress. Our nerves send pain signals to the brain, and the brain releases endorphins to basically block the nerve cells that receive the pain signals. Endorphins can also help with depression, anxiety, and can even contribute to weight loss. The more we exercise, the more endorphins the body will produce.

In addition, when we exercise, there is a nice gradual dopamine increase in the brain, and it stays up at a high level for several hours afterward. Dopamine is one of the major neurotransmitters in the brain that is directly involved with our feeling happy and motivated in general. Dopamine also helps with movement, memory, and focus. Low Dopamine levels is often associated with depression. Exercise helps us to have a nice gradual increase in dopamine that remains at a high level for quite a while.

And any type of aerobic exercise will be beneficial. You can use a stationary exercise bike, or ride a real bike around the block a few times. Ellipticals, treadmills, jogging outside, swimming (one of the best exercises, as it exercises all the major muscle groups of the body). Down hill skiing and cross country skiing, etc. *We need to move it, move it.* And by the way, the body doesn't know the difference between jogging back and forth in your living room, and going to the local gym and jumping on an expensive Peloton machine. It is benefited either way. Just keep moving.

There are other activities that can also lead to a nice gradual increase in dopamine, with lasting impact, such as listening to soothing instrumental music, going for a nice hike in the outdoors, and eating foods that are rich in tyrosine, such as almonds, fish, avocados, pumpkin seeds, bananas, and even soy. (Dr. Mohammed Saeed, MD, "How Does Dopamine Drive Our Behavior[83]?"

What we sometimes settle for are sharp dopamine *surges* with *Cannabis, alcohol and other substances, and pornography or casual sex,* which is often artificial, exciting, but not very substantive or meaningful, and missing the vital neurotransmitters of oxytocin and prolactin which only come in a committed relationship. The dopamine level without the oxytocin and prolactin drops below baseline, and starts picking off the dopamine receptors. Even consuming *chocolate* (which I love), and other *sweets, gambling, and chronic video gaming* will have a similar effect. What all of these activities have in common is a sharp dopamine increase or surge, *but it goes back down very quickly,* and when it goes back down, it actually goes *below baseline.* So we are worse off than before we started. Not the best[84].

And a lot of people keep at these activities for a whole afternoon or entire day. And every time that dopamine level drops back down, it goes further and further below baseline. So the person is in much worse shape than when they started, in terms of how they feel.

We should aim for the good stuff. We should aim for a nice healthy, gradual dopamine increase with lasting impact, associated with regular aerobic, cardiovascular exercise, and other wholesome activities listed above. This is being good to ourselves.

Even walking and even a nice conversation with someone you care about—especially if there is delicious food that you like happening—will result in a nice gradual dopamine increase. It won't go up as high as exercise, but it will stay up there for a while.

We also need *anaerobic* exercise. We need some kind of resistance training for our muscles, so they don't get flabby and begin to atrophy.

So, what we have here is a good foundation of sleep, wake, meals, and exercise. Another way of looking at these elements is *self-care*. These are some of the most important constituent parts of self-care, and being good to yourself. Now, if you are a spiritual person, you can easily put some reflection, prayer, medication, reading, etc. in this self-care foundation, in which case it would be sleep, wake, reflection, meals, exercise. If not, your self-care foundation is sleep, wake, meals, exercise.

If these elements of the self-care foundation are consistently happening, *everything else in your life will be a little more smooth, a little less chaotic, and a little more likely to actually happen.* If these elements of the self-care foundation are hit-and-miss, and not very consistent, *everything else in your life will be a little less smooth, a little more chaotic, and a little less likely to actually happen.*

Yes, this self-care foundation of the Intentional Set Routine is a big deal, and is extremely important for mental health, and physical health. Try to be consistent with this self-care foundation. You will feel much better in general, and you will have improved critical thinking, better response time, and healthier mood and disposition.

A Large Visual

The second aspect of an Intentional Set Routine is that we need a large visual with which to work. We need something that won't accidentally be erased or deleted; something that you can carry with you and keep handy. Yes, an electronic tool can work, but it is not as ideal or effective, for these strategic purposes. I have seen people use a tablet and a scheduling application, and this can work, as long as it gives you the ability to write in a check mark on the screen, when you follow through with something. But the problem with electronic versions of the Intentional Set Routine is that they can be accidentally deleted or erased, and that is not good. *What works best for these strategic purposes is a full-size paper schedule book or planner*—the kind that Staples makes, or Office Depot, or Office Max, and other fine office-supply stores (They should give me a kick-back, because I'm always sending customers their way, ha-ha).

This is what works best for an Intentional Set Routine, because it allows you to use all of your senses; it engages you fully; you can even smell the ink. That's what I'm talking about.

You need the kind of schedule book that when you open it up, you have a long column for each day, and on the two pages in front of you, you have the whole week at a glance.

Now, when you look at the page, use your imagination, and look into it as though it were 3-D; it has depth. It is *seven days deep.* You might remember the older *Willy Wonka and the*

Chocolate Factory movie, and the instance of a child reaching into a TV set and pulling out a chocolate bar, then munching on it.

That is what you can do as well, relating to the most important aspects of your week. When you look at the page in your planner, try to use your imagination and not only see this as being seven days deep, but it is also *very tall, and very wide.* It is an *infrastructure,* an apparatus of sorts. Sort of like a big ole' cantilever rack in a factory, row after row, that is very tall. And every once and a while a forklift comes along carrying a large load of, say, heavy sheet metal, and it carefully raises it up to the appropriate level, and places the load in the arms of the cantilever rack (I used to do just just that, back in the day).

That is a good picture of what the Intentional Set Routine actually is. You can reach in there and strategically, *intentionally,* place a task or appointment at 3:00 Thursday. Then you can do the same thing and place something of importance in a span of time from 10:00 am to 2:00 pm on Tuesday. Just think of it as an infrastructure.

So, you take your schedule book and a ball point pen (you want this to be relatively permanent—how's that for a phrase—so it won't fade, and you can look back in a few years and see personal growth, and progress).

You take your schedule book and pen on the weekend, and start punching things in there—just for the upcoming week. It's one week at a time. Start with your self-care foundation of sleep, wake, optional reflection, meals, exercise. Put those aspects in there for the upcoming seven days. Then, if you are working, put your work spans in there for all the days you will be working. Most of us have a beginning point and end point for our work, but this isn't always the case. Do the best you can with it, and obviously if you know your upcoming work schedule, it is much easier.

If you are a student (or you both have a part-time job *and* you take classes) you can place your classes in there for the week. Then place prep time for each class in there as well, so you will have ample time to prepare, finish assignments, or prepare for an exam. For work spans, you can even place a few priority bullet points on a particular day, if you know in advance that this will be a particularly stressful and full day. Then you can "be about" these priorities first thing that day.

Any important appointments go in there—medical appointments, counseling appointments, vet appointments, special lunch engagements or business or personal endeavors. They all should go in there. They are all important.

Ant try to place some "personal time" in every day—*chill time, relax time, do absolutely nothing time*—we all need this, and don't feel guilty about it—it's part of self-care.

If you are in a special relationship, make sure you place some quality time with your partner here-and-there in your week. If it's in there, it's much more likely to happen.

Even recreational pursuits, weekend activities, research time, family get-togethers, and other important aspects of your week should be placed in your Intentional Set Routine. Yes, it is important to be intentional about everything important—personal and professional—in your week. Be just as intentional about your personal life as you are with your professional life.

You don't need to put teeth-brushing time or shower time in there, unless of course either of these aspects have been a challenge for you to "be about" consistently. For the most part, just the major aspects of your week.

And every time you follow through with anything in your Intentional Set Routine, *check it off. Put a nice big check mark near that aspect.*

Every checkmark represents a success.

And at the end of the week, you will be confronted with a whole two-pages worth of successes! This does wonders for morale, and it also increases self-efficacy, which is a fancy term for our own belief in our ability to carry something through to fruition and to actually accomplish something. That belief—that confidence—is *increased* with an Intentional Set Routine.

If you have a tendency to be hard on yourself, or to kick yourself, or shame yourself, it will be even more helpful to "find evidence to the contrary" at the end of every week, when you see all those successes, and recognize all that you have accomplished. A worthless person wouldn't be following with much at all, and wouldn't even care. A failure of a person wouldn't even think to catch him/herself doing something right in the first place, and checking things off. You therefore must not be a worthless person or a failure.

This gives you the opportunity to constantly catch yourself doing something right, which is very healthy indeed.

Now, if something happens and throws off your whole morning, or your whole afternoon—and usually this is completely out of our control, and we have to scurry around, and reposition things—if this happens, obviously you won't be able to put many checkmarks there. Do not consider this a failure on your part. No, no. It is not a failure, but only a learning point. That's all it is.

And, its a good idea to add to your "short list of truisms" the idea that *"sometimes things happen that throw off my entire morning or afternoon, and leads me to make quick adjustments, and usually the timing is horrible, and it's completely out of my control, and I am okay with it."*

We should all have a short list of truisms—mine is called "David's Short List of Truisms." This can be a growing list of truisms which you can keep in your phone notes, or some place handy. That way, when something like this happens, you are not shocked, and it doesn't have to rattle you.

But, for the most part, try to check off everything that you indeed follow through with. This helps you to catch yourself doing something right, constantly.

Now, here is an important principle, and actually a good way to live, in general. T*ry to pour yourself fully into every next right thing in your Intentional Set Routine. Be fully immersed, fully engaged* in every next right thing, whether it be a meal, or work, or exercise, or when talking with someone. With blinders on to everything else. Nothing else matters except this one next right thing. Allow yourself to be fully in the moment, and pour yourself fully into every next right thing that you do.

This will result in improved productivity, and much more peace and satisfaction in general. Pour yourself into every next right thing. It's a new way of life. And when that next right thing involves talking with someone, you will be fully in that moment, full listening, fully attending, giving the gift of hearing to that person. This will greatly improve overall interpersonal communication.

The Challenging, Yet Powerful Part

Okay, we are now at the third aspect of an Intentional Set Routine. I will tell you what it is, and then I will unpack it and explain it. Here it is:

I follow through with every next right thing in my Intentional Set Routine,

regardless of how I feel.

You go to bed at that designated time that you have set for yourself at night, *even if* you are still wide awake, and have your second wind. Go ahead and go to bed anyway. Do it for the *right reason.* You have already spent time on your Intentional Set Routine. It's in there for a reason. Tell yourself, "This is healthy for me, this is important for me, this is in-line with wellness, this is a form of self-respect (you are the one that placed it there)—*do it for those reasons, and not based on how you feel.* Check it off robustly

You set your alarm for 8 or 9 hours later, and you get up at that designated time you have set for yourself, *even if* you are still tired, and you feel like hitting that snooze 15 times. Go ahead and get up, do some stretches, yawn, and check it off. You will be fine. You probably have slept sufficiently, so go ahead and get up because it's the right thing to do—not based on how you feel about it. Tell yourself, "This is healthy for me, this is important for me, this is in-line with wellness, this is a form of self-respect, this will help me be on time and keep my job—so many good reasons—*do it for those reasons.*

You do the same with breakfast. You eat a robust, healthy breakfast, even if this is the last thing you feel like doing. Maybe the mere thought of eating makes you feel nauseous. Go ahead, take some deep breaths, and have yourself a nice, robust breakfast. Do it because it's the right thing to do. Remember, "This is healthy for me, this is important for me, this is in-line with wellness, this is a form of self-respect, this will help me keep my job, this will help me to have sufficient energy—*do it for those reasons,* and not based on how you feel.

And when you do this—when you eat that robust healthy breakfast—it's like a shot across the bow (in naval terms). You are sending a clear message to your brain and your body—"*Let's do this! Let's grab life by the horns! Let's get it going—here's some fuel."*

And your body and brain will say "Thank you, thank you, thank you. We really needed this fuel." They will love you.

Don't allow yourself to get hung up in feelings. Always remember….

Feelings Follow Function

They will come. You will will feel energized, awake, motivated, ready to take on the day. But feelings are a BYPRODUCT, a RESULT of following through with the next right thing, in this case, breakfast. Don't worry about feelings, they will fall in line just fine.

I am not saying that emotions are not important. On the contrary, they are very important. We need to have a good deal of emotional intelligence—to be in tune with and aware of how we feel, and to be able to express how we are feeling to someone who cares. Make sure it's someone who cares. This is especially important in relationships and interpersonal interactions.

But feelings can also greatly interfere with productivity and follow-through. Big time. We can waste an entire day because of how we feel. Feelings are not *friendlies,* when it comes to productivity. So it is imperative that we do not allow them to slow us down, or to deter us from following through with what's important to us. This is why it is important to consider them as byproducts, and to keep moving forward with the next right thing, regardless of how we currently feel.

And this is how we should relate to *everything* in our Intentional Set Routine. We follow through with each next right thing, regardless of what it is, *regardless of how we feel.*

Now, two things. This will become easier and easier. It takes about a week-and-a-half to two weeks for the body and brain to start adjusting to the new routine you are setting for them. It can take a bit longer sometimes, so be patient with yourself.

But please remember that....

Success breeds success.
Momentum sets in.
And inertia happens—an object in motion
tends to stay in motion.

So, yes, your brain and body will adjust to your Intentional Set Routine, and they will resonate with it. Both the brain and the body love and crave routine and consistency.

But it just so happens that the energy involved with following through with the next right thing regardless of how we feel *is so opposite* from the low energy and yuck associated with depression, that it has a natural tendency to *pull a person right up out of depression.*

This is the single most powerful coping strategy I am aware of, to greatly decrease depression in a person's life, for that very reason. It appears that....

Intentionality is the antidote to depression.

Intentionality and depression just do not mix. They are like oil and water. They don't coexist very well. Intentionality definitely mitigates against depression. It feels so good to follow through with something, especially when we didn't want to do it in the first place. It feels extra good to check that thing off, and you just want to do it all over again, because it feels great. Success breeds success. And now every other next right thing in your day will be a little easier because you conquered this difficult thing that you didn't *feel* like doing, but did it anyway.

The intentional Set Routine will also help you to greatly decrease any anxiety in your life, because everything in your Intentional Set Routine is *automatically in your top circle*—it's all doable. An intentional Set Routine helps you to live in your top circle, where there is peace and productivity. It also helps you to constantly catch yourself doing something right, which is very healthy indeed. It helps you to have less distractibility, and a more meaningful experience.

This component of the "Intentional Set Routine" is very important, and actually includes aspects of *Behavioral Activation,* which is very effective with depression. This is my way of treating depression, because I understand just how powerful our actions and follow-throughs are. *Every action and every follow-through exerts a powerful influence on how we actually feel.*

Regarding ADHD

An Intentional Set Routine can also help a person to *manage* ADHD symptoms. I know just how interfering and time-wasting ADHD can be, because I have it, and I have been dealing with it for quite a while. But, I have learned to harness that ADHD energy, and I will show you how to do this as well.

Try to think of these ADHD distractions, thoughts and idea as *rabbits* who like to be chased. They are just cute little pesky rabbits. But if we chase them, we might end up in Zaire, or Paris, or New York, and we might end up wasting an entire morning or entire afternoon in the process.

So, if you have ADHD in the mix, when that rabbit comes around trying to get you to chase it, just say to that rabbit, "Hey there, little rabbit. You're really cute. Here's a nice juicy carrot. I can chase you, but I have to chase you in my next right thing. This thing is time-sensitive, and I need to get it done. I want you to help me with what I need to get done. We can do this together. I can still chase you, but chew on your carrot, and I have to chase you in this next right thing. I want to see that little cotton tail of your's hop, hop, hopping in front of me! Let's do this!"

Yes, the rabbit will cooperate, because they *simply want to be chased.* And yes, you can harness that ADHD energy and distractibility and *channel it right into that next right thing in your day.* I believe that a person with ADHD in the mix can be even *more* productive than a person who doesn't have ADHD in the mix. You can be hyper focused, fully immersed in the task at hand, and this is an ASSET, *not* a liability.

Rabbit Power. I will devote a whole discussion to Rabbit Power next chapter.

A Few Extra Points

Your Intentional Set Routine is a working document. You can tweak it, adjust it, as needed. It is your schedule, your plan. You are the architect. But your sleep time, wake time, meals, and exercise should be as consistent as possible however, because the brain and the body will get used to this routine fairly quickly.

Try to not be afraid to front-load the week with tasks and aspects that are difficult, challenging, something you have been putting off, or something you do not want to do at all. Thus, you can get them done early in the week, get them behind you, so that you can relax a bit, and enjoy the remainder of your week. This approach has truly helped me.

If you have accomplished something of importance that you have been either putting off for a while, or that took a long time to finish, or a big project that bas been completed, or a completed degree program or training program—*mark that progress with a special meal, or special date, or special activity of some kind.* It is significant, and it needs to be acknowledged in some way. Rewarded behavior tends to increase.

In the old days, people would put up pillars of remembrance or ziggurats, monuments, or totem poles, etc. to mark special occasions or progress. If we did that kind of thing nowadays, we would probably be violating several zoning laws. But we can still mark significant progress.

If you find yourself coming to the end of a work span, and you feel compelled to keep pushing on even past your normal shift end, try to make a decision in line with wellness, and resist that urge. Try to acknowledge that "this is enough" when you have taken a project or particular task as far as you can take it for today. This decision and redirecting will foster excellence, it is in line with personal accountability, and it will guard you from the *distortion* of excellence, which is *drivenness.* Drivenness involves stress, overworking, and leads to burnout.

Factor in interruptions, be intentional about them, and place cushions of time in-between the various planned activities for the day, to account for interruptions. If no such interruption occurs, you will just have a little extra time to work on something of import. If an interruption does occur, then you can be about it without the interruption bleeding into other planned time and activities.

Be sure to place a block of personal time in each day, to relax, to chill, to do absolutely nothing, or to even pick an ADHD rabbit to chase and do some exploration that is fun and meaningful.

And don't feel guilty about personal time--it's part of self-care.

Remember that even though you can put a task off till the end of the hour, it is better to get it done sooner more than later, thereby freeing up more time, and creating an intentional momentum that can have a reverberating impact on all other tasks in the day.

The Three Principles > Intentional Set Routine

We covered the three aspects of the Intentional Set Routine above. Here are the three *principles* of the Intentional Set Routine, or takeaways. Notice that the the third aspect is also the third principle, because it is so important:

1. Immerse yourself fully in every next right thing. Pour yourself into it, and be fully engaged in it, whether it is a a class, a work span, exercise, a meal, or getting together with someone. Be fully in the moment, with blinders on to everything else. And this really helps, by the way, with managing ADHD. It also will leave a lasting positive impression on the people with whom you converse, because you were fully in the moment with them. They don't get that kind of special treatment very often, and they are not likely to forget it any time soon.

2. Catch yourself doing something right continually, and check it off when you follow through with something. Success breeds success, and this creates momentum. Besides, it feels really good to catch ourselves doing something right.

3. Follow through with each next right thing for the right reason—"This is important for me, this is healthy for me, this is in line with wellness, this will help me move forward

in life", etc.—and NOT based on how you feel. Remember that *feelings follow function,* and are *byproducts* of following through. You might remember the original *Karate Kid* movie, and might remember when young Ralph Macchio was painting fences and waxing vehicles, and he was complaining because he thought that this work had nothing to do with his upcoming tournament. But he soon learned differently, that these basic, foundational movements were part and parcel of what he needed during that tournament. So remember that the best attitude to have with every next right thing in your Intentional Set Routine is "Yes, Sensei, as you wish. Wax on, wax off." This is actually a form of self-respect, because *you* are the architect of your Intentional Set Routine, and everything in there is there only because you put it there. You are both the Sensei, and the student.

Possible, Important, & Vital

It is prudent to have three categories, in terms of what we do and that which we are about. "Possible" can be anything, and definitely includes the direction that most ADHD rabbits want to pull a person. It's fine to put a "possible" item in personal time, or any other free time you may have. "Important" is a category for items that need to be executed, carried out, but are not necessarily *pressing* and will not culminate in distress or negative consequences, if not done.

"Vital" is a category for items, tasks, activities, or engagements that are *absolutely essential, time-sensitive, and cannot be put off without resulting chaos and definite negative consequences.*

With that said, try to fill your Intentional Set Routine with mainly "vital" items, and "important" items. You will need to place more importance and priority on any "vital" task in your day. You can sprinkle a few "possible" items in your week also —maybe a fun research or exploration, and the like. Try not to include recreational activities and entertainment activities in the "possible" category, because most of these activities are good for us, and help us to have a well-rounded existence. Be just as intentional about your weekend activities as you are about weekday activities. Use these three categories as a way to prioritize and simplify your week. This is the purpose of these three categories.

This will help you to not "get in the weeds" of what is possible, when ordering your day. Try to remind yourself that "Everything is possible, but not everything is necessary. Just because I *can* do something, does not mean that I should spend time and energy on it." Endeavor to be intentional about how you spend your time, and to use the Intentional Set Routine as an infrastructure for your life. This will help you to mitigate against the tendency to just go with whatever thought you are pondering in the moment. Thus, it will help you to minimize anxiety in your life.

Work-Life Balance

A healthy work-life balance is essential for peace, wellness, and relational vitality. Try to allow yourself to "take off fully your professional hat, fully close that professional door, then fully put on your personal life hat, fully open the door to your personal life, then fully close the door behind you. Try to have a *clear demarcation* between your professional life and personal life. This will help you to have a healthy work-life balance, to have peace in relationships or family, and to most likely have a little bit longer life span.

We need to get into the habit of turning unfinished work into *action steps* that can be placed in our Intentional Set Routine, with a specific day and hour (preferably the next morning). We should only continue to spend time on work-related business into our personal time if the task at hand is indeed time-sensitive and pressing. But as far as possible, train yourself to *turn any "leftover" tasks into action steps, and place these in your Intentional Set Routine with a specific day and hour.*

So, for instance, preparing for a return to a doctoral program while maintaining a healthy social life are not mutually-exclusive activities. You can indeed be about both of these endeavors concurrently, if you are careful, and if you are operating within an Intentional Set Routine. Your "ISR" will foster a healthy work-life balance, even in the most potentially challenging scenarios.

Everything can indeed......................*have its place.*

Passions

It is in line with wellness to identify your passions in life, and to try to find a place for them in your routine, as this will add meaning and substance to your life. We have basically three options, regarding allowing our passions to have a voice:

1. Enhance/amplify current job to allow your passions to be integrated (if employer permits)

2. Change careers/positions to facilitate working in a capacity which directly involves your passions

3. Continue working at current job, and creatively find a way to "be about" your passions "on the side" in your personal life.

But certainly try to have some reflection time, and to ascertain what your passions in life are. We need to be about them; they need to have a voice.

Summary and Conclusion

It is NOT about trying harder, but rather a complete change in approach. When you come to each next right thing in your Intentional Set Routine, get into the habit of doing something for the right reason—because it's important to you and vital—and NOT based on how you feel. This takes practice, but the brain and the body will cooperate.

And when you come to each next right thing, remember that you are coming to a "Y" in the road; you have a choice to make. You can either pour yourself 100% into that next right thing (which is consistent with productivity), or you can choose to engage in some other activity of interest. But it is in keeping with progress to *choose to be about the next right thing,* because you have already spent time in placing important items in your Intentional Set Routine.

So go ahead. Get yourself a schedule book, plug in all the self-care foundational aspects of your schedule, and all the other important aspects of your schedule, for the whole week. It only takes about five to ten minutes to do so. Then start fresh with a new week, and do things because they are the right things to do, regardless of how you feel.

This will become easier and easier as you practice it. True coping skills actually take practice and hard work, unlike medications and unlike substances. But true coping skills actually help you move forward in life, and they help you to meet *life on life's terms.*

Take these coping strategies in stride, and do be reasonable with yourself, as they take time and much practice.

So begin your success story. There is absolutely nothing standing in your way.

---

78. Kristen L. Knutson & Malcolm von Schantz (2018) Associations between chronotype, morbidity and mortality in the UK Biobank cohort,Chronobiology

International, 35:8,1045-1053, DOI: **10.1080/07420528 .2018.1454458**

79. Reference https://www.betterhealth.vic.gov.au/health/healthyliving/breakfast

80. Dye L, Lluch A, Blundell JE. Macronutrients and mental performance. Nutrition 2000;16:1021–34

81. Dr. Kerry Stewart, "Exercise and the Heart", *www.hopkinsmedicine.org*, Johns Hopkins Medicine, accessed 12/28/2022.

82. Heather Alexander, "Exercise and the Lymphatic System", *www.mdanderson.org*, The University of Texas MD Anderson Cancer Center, November 2019, accessed 12/28/2022.

83. Dr. Mohammed Saeed, MD, "How Does Dopamine Drive Our Behavior?", *www.intoactionrecovery.com*, Into Action Recovery Centers, accessed 12/28/2022.

84. Dr. Neil Nedley, MD, "The Two Roads", *www.youtube.com/watch?v=DrgcNeU9DG0&t=760s*, Michigan Conference of Seventh-day Adventists, June 2022, accessed 12/28/2022.

RABBIT POWER

This chapter is dedicated to a discussion on ADHD, and how to manage it. I am able to speak from experience, because I have struggled with ADHD symptoms for a long time. I used to hate it, loathe it, and consider it a liability. I have since learned that ADHD can actually be an asset, it can be managed, and it can actually help a person move forward in life.

Medications Vs. Therapeutic Interventions

Yes, medications can certainly help a person with ADHD. There are stimulant/controlled substance medications, and these are broken into three categories: Short-acting, Intermediate-acting, and Long-acting.

Short-acting stimulants include:

- Amphetamine/Dextroamphetamine (Adderall)
- Dextroamphetamine (Dexedrine, ProCentra, Zenzedi)
- Dexmethylphenidate (Focalin)
- Methylphenidate (Ritalin)

Intermediate-acting stimulants include:

- Amphetamine Sulfate (Evekeo)
- Methylphenidate (Ritalin SR, Metadate ER, Methylin ER)

Long-acting stimulants include:

- Amphetamine (Adzenys XR-ODT, Dyanavel XR)
- Dexmethylphenidate (Focalin XR)
- Dextroamphetamine (Adderall XR)
- Lisdexamfetamine (Vyvanse)
- Methylphenidate (Concerta, Daytrana, Jornay PM, Metadate CD, Quillivant XR, Quillichew ER, Ritalin LA)
- Mixed salts of a single-entity amphetamine product (Mydayis)
- Serdexmethylphenidate/Dexmethylphenidate (Azstarys)

There are also non-stimulant ADHD medications. These include:

- Atomoxetine (Strattera)
- Clonodine ER (Kapvay)
- Guanfacine ER (Intuniv)
- Viloxazine (Qelbree)

**Please make sure you consult your doctor or other medical provider before starting to take ANY ADHD medication, whether stimulant or non-stimulant. Your provider can explain the possible side effects of medications, and can tell you which medication would be best for your specific situation.

In addition, it is wise to have ongoing therapy while taking ADHD medications, because this tandem approach has proven to be quite beneficial in many cases.

The above medications can and do help many individuals who have ADHD. But therapeutic interventions can also be extremely beneficial, and quite effective. In fact, since 1999, there have been many research initiatives that have studied the positive impact that cognitive-behavioral therapy (CBT) can have on ADHD symptoms, and actually the majority of these studies have been conducted in the past 5-10 years, with significant results.

I recommend that a person first try solid coping strategies for not only ADHD but for most mental health issues, *before* going the medication route. You may find that you can learn to help yourself, and that symptoms can be minimized, even without medications. I have seen this happen time and time again.

Rabbit Power

You will remember that last chapter we talked about Rabbit Power in our discussion regarding the Intentional Set Routine. Most people with ADHD understand the concept of *hyper focus,* and can remember times when completing a task has been easy and incredible, and you are able to get a lot done in a short period of time. Rabbit Power is merely *intentional hyper focus.* You are choosing when to use it, and you direct it right into the next right thing that is screaming for attention. Rabbit Power actually works, and it helps a person to manage ADHD symptoms, transforming ADHD into an asset.

When your mind wanders, and an ADHD rabbit wants to pull you away, you have three options: you can enlist the aid of that ADHD rabbit and channel that energy and distractibility right into the next right thing that you are supposed to be about at the time. You can also give that ADHD rabbit a carrot, and say "No" to it and send it away, because you have way too much going on, with no time to converse with a rabbit. And thirdly, if that ADHD rabbit wants to take you in a direction that is important and substantive to you, you can easily open your schedule book, and give that idea or activity a day and hour, and actually be about it when the time comes. It's just a *timing* issue, in this case. You can tell that rabbit, "Look, rabbit, I like the direction you are trying to lead me, and I think it has some merit. But I can't do it right now. But I'll see you back here at 2:00 pm on Thursday. I can chase you then."

It's good to have options. But I would say that the *best* option is to enlist the aid of that pesky rabbit, and channel that energy right into your next right thing. This will increase productivity, and this will improve your self-appraisal, or what you think about yourself.

Dietary Factors

Yes, what we eat has a direct bearing on mental health in general, and how we feel. For ADHD, try to plan healthy, delicious meals for yourself that are as natural as possible, avoiding as far as possible *processed foods*. Try to eat a lot of fruits and vegetables (you can be creative, with fruit smoothies and haystacks and tostadas and stir-fries). Try to eat complex carbohydrates like potatoes, beans, oatmeal, whole-wheat bread, quinoa, sweet potatoes, barley, and the like. Protein-rich food helps with ADHD—I would recommend fish, lean poultry, low-fat dairy products, nuts and seeds (especially almonds), and soy. Try to limit your red meat intake as far as possible, as research has shown that regularly eating red meat and processed meat can raise the risk of type-2 diabetes, coronary heart disease, stroke and even certain cancers, particularly colorectal cancer[85].

Salmon actually checks off two ADHD-friendly nutrients: magnesium and omega-3 fatty acids. Other sources of omega-3 fatty acids are walnuts, chia seeds, and flax seeds. Also very helpful for ADHD are leafy greens, bananas, and whole grains.

Zinc has also been shown to improve symptoms of ADHD[86], particularly hyperactivity and impulsivity. Zinc is a "cofactor" in neurotransmission apparently, and it plays an important role in the healing of tissue and immune system functioning. Zinc also protects the gut barrier and blood-brain barrier.

Magnesium can reduce overall irritability, agitation and anxiety through its calming effect, which can be very helpful in helping ADHD children complete their tasks. In addition, vitamins B and C can be useful for alleviating symptoms of ADHD.

Try to avoid or limit your intake of dyes and sugar dumps, as these can definitely exacerbate your ADHD symptoms. Eating sugary foods can cause blood glucose spikes and crashes, which impact energy levels. Limiting refined sugar intake can also reduce the risk of diabetes, obesity, and tooth decay. Try to avoid or at least limit your intake of soft drinks.

It is a good idea to limit your intake of other simple carbohydrates, such as candy, white bread, white rice, white pasta, potatoes without skins, chips, soda, sports drinks, and french fries.

Be very careful with caffeine, especially if you are a young person. While it is true that stimulants in general appear to have an opposite or focusing impact on individuals with ADHD, stimulants like caffeine can actually intensify the effects of certain ADHD medications, and lead to adverse reactions.

For children with ADHD, removing artificial additives from the diet is a great idea. Artificial additives may also interfere with hormones, growth, and development. You are probably aware that many prepackaged and processed products contain artificial coloring, flavors, and preservatives. Examples include breakfast cereals, candies, cookies, soft drinks, fruit punches (100% fruit juice is better), and some vitamins for children. It is possible to find more healthful items that are more natural, and do not contain these artificial additives.

Lifestyle Factors

In an important study, a shorter sleep duration and less time spent in cognitively stimulating activities were associated with an increased risk of developing ADHD symptoms and behavior problems[87]. Getting at least eight hours of sleep (preferably nine or ten for children and teens) is very important for every one of us, but especially for those who struggle with ADHD symptoms. Engaging in **cognitively stimulating activities** is also very helpful for ADHD. These activities engage the mind, and include puzzles, reading, playing card games, drawing, chess, crossword puzzles, dancing, sudoku, word games, and number games.

Exercise is very important with ADHD management. Exercise can promote dopamine release, improve executive function, and alter BDNF signaling (a protein that promotes neuron survival and maintenance in the brain). If your doctor gives you the go-ahead, we need to "move it, move it" about three times a week, getting our heart rate up to about 75% of it's max, for about 15-20 minutes. This is actually better for us than pouring it on for five days a week for an hour at a time.

Please remember that **structure** and **routine** are extremely important and helpful for ADHD management. And yes, the "Intentional Set Routine" will provide both of these factors for you.

We also need to limit our screen time. Many studies have found a link between ADHD and excess screen time. Internet addiction can also contribute to more severe ADHD symptoms. And remember, screen time before bed can not only disrupt your sleep, it can also exacerbate ADHD symptoms.

If you are a parent of a young child with ADHD, encourage that child to read, and to engage in other fun cognitively-stimulating activities before bedtime (instead of screen time). You will notice the difference this simple change makes.

Summary and Conclusion

I believe that ADHD can be an asset, not a liability. If we can harness that ADHD energy and distractibility and stream it right into the next right thing at hand, we can actually *manage* the ADHD, put it to work for us, and be far more productive in the process. Rabbit Power actually works, and these ADHD rabbits just want to be chased. They don't care where they are chased, as long as they are chased. They don't mind being chased in our next task at hand. And remember that Rabbit Power is merely *intentional hyper-focus.*

---

85. Phong Hu, MD, "Is Red Meat Bad for You?" December 2, 2020, www.scripps.org/news, Scripps Health, accessed on 4/18/2023.

86. Doboszewska U, Wlaź P, Nowak G, Radziwoń-Zaleska M, Cui R, Młyniec K. Zinc in the Monoaminergic Theory of Depression: Its Relationship to Neural Plasticity. Neural Plast. 2017;2017:3682752. doi: 10.1155/2017/3682752. Epub 2017 Feb 19. PMID: 28299207; PMCID: PMC5337390.

87. Peralta GP, Forns J, García de la Hera M, González L, Guxens M, López-Vicente M, Sunyer J, Garcia-Aymerich J. Sleeping, TV, Cognitively Stimulating Activities, Physical Activity, and Attention-Deficit Hyperactivity Disorder Symptom Incidence in Children: A Prospective Study. J Dev Behav Pediatr. 2018 Apr;39(3):192-199. doi: 10.1097/DBP.0000000000000539. PMID: 29261536.

THREE LITTLE COUSINS, PART 3

PERSONAL INVENTORY
\<Let's Talk about Sleep\>

We come now to the third of the Three Little Cousins, the Personal Inventory. This is an accountability piece, but it is mainly a sleep aid. I consider sleep to be the number one factor when it comes to mental health. The importance of sleep cannot be overstated.

This Personal Inventory will help you catch yourself doing something right. It will help you tie up a couple loose ends, which is very helpful. It will help you to have a little bit better perspective on the day usually. It will help you put closure on the day. But most of all, it is a *sleep aid.*

Keep in mind that this activity is rhetorical in nature, and it does not involve any writing when you are doing it. It is a reflection time. It is a good idea to copy and paste this Personal Inventory onto a word-processing page, print it, and just keep it next to your bed, perhaps in a drawer.

Right before you go to bed, about 10 minutes before bedtime, while seated on the edge of your bed, reflect back on the day. Ask yourself the following questions, and answer yourself honestly:

Personal Inventory
By David D. Sullivan

1. Have I been fair and honest today? Only you know. But as you look back on the day, it's still fresh, and you can remember. Most of the time you will be able to admit to yourself, "I did all right with that one. Not a bad day."

2. Did I follow through with what I said I would do for someone; was I good for my word? This is all that people see, concerning us. They don't see our motives or our intentions, but they definitely see what we do, and our follow-throughs—especially that person who asked you to take care of something. That person will definitely know. As you look back on the day, you can tell how you did with this. If you find something that you did not follow through with, *simply turn that item into an action step,* open your schedule book or device that you use for your Intentional Set Routine, give that action step a specific day and time—give it a home—and BOOM! Let it go—just smile and wave like the penguins of *Madagascar.* You just tied up a loose end. It's done been dealt with; it's going to happen. Let it go.

3. Did I actually *hear* the people with whom I spoke today? Did I give people the gift of hearing? This is a gift that we give to people that is extremely valuable. Just to be in the moment with someone, to actually hear them, and not be thinking about what we're going to say next, or what will happen later in the day. You are focused in. That is a very valuable gift you are giving that person. You are validating that person, and are giving them a voice. And that person will not forget that any time soon, because it doesn't happen very often for most of us.

4. Did I cheat or cut corners?

Again, only you know. But as you look back on the day, you can tell how you did with this. Now, some shortcuts are just time-savers. Other shortcuts can be downright illegal, or violate company or school protocols. So it just depends, but as you look back on the day, you can tell which it is, and most likely it's not that big of a deal. You just saved some time, no worries. If it is the latter, and potentially damaging, you can make some adjustments, and get a plan going right away, to correct the situation. You can do what deputy Barney Fife (Don Knotts) said back in the day on *The Andy Griffith Show,* "Nip it in the bud." Feerless Fife. We can do the same. We can nip it in the bud, if we need to put a stop to some unwanted characteristic or pattern.

5. Did I purposely hurt anyone today, or cause emotional pain?

This is not talking about accidentally hurting someone's feelings. Sometimes that happens, and when it comes to our attention, we can make it right. We can talk to that person, and clarify what we meant, and be an agent of peace. No, this is talking about *intentionally* getting back at someone—revenge. It's mean, it's nasty, it's revenge and sarcasm and maybe some passive-aggressive aspects thrown in there. It's not good for you, and it's not good for that person. But as you look back on the day, you can tell which it is—either something you need to clarify, or some major damage-control in which you need to engage, with ownership and humility. But most likely, it's neither, and you can again say, "Not too bad of a day."

6. (For those with substance issues) Did I have any thoughts of using my substance of choice

today? If so, what did I do with those thoughts? Now, it just depends on the person. It's relative. You can have two people standing next to each other, person A and person B, with the exact same substance of choice, and the exact same usage history. Person A might be sick and tired of being sick and tired, and they might be weary of the lethargy, the amotivation, the decrease in critical thinking, or feeling like a trainwreck the next morning. This person just wants to put distance between self and that substance, or be in recovery. Person B might say, "Oh, it's okay. I got this. I got this. No worries." It depends on the person. But for anyone that is wanting to cut down or be in recovery, this is one of the basic principles of recovery: If we can *get ourselves busy doing something*—preferably something that is indeed under our control—these urges to use substances usually do not last very long. They will go away in a short time usually. It's only when we give those urges, those thoughts, the time of day, and *entertain* those thoughts, that they become problematic, and those thoughts develop feet that walk to the corner store, or the local dispensary, or call someone up to make a connection.

7. Did I appreciate the people and the blessings in my life today?

An attitude of gratitude. If we just open our eyes, there are decent people and practical blessings in our day. And it's all right to give someone some feedback when appropriate. Basically catch that person doing something right. You can tell that person, "I like the way you followed through with that. I don't think I could have done it that well. You rock." You just validated that person, and caught them doing something right. And that person will not forget that any time soon, because unfortunately it doesn't happen often.

8. (For those with children, or who work with children) Was I present and giving full attention

to the children in my life today? There are youngins everywhere, even if you do not have children of your own. Just to be in the moment with them, and let them tell their stories. They will talk about all kinds of things. They will talk about what they just learned, or the new contraption they just got, or their triumphs or their letdowns. Just be in the moment, listen, catch them doing something right if appropriate. This is a gift of *validation*, and you are *facilitating that young person having a voice,* and feeling like they *actually matter.* They may not even have that at home, but this is something we can give to our children or any children every day, and it will have a lasting positive impact on them throughout their years.

9. Did I accomplish what I set out to accomplish today? If not, can I peacefully let it to until tomorrow, or another day, and not stress about it? So, if this happens, and you didn't get every little thing done in the day that you wanted to, don't think it strange. This happens to all of us at times. Just *turn that item into an action step,* open your schedule book or whatever you use for your Intentional Set Routine, give that action step a specific day and hour (give it a home), and BOOM! Let it go--just smile and wave like the penguins of *Madagascar*. You just tied up another loose end. It's done been dealt with; it's going to happen. Let it go.

10. How did I impact and influence the people in my life today? Did I help or hinder? We are always influencing people, whether we like it or not. We rarely leave anyone in a neutral state. We are either enhancing someone's life, or we are dragging them down. It's good to be mindful of our influence, and aware of our impact, because it's always happening.

11. Did I use my time wisely, or did I waste valuable time? Only you know. But as you look back on the day, you can tell if it was no wasted time, a little wasted time, or a whole wheelbarrow full of wasted time. If you need to, you can make some adjustments, and carry on. This Personal Inventory helps you to catch something *early.*

12. Did I have some personal time today? Yes, we should have some personal time in every day—chill time, relax time, do absolutely nothing time, chase a rabbit time, research/exploration time, power nap time. And don't feel guilty about it, it's part of self-care.

13. Did I accomplish any significant personal goals today that I have set for myself? Have I had any insights today that are noteworthy, and did I write these insights down somewhere? Maybe it's something you have been working on for some time, like a project or important task or a degree program or certificate program or training. Or maybe it's something you have been putting off and procrastinating forever, and you finally had the determination to get that thing done. *It is significant, and you need to mark and showcase this time.* Back in the day, they would put up pillars of remembrance, and later there were ziggurats and obelisks, and totem poles and such, to mark special progress, events, and passages. You do that kind of thing nowadays, and you'll probably violate several zoning laws. But you can still mark that occasion or significant progress with a special meal, a special date, or special weekend activity. It is significant. Rewarded behavior tends to increase.

Secondly, if you had any insights today, and you haven't already written them down, you can do so now. The best time to keep track of an insight is when it happens. Just put it in your phone notes. But if you haven't yet written it down, this Personal Inventory gives you one last look at the day. You can write it down now. These insights are going to come in handy. It might be just the thing you need for any upcoming presentation, or interview, or date, or podcast, or even a book. I believe that everyone has at least one book in them. So, go ahead and write it down, because it's going to come in handy.

14. Is there anything still on my mind, or still a concern of mine, at this time? Then ask yourself, "Is there anything I can do about this? Anything at all?"

And if the answer is yes, in other words, this is in your top circle, again, *turn that item into an action step,* open your schedule book or whatever you use for your Intentional Set Routine. Give that action step a specific day and hour in your schedule (give it a home), and BOOM! Let it go. Just smile and wave like the penguins of *Madagascar,* and let it go. It's done been dealt with. You just tied up another loose end. It's going to happen, just let it go. Smile and wave. *Then go through that sequence one more time.* Ask yourself, "Is there anything still on my mind, or still a concern of mine, at this time?" Then ask yourself, "Is there anything I can do about this? Anything at all?" And if the answer is no, in other words, this is in your *bottom* circle, and there's not a thing you can do about it. And if you spend any time on it, you'll just be spinning your wheels, and this will lead to anxiety and sleep disturbance.

So, what I tell people when there is something pressing and important that is on our minds, and it's in our bottom circle, and there's not a thing we can do about it. I say, that is the kind of thing you pray about, meditate about, or forget about, *but you cannot take that thing to bed with you, because this is precisely what causes sleep disturbance. It's unfinished business.*

So you have to let it go. Just smile and wave, like the penguins of *Madagascar,* and let it go.

Now, if you are a person of faith or a spiritual person, you can pray that matter right into the hands of the God of your understanding, or you can meditate or engage in some other activity that is helpful. Let it go. But even if you are not a spiritual person, you still need to let it go. Now, if you are a visual person, and you need something tangible to help you let it go, you can convert an old shoe box, and put some nice interesting contact paper on it that you like. You can put a slit in the cover, and keep some small pieces of paper handy, so that when you have something pressing on your mind at night that is in your bottom circle, you can write it on the paper, fold it, and stick it in the shoe box. Then you can put the shoe box in the closet or in the basement, so you don't have to look at it constantly. If that helps you to let it go, then so be it. But either way, you have to let it go, because if not *it will become a form of unfinished business, will follow you to bed, and cause sleep disturbance.*

Now, don't be surprised if initially you find yourself waking up in the middle of the night with something on your mind, and you think "Wait a minute, I already let this thing go" or "I already tied up this loose end…what the deal?" Try to think of it as *quality control.* The brain is an organic super computer. Sometimes we train our brains to get used to reacting, and just going with whatever thought is going through our heads.

When we actually start to *process* things, the brain takes notice. And sometimes it just wants to make sure we are serious about actually letting something go, or actually tying up a loose end. And we will wake up, thinking about it. Do not be alarmed, it's only quality control. Think of the person in the white hat in a factory or shop who comes around once in a while to your machine, and says, "We just noticed you were a little off in readings in the office, and I just need to make this little tweak right here. There, you should be good to go. Keep up the good work."

It's just quality control, and that is what your brain is engaging in, in the first week or two when you are trying to help yourself, and improve your sleep. If that happens, tell your brain, "Yeah, I'm serious about it. Now, leave me alone." *Go right back to sleep. Don't start looking at your phone, or turning on the TV, etc. If you do this, every system in your body will start to wake up, and even pain receptors will become more active. If you wake up in the night, go right back to sleep, while you are still in a semi-sleep state.*

15. Am I getting in the weeds with my thinking, and getting distorted?

Sometimes in the day we start to become anxious, but we do not have time to correct that self-talk to something true, valid, and reasonable. There's just too much going on. But in this Personal Inventory right before bed, you have one more opportunity to process this anxiety that started earlier in the day. That anxiety is most likely still there, because it has not yet been processed. But you can still process it now, after the fact. Ask yourself, "What's the truth here? Okay, I'm going with that. What's the valid thing here? How can I have a voice in this situation? What does that look like? Okay, I can have a voice in this situation. I have a voice. I be jammin'. And what is the reasonable thing here? Okay, I'm going with that. I am *out of the weeds; I be jammin'.*"

Now you have corrected that self-talk, and you have processed that earlier situation. This is important to do, because if we do not process anxious thoughts, that anxiety will still be there, and it will follow us to bed, and will become *yet another form of unfinished business.* It will disrupt our sleep. It needs to be processed before going to bed.

So there is nothing left. You have put closure on the day. You have caught yourself doing something right. You have tied up a few loose ends. You have let a couple things go. You have sized up that day, and put it to rest. Now *you* can rest. It's either already been done, or it will be done, or you've let it go. There is nothing left. The only task left is to sleep. Give yourself permission to actually rest. Think of your happy place. For me, it's a hammock between two palm trees, on a white sand beach in the Philippines. It's 87 degrees out, I'm in the shade, I can smell the salt in the air, I can hear the waves coming in, I can hear the seagulls up above—yeah, I can sleep in that setting. Just think of your happy place, and sleep. All is well.

The Tripartite of Sleep

Sleep is so important, I have developed three ways to prepare for it:

>Strategic Journaling

As a meaningful segue between the professional part of your day and the personal part of your day, this *Strategic Journaling* brief activity can provide just such a peaceful doorway. *Strategic Journaling* is a concise, specific way to journal that takes only a few minutes and captures a few basic components of the day.

So as you end the professional (work, classes, training, etc.) part of your day, imagine fully taking off your professional hat and hanging it up. Then imagine opening the door to the personal part of your day. Try to take a seat close by, and then quickly cover these five components of your day thus far. You can easily just put these in your phone notes, using your microphone:

1. Write down or think about the *stressors* you encountered in the day, and *how you handled them.* Just a couple examples.

2. Then write down or think about any instances of *correcting your self-talk* and getting yourself out of the weeds. Again, just

a couple examples, if it indeed happened. The first sentence can be what the situation was. The second sentence can be what you did to help yourself. The third sentence can be what the result was, or how you felt afterwards. Done.

3. Then write down or think about any *insights* that you had today. Write them down, and keep track of them, while it is still fresh in your mind. These insights are going to come in handy in some way, at some time. The best time to write down insights is when they actually happen. But you can still do so now, during this *Strategic Journaling* time.

4. Then do a quick spot check on how you are currently *feeling*, and write down just a couple sentences about this. This will help you to increase emotional intelligence.

5. Then do a quick spot check on what you are currently *thinking*, and write down just a couple sentences about your thought process at present. It's good to think about what we are thinking.

And you are done! That's it. This is a smart way to journal, because you are capturing a significant part of the day, in terms of substance. *And you are already starting to put some closure on the day.* This is why *Strategic Journaling* is part of this *Tripartite of Sleep.*

>Pre-Sleep Preparation Hour

The second leg of the *Tripartite of Sleep* is the *Pre-Sleep Preparation Hour.* The last hour that you are up before bedtime should be considered a pre-sleep hour. As far as possible, try to "wind down" and relax during this time, avoiding mentally-taxing activities. It's best to do some *reading* during this time. Most of us have a book or two that we have been meaning to get back to. Well, this is the perfect time for getting that book off the shelf, or accessing it on your phone, etc. You may have noticed this, but *reading tends to have a sedative effect when it's done during the night.* You will probably start yawning—I wouldn't be surprised. Reading is perfect, as a way to wind down and prepare for sleep. You can even take turns reading paragraphs with your partner or friend or family member. Even if that person is not with you, you can have a video chat or phone chat with the speaker on. This way you are killing two stones with one bird (I say it that way, rather than the regular way, because I am quite fond of birds). You can increase quality time with someone *while* winding down.

There are other activities you can engage in during this pre-sleep hour. You can engage in crossword puzzles, circle-word puzzles, Sudoku, or chess. What all of these activities have in common—including reading—is that they are all *cognitively-stimulating activities.* They involve the imagination (imagine that), and have a *relaxing* effect on us.

Try to avoid screen time, and video-gaming, or watching movies during this pre-sleep hour. The rapid scene changes and artificiality of these activities can wreak havoc on the brain, thereby mitigating against the winding-down process. It is especially important to avoid screen time right before bed *when ADHD is in the mix.* Screen time can exacerbate ADHD symptoms when right before bed.

This second leg of the Tripartite of Sleep will help you to wind down and relax, which helps you to prepare for sleep. So do some reading.

>**Personal Inventory**

Then right before bedtime, just sit on the edge of your bed, and use the Personal Inventory to put some closure on the day, to tie up a couple loose ends, and most importantly to help you to *avoid taking any unfinished business with you to bed.*

These three ways to prepare for sleep can truly help you to improve the quality of your sleep, which will positively impact every part of your life.

Inverted Sleep-Wake Cycle

Although it is not ideal nor in the best interest of overall wellness, sometimes a person has to work a third shift, or some other similar setup. Whenever possible, we should try to have a daytime operating schedule, so we can preserve a healthy Circadian rhythm and sleep-wake cycle.

If you must have an inverted sleep-wake cycle, try to still have a robust first and second meal and lighter third meal. Your first meal will probably be in the late afternoon. Try to still use the *Personal Inventory* right before bedtime to put closure on the day and to avoid taking any unfinished business with you to bed. Try to darken your sleep room and quiet the room as far as possible, and consider using a white noise machine that you set right outside your door. Also consider using a blue light therapy device before bed, which can help your brain and body get accustomed to a daytime sleep schedule, thereby *simulating nighttime.*

Most employers will allow a person to have a couple of breaks during their shift so that the worker can still eat a robust second meal and lighter third meal. This third meal will probably take place in the early morning hours, about 4-5 hours after the second meal. You can still be intentional about the short amount of time you have when you get home, and you can be intentional about the short amount of time you have after you wake up. You have to be creative and specific about your time usage, when there is an inverted sleep-wake cycle in place. But it can be done. Just make sure you are still getting 8-9 hours of sleep when you sleep.

Happy slumbers.

AS A PERSON THINKETH...

"As a man thinketh in his heart, so is he." (Proverbs 23:7, Solomon)

"But the things that proceed out of the mouth come from the heart, and those defile the man." (Matthew 16:18, Jesus Christ)

"I think, therefore I am." (Rene Descartes)

"The more man meditates upon good thoughts, the better will be his world and the world at large." (Confucius)

"A man is but a product of his thoughts. What he thinks he becomes." (Mahatma Gandhi)

"Thought is the sculptor that can create the person you want to be." (Henry David Thoreau)

"Our thoughts are the architect of everything we do and feel.....better guard your thoughts." (David Sullivan)

It is not the words of people, or the circumstances of life, that cause us to experience symptoms of depression and anxiety. It is how we interpret what comes at us—what we tell ourselves about it—what we choose to believe about it.

And we must also avoid cognitive distortions, as far as

possible.

The Most Common Cognitive Distortions

In 1976, psychologist Aaron Beck first proposed the theory behind cognitive distortions, and in the 1980s, David Burns was responsible for popularizing it with common names and examples for the distortions.

1. Filtering

A person engaging in filtering (or "mental filtering") takes the negative details and magnifies those details while filtering out all positive aspects of a situation. For instance, a person may pick out a single, unpleasant detail and dwell on it exclusively so that their vision of reality becomes darkened or distorted. When a cognitive filter is applied, the person sees only the negative and ignores anything positive.

2. Polarized Thinking (or "Black and White" Thinking)

In polarized thinking, things are either "black-or-white"—all or nothing. We have to be perfect or we're a complete and abject failure—there is no middle ground. A person with polarized thinking places people or situations in "either/or" categories, with no shades of gray or allowing for the complexity of most people and most situations. A person with black-and-white thinking sees things only in extremes. By the way, it's most often "both/and" rather than "either/or." Try to avoid false dichotomies.

There is an exception to this however. A person's convictions involving deeply held truth can be constant and abiding. People of faith are more likely to adhere to such abiding and timeless truth on the level of principle, and this should not be criticized or denigrated.

3. Overgeneralization

In this cognitive distortion, a person comes to a general conclusion based on a single incident or a single piece of evidence. If something bad happens just once, they expect it to happen over and over again. A person may see a single, unpleasant event as part of a never-ending pattern of defeat. This is "awfulizing."

For instance, if a student gets a poor grade on one paper in one semester, they conclude they are a horrible student and should quit school.

4. Jumping to Conclusions

Without individuals saying so, a person who jumps to conclusions knows what another person is feeling and thinking—and exactly why they act the way they do. In particular, a person is able to determine how others are feeling toward the person, as though they could read their minds. Jumping to conclusions can also manifest itself as fortune-telling, where a person believes their entire future is pre-ordained (whether it be in school, work, or romantic relationships). You just *know* what's around the bend (right).

For example, a person may conclude that someone is holding a grudge against them, but doesn't actually bother to find out if they are correct. Another example involving fortune-telling is when a person may anticipate that things will turn out badly in their next relationship, and will feel convinced that their prediction is already an established fact, so why bother dating. For certain, all of these cognitive distortions can interfere with our moving forward in life.

5. Catastrophizing

When a person engages in catastrophizing, they expect disaster to strike, no matter what. This is also referred to as *magnifying*, and can also come out in its opposite behavior, *minimizing*. In this distortion, a person hears about a problem and uses *what if* questions (e.g., "What if tragedy strikes?" "What if it happens to me?") to imagine the absolute worst occurring.

For example, a person might exaggerate the importance of insignificant events (such as their mistake, or someone else's achievement). Or they may inappropriately shrink the magnitude of significant events until they appear tiny (for example, a person's own desirable qualities or someone else's imperfections). This can be particularly harmful when "sizing up" a potential partner who has inappropriate or unhealthy attributes or patterns of behavior, and minimizing the obvious, just to keep the peace, or to hang on in desperation.

With practice, you can learn to answer each of these cognitive distortions. Any distorted thought can be corrected.

6. Personalization

Personalization is a distortion in which a person believes that everything others do or say is some kind of direct, personal reaction to them. They literally take virtually everything *personally*, even when something is not meant in that way. A person who experiences this kind of thinking will also compare themselves to others, trying to determine who is smarter, better looking, etc. Comparing ourselves to someone is simply a *distortion* of something benign or neutral—admiring or acknowledging.

A person engaging in personalization may also see themselves as the cause of some unhealthy external event that they were not responsible for. For example, "We were late to the dinner party and *caused* everyone to have a terrible time. If I had only pushed my husband to leave on time, this wouldn't have happened."

7. Control Fallacies

This distortion involves two different but related beliefs about being in complete control of every situation in a person's life. In the first, if we feel *externally controlled*, we see ourselves as helpless victims of fate. For example, "I can't help it if the quality of the work is poor, my boss demanded I work overtime on it."

The fallacy of *internal control* has us assuming responsibility for the pain and happiness of everyone around us. For example, "Why aren't you happy? Is it because of something I did?"

8. Fallacy of Fairness

In the fallacy of fairness, a person feels resentful because they think that they know what is fair, but other people won't agree with them. As our parents tell us when we're growing up and something doesn't go our way, "Life isn't always fair." People who go through life applying a measuring ruler against every situation judging its "fairness" will often feel resentful, angry, and even hopeless because of it. Because life isn't fair—things will not always work out in a person's favor, even when they should. *Ahhhhh, but we can still be an agent of fairness, even in an unfair world.* We can still live in our top circles. Nothing is keeping us from doing that.

9. Blaming

When a person engages in blaming, they hold other people responsible for their emotional pain. They may also take the opposite track and instead blame themselves for every problem—even those clearly outside their own control. For example, "Stop making me feel bad about myself!" Nobody can "make" us feel any particular way—only we have control over our own emotions and emotional reactions. Yes, people can *contribute* to how we feel. But the buck stops with us. We can decide how we will relate to the situation, and how best to move forward.

10. Shoulds

Should statements ("I should pick up after myself more...") appear as a list of ironclad rules about how every person should behave. People who break the rules make a person following these "should" statements angry. They also feel guilty when they violate their own rules. A person may often believe they are trying to motivate themselves with shoulds and shouldn'ts, as if they have to be punished before they can do anything. For example, "I really should exercise. I shouldn't be so lazy."

Musts and *oughts* are also offenders. The emotional consequence is guilt. When a person directs *should statements* toward others, they often feel anger, frustration and resentment.

Again, there is an exception. For instance, when we have an Intentional Set Routine, the items in our schedule have been hand-picked intentionally by us, and are therefore important. It is safe to say that these items are important and that we should follow through with them, whenever possible. But if we are not able to follow through for whatever reason, it is not to be considered as a failure, but only a missed opportunity or learning point. We can try to do it better tomorrow. And we can easily tie up a loose end, and give that item a specific day and hour in our schedule.

It should also be kept in mind that for persons of faith, there could be some significant *shoulds* or *oughts* that one holds deeply on the level of *conviction*. In other words, *abiding truth* that rises above the wax and wain of unpredictable societal pressure or passing ideology or fad. These persons of faith "should" not be *denigrated* or *cancelled* or *devalidated* simply because they happen to believe deeply in several *oughts* or *shoulds.*

Having said that, for persons of faith, try not to superimpose your belief system or convictions on anyone else, as this is not ethical. We are all free to move about the cabin with conviction and belief.

And parents, remember that our children truly need guidance. They are learning primarily through the example we give them. But they also are looking to us to counter or confirm the loud blaring cacophony of societal noise which bombards them constantly. Don't be afraid to teach and guide your little ones.

11. Emotional Reasoning

The distortion of emotional reasoning can be summed up by the statement, "If I feel that way, it must be true." Whatever a person is feeling is believed to be true automatically and unconditionally. If a person feels stupid and boring, then they must be stupid and boring.

Emotions are extremely strong in people, and can overrule our rational thoughts and reasoning. Emotional reasoning is when our emotions take over our thinking entirely, blotting out all rationality and logic. The person who engages in emotional reasoning assumes that their unhealthy emotions reflect the way things really are—"I feel it, therefore it must be true."

12. Fallacy of Change

In the fallacy of change, a person expects that other people will change to suit them if they just pressure or cajole them enough. A person feels a need to change people because their hopes for success and happiness seem to depend entirely on those people.

This distortion is often found in thinking around relationships. For example, a girlfriend tries to get her boyfriend to improve his appearance and manners, in the belief that this boyfriend is perfect in every other way, and will make her happy if he only changes these few minor things. It is healthy to understand one's expectations for a relationship, and one's partner's expectations. But this can become distorted if our whole focus is on *changing that person,* rather than taking an objective look at reality.

We will talk a lot more about this in the upcoming chapter for couples.

13. Global Labeling

In global labeling (also referred to as mislabeling), a person generalizes one or two qualities into a negative global judgment about themselves or another person. This is an extreme form of overgeneralizing. Instead of describing an error in the context of a specific situation, a person will attach an unhealthy universal label to themselves or others.

For example, they may say, "I'm a loser" in a situation where they failed at a specific task. When someone else's behavior rubs a person the wrong way—without bothering to understand any context around why—they may attach an unhealthy label to him, such as "He's a real jerk."

Mislabeling involves describing an event with language that is highly colored and emotionally loaded. For example, instead of saying someone drops her children off at daycare every day, a person who is mislabeling might say that "She abandons her children to strangers."

14. Always Being Right

When a person engages in this distortion, they are continually putting other people on trial to prove that their own opinions and actions are the absolute correct ones. To a person engaging in "always being right," being wrong is *unthinkable*—they will go to any length to demonstrate their rightness.

For example, "I don't care how bad arguing with me makes you feel, I'm going to win this argument no matter what because I'm right." Being right often is more important than the feelings of others, with a person who engages in this cognitive distortion, even loved ones.

15. Heaven's Reward Fallacy

The final cognitive distortion is the false belief that a person's sacrifice and self-denial will eventually pay off, as if some global force is keeping score. This is a riff on the fallacy of fairness, because in a fair world, the people who work the hardest will get the largest reward. A person who sacrifices and works hard but doesn't experience the expected pay off will usually feel bitter when the reward doesn't come.

So, try to do things because it is consistent with your values, and for the right reason. Don't do things as an effort to gain a reward. There is satisfaction in following through with meaningful activities, and in being true to our word. That is reward enough.

And for people of faith, yes, it's okay to remind oneself that *Someone a lot bigger than me notices everything, looks at the heart of a person, and operates in unconditional love and fairness.*

So, if that is you (above), just keep in mind that doing things for the right reasons is always best, and is in line with wellness.

A Word About Assumptions

Assumptions are not very reliable, and they are frequently wrong. So try not to make them. There are certain situations in which assumptions can be very important and necessary. If you are standing in a bank and waiting in line to see the teller, and two guys walk in with ski masks on and Uzis in their hands, and yell "Get on the floor dirtbags!" you probably should get down on the floor, and assume that it is a very dangerous situation. Most likely, they will get their cash, the ink will explode, and they will get caught. But you will live to see another day. Similarly, if you are involved in a house fire, you should assume that this is a very dangerous situation, and try to get all the people and pets out of the house as soon as possible. Again, try to live to see another day.

But most of the time and on most days, *assumptions are very unreliable and should be avoided as far as possible.* It is better to tell yourself the *truth* about a situation.

Challenging Negative Thoughts

Answer the following questions to assess your thought:

Is there substantial evidence for my thought?
Is there any evidence contrary to my thought?
Am I attempting to interpret this situation without all the evidence?
What would a friend think about this situation?
What is the truth about this situation?
How can I have a voice in this situation?
What is the reasonable thing about this situation?
If I look at the situation positively or objectively, how is it different?
Will this matter a year from now? How about five years from

now?

Three Scenarios (check for distortions, apply above questions)

1. Your boss comes to you and seems to be upset. He tells you that you can't seem to get it together, and that you are always late for work. He says that he doesn't have much time right now, but that soon you and him will have to sit down and draw up a corrective plan.

2. Several bad things happened to you in rapid succession: your cousin, with whom you were very close, just found out she has terminal cancer; your dog ran away and you can't find him; you are late paying the rent again, and the landlord has already warned you about it; and now you just discovered that you will have to pay $820 for a major car repair. You tell yourself, "I can't do anything right. I'm a loser. Why does everything have to happen to me? What's the point in trying anymore?"

3. You have suffered with intrusive thoughts and voices for quite a while. Sometimes these thoughts/voices are very mean, and say things like, "You know it will never get better," "You should cut yourself," "You are no good, worthless!" "Kill yourself."

In the above scenarios, there are a variety of cognitive distortions, complete untruths, and dangerous extremes. Always remember that the moment you start to feel anxious or tense, take a step back, take some deep breaths, and *correct that self-talk to something true, valid and reasonable.* This will have a calming effect on you, and will get you out of the weeds. You can then go on with your day.

But the above bulleted questions are good to keep in mind.

Three "Remembers"

Remember to be kind to yourself, and reasonable (after all, this is how you would relate to someone else, right?) So extend the same courtesies to yourself.

Remember that assumptions are generally wrong, and unreliable.

Remember to pause and process, not react (dogs react; people can think about what they think, and choose what they focus on).

How to Not React

Pause and reflect. Ask yourself:

Is there any truth to what was said/what happened?

Can I have ownership and apply to my life the one little piece of what was said or what happened that is true, and apply that to my life, and discard the rest?
Does this person deserve to have power over me right now? (If I react, I'm giving this person power. Do they really deserve it? And do I really want to be controlled?).
Can I safely take a short break away from this situation?

We get so used to reacting. It becomes part of our basic routine. Those neural pathways involved with reacting and going with whatever thought that comes along have become very wide and well-worn—like a super highway—because we are so used to going down that road. It seems to be automatic now (it's the same for assumptions, negative self-talk, and addictive thinking).

Make sure what you tell yourself about situations and about people's words is true, valid and reasonable. A lot of what we tell ourselves is not very true, and not very reasonable.

You can think of your self-talk as the rudder of a huge ship.

That little rudder actually guides the direction of the big ship. Our brain and our body will generally travel in the direction we are focusing on. So be careful what you focus on.

When we begin the process of being truthful and gentle with ourselves, and stop ourselves from reacting, we start a new neural pathway that begins as a small little path. But it's an important path. You are setting the tone for yourself that is healthy, and in line with wellness.

We need to replace reacting with being *intentional.* This involves pausing, reflecting, *processing,* and asking ourselves if there is anything we can personally do, regarding that particular stressor. We might be able to turn this into an action step.

Changing Personally Damaging Statements to Personally Helpful Statements

> "I'm trying" rather than "I'm lazy"

> "There's room for improvement in my interactions with others" rather than "I'm not very nice"

> "I can give back to others as opportunities arise" rather than "I've been a mooch"

> "I can intentionally take a class or two/finish my program/get caught up on latest research" rather then tell myself "I've wasted people's time and money"

The above comparisons are merely examples of how we can change our own self-appraisal from something damaging to something helpful. Again, this is consistent with "true, valid and reasonable" and helps us to extend the same basic courtesies we extend to others, to ourselves.

A Word on Anger

Anger is simply a human emotion. It is no better or worse than any other emotion. And there are probably some things happening in this world that it is even appropriate to be angry about. But we have to manage anger, not let it manage us.

**There are three main causes of anger:
compromised values,
unmet expectations,
and unmet needs.**

If you start to become uneasy, frustrated, or angry, *first check your values*, and see if any of them are being compromised. This is the main cause of anger, so keep your values handy, such as in your phone notes, for easy access. And if you ascertain that one or more of your values is being trampled on or being compromised, this should be a *huge red flag* to you, and should truly get your attention. You will probably need to take a step back and put some distance between yourself and that person, or that particular situation. There shouldn't be business as usual. This is being good to yourself, and having self-respect. It is a big deal when someone or some situation is continually compromising our values.

In addition, always remember that it is healthy for us and in-line with wellness to allow our values to inform and impact our daily living and decision-making. Life will be more peaceful for us if we do this, and we will be more in-sync with who we are.

In addition, *unmet expectations* in a relationship or situation can also lead to anger. This is why it is so important to understand what our expectations are *before* entering a relationship or beginning to take part in a situation. Explore your expectations, and what you would like to see happen in the various areas of that relationship or situation. And of course give these expectations a voice, and actually articulate them to the individuals involved. This too is having a voice, and it will also help that other person to know where you stand.

And thirdly, *unmet needs* in a relationship can sometimes lead to the emotion of anger. So communicate with your partner what you are needing in the relationship. Have a voice. Now, in a situation such as financial stress or believing that your basic needs will not be met, there can indeed be a whole range of emotions, including anger. So turn your concern into an action step of some kind, find a specific time and place for it in your Intentional Set Routine, and then *pour yourself into that exploration or research* when the time comes. We can often think or plan or strategize our way out of frustration and anger by *doing something that is clearly under our control.*

And keep the communication lines open. Have a voice, and communicate your wishes. If there is not openness or a receptive attitude on the part of the other person, maybe it's time to make a change, socially or professionally.

Remember that anxiety and stressors can be cumulative in nature, and that it is likely that pent-up frustration and unprocessed events and concerns have coalesced in such a way that you finally *let out all this emotion and frustration and anger at one time.* This can be damaging to relationships, friendships, and even work interactions. It is better to process as we go, to let that steam out *gradually,* to have a voice, and when possible to *do something about it* or *communicate.* When we do this, it helps us to calm down, it empowers us to exert an influence on our surroundings, and it creates a safe place for others to network with you and collaborate with you.

You can set the tone for those around you. Yes, your example, and your having a voice, can impact others in a remarkable fashion. It's a ripple effect.

A Word on Psychosis

Try to relate to scary or frightening thoughts related to psychosis the same way you relate to anxious thoughts, or other intrusive thoughts, *by telling yourself the truth, having a voice, and being reasonable about the situation.* In the moment, you can tell yourself that the truthful thing is that you are important and actually matter, and that the reasonable thing is that instead of hurting yourself, you need to be helping yourself, and engaging in activities that will promote health and wellbeing.

These bad dreams you've been having are either related to previous traumatic events you have experienced, or are related to overall uncertainty or fear in your present life, or are simply part of the disease component of psychosis. It is not a character defect to have such a disease, just as a person with a weak hand or chronic cough is not necessarily a bad person simply because of the existence of a disease. So, focus on your career, and your future. Try to view yourself as a successful person and a person who is definitely moving forward in life, despite ongoing symptoms.

I have successfully used cognitive-behavioral strategies with clients who have had thought disorders, auditory or visual hallucinations, paranoia, fear, or the overwhelming notion that the "system" or the government is "out to get me."

Even psychosis involves the thought world. It involves cognitions. So, if you or anyone you know struggles in this area, the principles and strategies found in this book will still be very helpful, and possibly life-changing.

Summary

Being mindful of what we are thinking and what we are telling ourselves is the beginning of a more peaceful experience. We can indeed avoid chaos and confusion, if we are truthful and reasonable with ourselves, and we are actually having a voice in the situation.

And that is my closing thought.

THE POWER OF REFRAMING

Transitions

Transitions are a part of life. There are different types of transitions: job loss and job change, relocation, graduation and beginning a career, the divorce process and transition to singlehood, getting married, loss of a close loved one, losing one's parental rights, a young person being placed in a foster home, recovery and rehabilitation after surgery or injury, reaccclimation to society after long-term incarceration, and yes, transitions related to a worldwide pandemic.

In fact, I have often said that because of the recent worldwide pandemic, it's as if the entire world were in the midst of a huge collective adjustment disorder. People of all ages have struggled with anxiety and depression, including young people.

There is no doubt about it. Transitions, even positive ones, produce stress, and can often result in increases in both anxiety and depression. In short, transitions are extremely difficult sometimes, and can really do a number on us.

> **But transitions can actually be incredible *seedbeds*
> for personal growth and creativity,
> if we can harness that energy and angst,
> and put them to work for us.**

We can indeed be architects of our present tense; architects of our transitions. And the way this happens is through *reframing*.

Reframing is extremely important in life, because **if we do not reframe, we stagnate,** and fade into the malaise of depression and perpetual frustration. Simply put, *reframing is looking through a different pair of lenses at the situation.*

I am not suggesting a pie-in-the-sky fantasy world or utopia. Reframing is actually a very powerful and practical cognitive skill that we can use to help ourselves move through a transition period safely, and meaningfully.

And so for the remainder of this discussion, I will be describing how the reframing process works.

It is important to view a transition period as a catalyst of time that can propel you forward. Transitions are incredible opportunities in which to discover who we are, why we are, and where we are going. Transitions are powerful avenues for new knowledge, new skills, new strategies, and new awareness.

Personal Assistants

If you are currently in a transition, I want you to understand that every person in your life right now is your **personal assistant, who is simply there to help you move forward in life.**

Take a moment to let that sink in a bit . . .

If you are on probation, your probation officer, the judge, the supports you have in place such as relatives and friends, any counselors or clinical people in your life, your doctor, possibly your neighbors, your boss, your coworkers, your significant other—all of these people are your personal assistants who are simply there to help you move forward in life.

Just insert your specific situation into the equation. If you can look through these lenses—if you can look at each person, each player in your life at present as your personal assistant, you can not only survive your transition; *you can actually be propelled forward by your transition.*

I remember, as a part of my regular duties at a community mental health agency, working as a jail liaison at the local jail. I would regularly meet with individuals who were at various phases of their legal experience, and some of whom were frantic and full of uncertainty and beside themselves with anxiety. I would help them to view all of the corrections officers, jail nurse, jail physician, their court-appointed attorney that they hardly ever saw, myself, their significant other and any supports they had, that sergeant sitting over there at the desk, the judge, the DA who threw the book at them, and even cell mates as their personal assistants, who were simply there to help them move forward in life. Yes, even in that horrible situation, a person can reframe and move forward in a meaningful manner.

I would help inmates to make progress in their career track, learn a new skill, learn a new language, or even complete a certificate program, while incarcerated. These individuals learned to embrace the process, to view everyone in their life as their personal assistants, and to better themselves even in the midst of upheaval and uncertainty.

Yes, reframing even helps people who are in the midst of extreme emotional turmoil, fear, and uncertainty. Reframing is healthy, beneficial, and very consistent with everything I have shared previously.

In other words, reframing helps us to determine our personal focus at the moment, helps us to not borrow trouble, helps us to avoid making assumptions, and helps us to live in our top circle and involve ourselves in strategies and activities that are clearly under our control.

So go ahead. View the various people and players in your life at present as your personal assistants, who are simply there to help you move forward in life. You can think of personal assistants as the little rollers and tabs that you push to help a pinball move all over the place in a pinball machine. Personal assistants function to propel us forward in life in a meaningful way, if we are being careful to be intentional, and to allow ourselves to be architects of our present tense.

Now, mind you, it is likely that the people in your life who are serving as personal assistants may not be aware of this role that they have. And that is okay. You are the one who is reframing, not them. What matters is that *you are seeing them as aides to your personal growth and creativity.*

Here are some important questions you can ask yourself when in the midst of a difficult transition:

Reframing a Difficult Transition

1. What is the difficult transition about? What does it involve? How is it impacting my life?
2. What am I telling myself about this transition and my ability to handle things, and how likely is it that I will survive this?

3. Who are the specific people or players in my life during this transition?

4. Am I willing to start viewing all of the above people as my personal assistants, who are helping me to move forward in my life?

5. What will my life at present look like if I start seeing my transition as a seedbed for personal growth and creativity, and start seeing all the people in my life as my personal assistants? What action steps and explorations and discussions and research come to mind?

Yes, architects can function even in the midst of turbulence, difficulty, and uncertainty.

When you reframe, you look "through the lens of what can enhance me rather than hurt me, what can sharpen me rather than demoralize me, what can promote peace and wellness rather than destroy or depress me, and how to look at everyone in my life as my personal assistants, who are simply there to help me move forward in life."

You can think about the past, learn from the past, and *extract whatever you can learn from that past memory—that past hurt— extract and learn and be sharpened by as much as you can from that previous hurtful experience,*

> *leaving only an exoskeleton of that previous hurtful experience,*
> *that can easily be blown away with the wind.*
> *Just let it go,*
> *let it be blown away with the wind.*

Reframing helps us to *see through the transition* to the other side of it. Reframing helps us to be proactive and intentional while in the midst of a transition. Reframing also helps us to start something new, to try something different, to attempt something challenging.

Packaging

I use the term "packaging" for the way we set ourselves up, the way we prepare for anything upcoming. We can set ourselves up for defeat, or we can set ourselves up for success. Ownership for one's actions is important, and accountability is important. But self-shaming and self-degradation are distortions, and are damaging.

We have to be careful how we prepare for an upcoming event of any kind. We have to be careful how we *package* it. We can decide ahead of time to be true, valid and reasonable with our self-talk (how we are relating to it), thereby *setting ourselves up for a peaceful experience.*

We can remind ourselves that we cannot control the attitude, responses, or decisions of anyone else, and that we can prepare ourselves ahead of time to be mindful of that and to be okay with that, thereby setting ourselves up for being *fully in the moment.* We can choose ahead of time how we want to act, to talk, to listen, to relax.

Having a Voice/Remaining in "____ville"

It is important to have a voice in life. When we have a voice, we are remaining in "____ville," our values are surrounding us and guiding us, we can stand up fully in our own two shoes, and we can say what we mean and mean what we say without pouring gas on the fire. This is as good as it gets, and is quite consistent with assertive communication.

So insert your name there. For me it's "Davidville." For you it may be "Katrinaville" or "Robertville" or whatever your name is. So let's just make up a fictitious person named Susan, for sake of illustration. There is PEACE in "Susanville" and there is strength in "Susanville." In "Susanville" you can embrace the process, you can make sound decisions, and you can communicate freely. You don't have to ever leave "Susanville" to go anywhere—to work, to class, to a family get-together, to go hang out with friends, to show up at an event, to give a presentation, to go on a date, or to clarify something or confront someone. You are still there, your values are still surrounding you, and you can make an informed decision about your choice of words, your tone of voice, and your volume. Remain there, and you have no need to leave there. It's a peaceful place. It's a healthy place.

This way of relating to life can help you in a variety of ways. When we have a voice, it takes away our fear. And *decent people will adjust to us, and will notice and accept the personal growth that is happening in our lives.* They will embrace this change, and will be happy about it. People who are either not considerate or not interested at all may not notice, or they may indeed notice, but not say anything. No worries.

So if you are preparing for a get-together, you can be careful how you package it. You can remain in "____ville" (insert your name) when you are there, and reframe the situation as an opportunity to enjoy yourself, to spend quality time with children, partner, other family members, or friends, or even complete strangers. Again, when we are remaining in "____ville," *decent people will adjust to us, and will notice and will accept the personal growth that is happening in our lives. They will embrace this change, and will be happy about it.* They will be more likely to relax and be in the moment if YOU are. YOU set the tone for everyone around you, when you remain in "____ville." While you cannot control how anybody else responds to you, or how anyone else processes anything, you can still be on top of how YOU respond, and how YOU process what comes at you. This is having a voice, and this is remaining in "____ville."

So, if you are preparing to have a discussion with your partner, operate from "____ville" (insert your name), be authentic, have a voice, be honest, and be fully in the moment. You can have self-respect, and come at this relationship from a position of health, peace, and strength. Your partner will notice your authenticity, and will either resonate with it, or (if not careful) will be intimidated by it. No worries. In "____ville" you can clarify when you need to. The main thing is to actually have a voice, and to remain in "____ville." Your partner can do the same. That partner will adjust, as will everyone else. You are setting the tone for everyone around you.

"____ville" is a peaceful place; Conjectureville is a chaotic place. Give yourself permission to show up, be authentic, to listen, to have a voice—that is as good as it gets.

There are many ways to have a voice. Just by getting out of bed in the morning you have a voice. Whenever you state your opinion or position on something, you have a voice. Whenever you follow through with something that is truly under your control, you indeed have a voice (and if you have not yet set up your Intentional Set Routine, please do so right away. It can revamp your whole life). Whenever you choose to go out on a date or attend a function or a get-together of some kind, you have a voice. Whenever you speak a specific boundary into existence, and draw a line in the sand with someone, you truly have a voice. Whenever you *maintain* a previously created boundary, you have a voice (more on this later). Whenever you choose one class over another class, or one job over another job, you have a voice. Whenever you decide to discontinue any substance usage, you have a great big voice (not one of them is actually good for you—more on this later). I'm just getting started!

There are many ways to actually have a voice, and to remain in "____ville." Remember, when you are remaining in

"____ville," your values are surrounding you (so you need to know what they actually are). You can stand up in your own two shoes. You can have self-respect. You can focus on the personal goals that are most important to you. You can also say what you mean and mean what you say, without pouring gas on the fire. And yes, this is as good as it gets, and yes, people will take note that you are having a voice, and will want to *emulate* you.

Several Scenarios

1. "<u>I don't want to be alive sometimes; I see no future. I end up normalizing these ideas in my head, and it's like I try to hurt my future self.</u>"

First of all, if you are actively suicidal, and feel at-risk of harming yourself, you need to immediately call someone who cares, or a suicide hotline (they are everywhere), and a person on the other end will help you and listen to you and guide you to a safe place, even if it's your own home.

But sometimes a person can have *passive ideation*, with just an ongoing, debilitating sense of "What's the point?" or "It will always be like this, I don't really care what happens." Regarding the statement above, this is a macro form of self-sabotage, and even though it is passive suicidal ideation, it is still very damaging to a person, because "the brain and body will always travel in the direction we are focusing on." This person can reframe his current situation as a learning opportunity, and as an experience that will sharpen and enhance him, as he prepares for resumption of his degree program.

2. "<u>It's engrained in me not to care about the future—the depression won't let me.</u>"

Although clinical depression is debilitating and drains one's energy and motivation at times, it can indeed be greatly reduced. And this depression is only one minute part of who you actually are; there is so much more to you than a mere diagnosis or a set of symptoms. Your values, your personal goals, your convictions, your passions in life, your dreams, your talents—these come to mind. Be careful how you define yourself. More on that later.

3. "My current job, future career, having a family, settling down, having peace—it just doesn't seem like any of it will happen, and I can't accept it."

You can reframe your current life as a preparatory stage, and that even your current restaurant job will contribute to your future role as an IT professional. Resist the temptation to make assumptions or over-generalizations, but rather ask yourself, "What is true, valid, and reasonable as I think about the future and how it will be for me? How can I actually have a voice in what happens?"

Think of your preferred career track and actual preferred position or role. BE THAT PERSON in the present tense. Carry yourself, dress yourself, have the mindset and attitude of that role, and arrange your current workspace or office similarly to what it will be once your are in that role (you may have to do this at a home office or other room, rather than the restaurant).

This way of thinking/living will help you to derive much more meaning from your current experience, and will help you to be much more intentional about everything you do. Every act and experience has meaning, and there is no wasted experience, education, or endeavor. It will ALL come in handy, and will sharpen you and mold you into the person you want to be. More on this later.

4. "I just had carpal tunnel surgery on my wrist, and it's hard to

do much of anything with my violin. I feel lost and like I have no purpose anymore."

Relate to your violin as a child with wide-eyed wonder and awe. Spend time holding your violin, holding your bow, listening to violin music. Then consistently, gradually, and happily begin to practice playing your violin; to embark on a musical/manual Renaissance of sorts. Embrace the process, catch yourself doing something right, and enjoy the journey. Resist the thought to assume that it will never be as good as it was. Dismiss that. Instead tell yourself, "It will probably be different, *but it can be an even better, even more robust of an experience for me, as I incrementally move forward."*

5. Let's say you have a desire to return to your collegiate program, but the mere thought scares you, and so you put off doing anything about it.

Well, select a return date for your program, such as next Fall, and then write down several components you should include in your preparatory process, including self-care, professional development, social, financial/budgetary, and wellness/mental health. Put some meat on the bones, and think about some action steps that you can place in your Intentional Set Routine, and one-by-one take care of these important items. You will thus be preparing yourself for your return to school, you will be remaining in "____ville," and you will have a voice in this whole process.

6. "It's a very unfair world, and it seems that bad things continue to happen to me that don't seem right or fair."

Well first of all, I want to express my condolences. But I also want to encourage you to adopt this frame of mind: *"It's an unfair world, but I can still be an agent of fairness, even in an unfair world."* You can live your life in such a way that your values are given a voice, and *fairness* and *courtesy* and *respect* and *integrity* can ensue. In this way, you will be setting the tone for everyone around you, and you will be remaining in "____ville" and will have a voice in a very big way. You can plan specific action steps for yourself that are consistent with your values and with fairness, and you will be creating a significant "fair zone" all around you which positively impacts others. The people in your life will sense that when around you they feel safe, and they feel respected. This will then help you to move forward in your life, with one *fair* baby step at a time.

7. "I get so bogged down in this divorce process. It's always on my mind, and I can't seem to relax or enjoy much of anything."

Moving forward with this divorce process, and permitting yourself to relax and to have adequate personal time, *are not mutually-exclusive* undertakings. They can live harmoniously together. As is usually the case, it is not either-or, but rather both-and. Beware of false dichotomies. Utilize your Intentional Set Routine, be intentional about self-care, professional life, personal life, appointments, recreation, and the like. Your life need not come to a halt just because of this difficult transition that is happening. You can indeed be an architect, having a specific time and place for everything that is important to you. You can actually thrive through this transition, and develop yourself in ways that will propel you forward, if you are careful. Indeed, this divorce process could be the ignition that your life actually needs at this time.

Again, it is so important for us to reframe. If we do not reframe, we stagnate.

Locus of Control

Developed by Julian B. Rotter in 1954, people who have an "internal" locus of control believe that they can actually exert an influence on their surroundings or environment, and that their success in life largely depends on their own efforts.

People with an "external" locus of control believe that circumstances, luck, and fate pretty much determine what happens in their lives, and the degree to which they can be successful.

Yes, there is a world of difference between these two perspectives. Can an "external" locus of control person become more like an "internal" locus of control person? Certainly, and fortunately.

Of course, I call this *having a voice.* When we live in "____ville" we can have a voice, be comfortable in our own two shoes, and we can indeed exert an influence on our surroundings. Instead of being stifled and debilitated by circumstances, *we can actually view those obstacles and impediments as OPPORTUNITIES that will simply serve as springboards, propelling us forward.* In other words, we can steer safely *through* the obstacle, and get to the other side of it.

And the Intentional Set Routine will help you to do this. It helps you to be an architect, to plan meaningful activities and endeavors for yourself, to remain in "____ville" and to embrace the process.

So, try to move towards an internal locus of control, and view circumstances for what they are—circumstances—and concentrate on your personal values, personal goals, an personal passions in life. See circumstances as opportunities for personal growth that will enhance you and sharpen you, and help you move forward in life. And no worries—this is not the same as the "Control Fallacy" cognitive distortion, which has more to do with believing that you are responsible for the problems and circumstances of other people. Having an internal locus of control is having a voice, and learning to move forward, be empowered, and to exert an influence on your own life. This is quite healthy.

You Can't Get No Satisfaction?

I have had many clients who present as being malcontent, or miserable, or bored stiff, or super unhappy, or feeling like their life is at a standstill and going nowhere.

Well, there are several elements of satisfaction in life, with the existential piece being more in-depth and worthy of exploration. Let me say this, if you have a spiritual or religious inclination, or even a philosophical bent, this can facilitate a healthy exploration on your part. This might involve some meaningful reading or exploring, but can be a very robust way to expand yourself and put the pieces together in your life a bit easier.

Try to think of happiness and satisfaction as byproducts of living and working and making decisions in such a way that is congruent with your personal values, personal goals, passions in life, convictions, beliefs and preferences. When we live consistently with our values and personal goals and passions, we will most likely be more satisfied and more at peace with ourselves.

So, let your values have a voice and guide you. Pursue your personal goals actively and intentionally, and don't be afraid to "be about" your passions. You will thereby have more peace, and more general contentment.

And no, peace and contentment do not come from substances. This is a farce. Truly lasting peace and contentment come from living consistently with who we are, and embracing the process.

Summary

Reframing helps us to see through the transition to the other side of it. Reframing helps us to be proactive and intentional while in the midst of a transition. Reframing also helps us to start something new, to try something different, to attempt something challenging.

You will indeed get through this . . .

So put on a pair of new glasses.

They will look great on you.

CAREER CONSIDERATIONS

First Principles

It is best to start with the basics, and to set yourself up for a substantive and meaningful journey, when embarking on a career exploration process.

Values

You already have spent some time ascertaining your values, or what's most important to you in life. If you have not yet done so, just see chapter 1 for guidance. This by far is the most important aspect of the "3 Ways," as I call them. Allow your values to guide you and protect you and inform you, as you begin the process of exploring career options. This will lead to peace, and will keep chaos away from you.

3-Year Preferred Scenario

Just start writing down some important questions and truthful responses:

1. What do I see myself doing three years from now?
2. What's the general direction I see my life going over the next three years?
3. What does life look like at that time? What would I *like* it to look like?

4. What kind of work am I doing, and what kinds of activities are going on? What's going on day to day?

5. Do I see myself alone or with someone? What kind of person am I with?

Reflect, and write down your meaningful responses to these questions. This exercise will help to guide you in your career exploration journey.

Passions

Try to identify your passions in life, and to try to find a place for them in your routine, as this will add meaning and substance to your life. You basically have three options regarding allowing your passions to have a voice:

1. Enhance /amplify current job to afford passions being integrated (if employer permits).

2. Change careers/positions to facilitate working in a capacity which directly involves your passions.

3. Continue working at current job, and creatively find a way to "be about" passions "on the side" in your personal life.

But one thing is for sure. It is in line with wellness to allow our passions to inform what we do and plan. For someone starting out, or in the midst of a career transition, it is an opportune time to selectively choose a career path or job in which at least one of your passions can have a voice. You can do this, if you are careful. And then you will enjoy going to work every day, and it won't be drudgery.

Build Yourself a Personal Budget

This is absolutely important. I would not dare to go about my month without first putting together a realistic, accurate budget. I put my monthly budget together during the last weekend before a new month starts. Whether you get paid once a month or biweekly, go ahead and pick two specific dates that are two weeks apart, and use these two dates as your two headings for your two columns. And by the way, you can type this or use a spreadsheet or even write it on the back of a recent bill envelope or piece of paper, and take a photo of it. That is typically what I do actually. Leave some ample space in-between these two dated lists.

Now, this budget needs to include all of your recurring bills and expenses that happen every month. It also needs to include any quarterly bills or yearly bills that just happen to be timely and important for this particular month. Put it all in there, and spread things out in two clumps or groups, separated by two weeks. This is the way of peace.

Make sure you include ongoing grocery line items, anticipated fuel costs, utilities, loan payments, any auto debit items that will occur in that month, and any anticipated restaurant, entertainment, or recreation costs. Be intentional about what you anticipate for that month. And if you can, include a line item for gradually transferring some funds into a side savings account or something similar for an emergency fund. This is wise, if you can do it.

When you have both of your two dated lists of bills and expenses completed, in-between these two lists write down your anticipated income for that coming month, and be specific about it. Then total bills and expenses, then total anticipated income, and hopefully you will be solvent and not be in the red. If there is a deficit, then you either need to remove one or more line items, or tweak one or more line items. You may have to move one particular bill to later in the month. You may have to sacrifice some fun activity or night out.

DO WHATEVER IT TAKES TO ABIDE BY YOUR PERSONAL BUDGET, AND STAY WITHIN IT. I cannot overemphasize just how important this is. This will help you move forward in whatever endeavor you are planning for yourself, *in a fiscally sound manner.*

Train yourself to think of what is actually "necessary" and not merely "possible," and be aware in the moment that you can make a healthy, strategic decision that is in line with your budget. This is a form of self-respect, because you designed your budget. This will also keep your head above the water, avoiding financial train wrecks.

Career Exploration Instruments

> Strong Interest Inventory

Many in the career counseling field consider this to be the gold standard of career assessments. This instrument is based on the work of E. K. Strong, Jr., who published his interest inventory in 1927. Today the Strong Interest Inventory also includes John Holland's Theory of Career Choice (RIASEC), and maintains that in choosing a career, people for the most part prefer to be around people who are similar to them in interest and outlook. The Strong Interest Inventory compares your responses to the responses of hundreds of other people who are in a huge variety of different career tracks. The results can be very helpful and useful, and will give you lots of options to consider, regarding career. This particular instrument needs to be administered by a career counselor who has been trained in administering and interpreting the Strong Interest Inventory. But you can easily find someone to give you this test at a local community college or four-year college. There is usually no charge for this.

> Intelligent.com

This site is fabulous because it contains links to several robust and helpful career assessments that you can complete on your own—and all of these appear to be free! This site gives you access to:

- 123test - Career Aptitude Test
- My Next Move - O*NET Interest Profiler
- Truity - Career Personality Profiler
- Career Explorer by Sokanu - Career Test
- Career Fitter - Career Test
- The Princeton Review - Career Quiz
- Career One Stop - Interest Assessment
- Your Free Career Test - Free Career Test
- Rasmussen University - Career Aptitude Test
- Minnesota State University - Career Cluster Interest Survey

Here is the link to the actual page. If you cannot click on this, just copy and paste it in your web browser[88]:

https://www.intelligent.com/best-free-career-tests-and-quizzes/#:~:text=Truity%20–%20Career%20Personality%20Profiler,and%20a%20Photo%20Career%20Quiz.

Weighted Factorial Analysis

This is what I suggest for anyone who is trying to decide either what career to pursue, or what job to select, or what geographic area to pick for relocation. I call this a "Weighted Factorial Analysis" and it is a simple but more-or-less objective way to compare options and to decide on your best option. So, get a blank piece of paper out, or start typing in a word-processing document or spreadsheet.

You first need to brainstorm with yourself and select 3-5 viable options for career, job, or location. Once you have these contenders in place, write these across the top of your paper, left to right, with a little space between.

Then take a little time to decide on important factors, and write these from top to bottom on the left-hand side margin or side of your page. These factors can be salary range, job satisfaction/feedback from people in these occupations, typical day, market demand, relocation necessary?, further indebtedness/education?, how does this occupation facilitate a healthy work-life balance? ("Work-life balance"), and any other important factor.

If it is about relocation, your factors might be housing costs, climate/weather, cost of living, crime rates, schooling quality, demographics, proximity to oceans/lakes/mountains, etc., and the like.

Once you have your decided-upon options going across the top, and your important factors vertically on the left, then assign a value between 1 and 10 for each of your factors, taking one option at a time. So, let's say your first option up on top is "Underwater Basketweaving," research and explore what the salary range is for underwater basketweaving where you live, or where you would like to live. Then decide if this salary is fantastic (10) or abysmal (1) or so-so (5) or mostly good (7 or 8), and write this number for "salary range" under "Underwater Basketweaving."

Then type "typical day for underwater basket weaver" in your web browser, and boom you will see immediately what a typical day looks like for this particular profession. Assign the appropriate number to this factor under "Underwater Basketweaving." Do the same with market demand, relocation necessary?, etc. Go through all of your factors for that particular career or job option, assigning appropriate values to each of them. Then start on the next career or job option, and do the same with each of your factors. These are simple web searches that take maybe a few minutes each.

When you are finished with all of your options and have assigned values (1-10) for each of your factors for these options, total up each column for each option. You may be surprised, as this is often the case. You might have a larger total for an option that you did not anticipate. Maybe you thought it would surely be "Underwater Basketweaving" but the biggest total ended up being "Certified Box Stretcher" (in case you haven't noticed, I have a warped sense of humor). *This is a way to more-or-less have an objective sense of what the best path forward is.*

Going through this meaningful process also helps you to have a voice in big way. It helps you to exert an influence on your surroundings, on your life. It facilitates your careful, intentional decision-making, it empowers you, and helps you to move forward in life in a meaningful fashion.

This is a somewhat objective way to arrive at the option that is most conducive to wellness, and which is most congruent with your goals and preferred future.

A Baby Changes Everything

Yes, if you happen to have little ones, or not-so-little-ones, or have one on the way, this will definitely impact everything you plan, and will broaden your perspective. No doubt. So, put your budget together with this in mind. What kinds of expenses will be in place with this little one in the mix? How will having this little one impact where I/we live, and how life looks, in terms of income needs and available resources, including schooling?

As you can see, the existence of children will also impact how you put your "Weighted Factorial Analysis" together.

Single Parents, Non-Wealthy Folks & Job-Seekers

Yes, it's not easy to be a single parent, and it's not easy to be barely making it. This is actually a situation in which a lot of people find themselves. But you can still use the "First Principles" and budgeting and "Weighted Factorial Analysis" to help yourself to creatively find a way to move forward.

And if you are desperately trying to find an appropriate job, turn your job-seeking into a part-time job of sorts. Set for yourself a specific number of resumes or applications you want to submit in a week, and put these blocks of time in several places in your week, using your "Intentional Set Routine." Keep track in your phone notes where you are applying, what the position is, and the date. You can update this as time goes by. Then, make sure you are completing a follow-up call to each employer one week after applying, just to check on the status of your application. This is good for you, but it also helps that HR person on the other end of the line to know that *you mean business, and you are ready to roll.*

I have told people often that it is best to avoid debt whenever possible. But I always qualify this with these four exceptions: to buy a house, to buy an automobile, to finance one's education, or to establish credit when no credit exists.

In all of the above scenarios, you are actually making an investment in yourself, and in your future. And remember, guaranteed student loans do not become payable until six months after you graduate, and they remain at a low interest rate usually.

But if you do not want to take out a student loan in order to complete your degree, you can still continue to work, and take one class at a time, *paying as you go.* Nothing at all wrong with that. Most schools will allow you to make payments over the course of the term. And you are still *incrementally* making progress towards completion of your degree. Yes, it takes longer, but you are still moving forward. Enjoy the journey.

When Planning to Relocate for Work or Any Other Reason

First, make sure you have completed what I call the "Three Ways" to know yourself a lot better (Values, Temperaments, Love Languages). This enhanced self-understanding can help you to be grounded in the present, and to navigate a little easier in life.

Make sure you have a good understanding of what your "3-Year Preferred Scenario" is, in terms of how you would like life to be like in the near future. Then consider completing the "Weighted Factorial Analysis" because it can definitely help you to narrow down your life choices to something that is objective and meaningful to you.

Then you can further narrow down your preparation for relocation to a particular area. So, let's just pick Chicagoland as an example place for relocation. Research job salary ranges for the job you have in mind for Chicago, and pick a number towards the bottom of the salary range. Then put together a careful projected Chicagoland budget, including researching average housing costs, utilities costs, cost of living in general, and using your current personal budget as a guide for categories and line items in your projected Chicagoland budget.

Then you can put together a one-year preferred scenario for Chicagoland, including aspects such as lifestyle, entertainment, and living situation/arrangement. You can attach a monetary value to each of these aspects, and include them in your projected Chicagoland budget.

This is a smart way to prepare for a relocation, as that new location will be different in several ways.

Preparing for Tests and Exams

I suggest this four-pronged approach as a helpful way to prepare for upcoming exams:

1. Take excellent notes, and pretend you have to present that same material to another class next period. I bet you you will take careful notes and write down all the salient points that the prof is making. You won't be able to field any questions, but you can probably present the material. This is the most important way to roll, when taking any class. Let the smoke rise from your writing or typing. The importance of this one habit cannot be overemphasized.

2. Underline or highlight significant portions or concepts in your text book, remembering the areas or concepts that the professor has emphasized.

3. Pay attention to and be consistent with your self-care foundation of sleep, wake, meals, and exercise, so you can be in the best possible physical and mental shape for this test.

4. Tell yourself the truth about the upcoming test, and be reasonable about it. For instance, "The truth is, I've done well on previous tests, and I have studied well and continue to study well for this test. The reasonable thing that I will do fine on this test, because of my hard work and study, and my attention to self-care. I can arrive at this test in peace, and I can have a voice. I don't have to leave ____ville (insert your name) to do so."

Work-Life Balance

It is vitally important to have a clear demarcation between the professional part of our day, and the personal part of our day. So, when you are done with your work for the day (and if your work continues on into the evening, you need to re-think that. More on this in a second). When you are done with your work for the day, fully take off your professional hat, hang it up, fully open the door to the personal part of your day, fully close the door behind you (resist the urge to check work emails and such), and fully put on your personal life hat, and fully enter in to the personal part of your day.

This is so important, to have a clear demarcation between work and personal life. If you happen to have a job that requires you to continue to work into the evening, even after you've already spent a full day on the job, *it's time to consider getting a different job.* That job will lead to burnout, it will continue to disrupt your personal and family life, and will ultimately become a wedge between you and your partner.

We are all free to move about the occupational landscape; free to explore options; free to select a career track or position that is congruent with our values, personal goals in life, convictions and beliefs, and passions in life. Try to place yourself in a career track or job that allows you to have *a healthy work-life balance.*

This is in your top circle.

And yes, it is quite all right to communicate with your team that you value your personal time, and that you will not answer emails and texts when not working. Then give yourself permission to fully take off your professional hat, and fully put on your personal hat, and then fully immerse yourself in your personal time. This is an example of what I call a general boundary—a basic limit that we place on ourselves, that is very healthy for us, and which sometimes directly involves other people.

You are an architect of your time and roles. Try to make healthy decisions for yourself, because these decisions will also impact the people you care about in your life.

You should not be working 60 or 70 hours in a week. That is a recipe for severe anxiety, decline in health, and relational demise.

Be good to yourself. There are plenty of careers and jobs out there that *are* actually conducive for a healthy work-life balance. *Pick one.*

"Do it, Mon!"

Parenting One's Parents

It's just a matter of time for some of us. The tables sometimes turn, and now we get to provide for, guide, safeguard, and facilitate the health and happiness of our parents. In some cases the child becomes the parent, and we get to "give back" in a meaningful way.

Sometimes when an individual is coming into the sunset years, they arrive at what I call the "Existential 'No.'" What I mean is, sometimes a person has a great deal of turmoil or internal turbulence because they realize they are getting older, and yet they haven't accomplished what they wanted to accomplish, or they have unfinished business in terms of regrets or even passions that they have not been able to "be about."

It is so important to facilitate our older parents' ability to have "integrity versus despair" in their present experience (borrowing from Erik Erikson). Integrity includes acceptance, a sense of wholeness, lack of regret, having peace, having wisdom, and having a sense of success. This is a whole lot better than looking back on life with feelings of regret, shame, or disappointment.

Yes, you can help your older parents to "be about" something that is important to them. You can help them to plan meaningful activities, and to be intentional about their time. And you yourself can strike the balance between acceptance and emphatic economy of time, when planning activities and get-togethers with them.

We can help our parents to *finish strong.*

Post-work Scenario

I prefer to refer to retirement as a "Post-work Scenario" because this is less demeaning, less potentially demoralizing, and it hints at proactivity. So often people tend to decline in health and overall wellness and vitality in retirement. This need not be.

So if you, or someone you know, is getting ready to retire (or you already have), *listen up.*

It is so important to be intentional about planning for retirement. You have to take your personal and familial needs, personality, and lifestyle into consideration when planning a "Post-work Scenario." It does not have to be a decline or demise. It can be *even better now, because you can focus on what's most important to you.*

Plan in such a way that you can hit the ground running, with a *similar activity level and similar engagement* to that which has been going on for some time. This is good and this is important for us. Sure, you can have more free time and explore more and even relax more in your "Post-work Scenario." But you can be even MORE intentional about what you plan for yourself, and even MORE congruent with who you are, and how you are put together in terms of passions and aspirations.

**This phase of your life can be
the BEST part of your life!
You can get ALL THE IMPORTANT STUFF DONE NOW!**

FINISH STRONG!

With this in mind, I recommend the following aspects/components to be present in your "Post work Scenario":

1. Research and exploration that are either personally or professionally meaningful for you.

2. Seminar/training attendance.

3. Outdoor activities that are planned and intentional.

4. Ongoing "Intentional Set Routine" that includes self-care foundation of sleep, wake, meals and exercise, in addition to any important appointments, get-togethers, quality time with partner or others, and recreational pursuits.

5. Bonding experiences and trips with partner, if appropriate.

6. Variety.

If you have a partner, it's good to start putting your "Post-work Scenario" together with your partner, so that you can plan together. Also, if appropriate, strategize with your partner about the timing of your "Post-work Scenario."

It is so important to have a smooth transition into this "Post-work Scenario," with a *similar level of overall engagement and activity happening* even after your regular work time is done.

Only more meaningful.

---

88. https://www.intelligent.com/best-free-career-tests-and-quizzes/#:~:text=Truity%20%20Career

%20Personality%20Profiler,and%20a%20Photo%20Career%20Quiz

EMBRACE THE PROCESS

For many years I balked at the idea of a "process." I didn't like it one bit. I guess there's just enough Choleric in me to want to be done with it, anyway! Get that thing behind me, and plow forward. Forget that silly process, just get it behind me.

Yeah, right.

Thankfully, I have since learned to actually *embrace* the process, and I must say that life is a lot more smooth and manageable.

Incremental Resolution

Everything is a process. I mean just about everything, from brushing our teeth, to taking a shower, to putting one's shoes on. Yes, even when picking up my water bottle, and taking a drink of water. I first have to have the acknowledgement that I am thirsty. Then I have to think "I need a drink of water." Then I have to turn my head in the direction of my water bottle. Then I have to reach out my arm in the direction of my water bottle. I have to make sure my hand is open, and not a closed fist. I then have to work against gravity, and pick up said water bottle, and bring it towards my mouth, and finally drink.

It's a silly process, and it happens quite fast. But it's an important process nonetheless.

Not only is just about everything we engage in throughout the day a process, but *we* are all *in process* as well; every one of us. Nobody is perfect, and not one of us has "arrived." We are all *in process.* This is not only the case for us developmentally or existentially. Every system inside of us is also a process, and (usually) happens over and over again, routinely and consistently. And of course when we are very young we grow quickly and the changes are obvious. Then throughout the years we have the maturing process (I think this sounds better than "aging").

Think of the mentors or helpful people in your life who have guided you, encouraged you, and helped you along life's path. If you were to sit each of these people down, and ask each of them if they have "arrived," I am sure that every one of them would laugh, and say something like, "Oh, don't ask me that, don't go there, no, no, I am still learning, I am still growing, I'm on a journey, I'm learning from you right now! No, I haven't arrived, but it's okay."

Think of some of the powerful thought leaders and movers and shakers in society, in terms of insights and general helpfulness to others. I'm thinking of Mother Teresa, Gandhi, Zig Ziglar, Tony Robbins, etc. If you were to sit each of these individuals down, and were to ask them if they have "arrived," their responses would probably be similar to those of your mentors, above. I imagine Mother Teresa would say, as she already has said, "Intense love does not measure, it just gives[89]....Our progress in holiness depends on God and ourselves—on God's grace and on our will to be holy[90]."

I imagine Gandhi would perhaps say it a bit differently, but I am certain that he would not think of himself as "arriving" at perfection. Indeed, we already know his view: "Live as if you were to die tomorrow. Learn as if you were to live forever.....believing as I do in the theory of reincarnation, I live in the hope that if not in this birth, in some other birth I shall be able to hug all of humanity in friendly embrace[91]."

Try to think of yourself as *in process, on a journey, always learning, always growing.* And it's helpful to remind yourself that you are in process, when you are down on yourself, or shaming yourself.

With this in mind, try to be decent with yourself, and reasonable. After all, you probably try to be decent and reasonable with others, right? Try to extend the same courtesies to yourself as you do to others. If you didn't follow through with something that is very important to you, don't view it as a failure, but rather as a learning opportunity. That's all it is. You can do better tomorrow.

I recommend that you adopt the principle of "Incremental Resolution" in which you realize that every person and indeed all of life is "in process," and that it is all right to "tackle one meaningful piece of a task or project for today, and to be satisfied with it."

Think about it. When a general contractor gets a contract for a huge apartment complex, that contractor usually has a budget in place. That contractor is getting personnel in place —plumbers, electricians, framers, etc. That contractor has a budget with which to work. But at present that contractor is getting the big Tonka toys out there, moving dirt around. That contractor is getting the surveyors out there as well. That contractor knows that the lay of the land needs to be just right, so that this huge structure can be secure and viable. This is where the focus is at present. It's all about the foundation right now.

That contractor is not yet thinking about the roof, and he/she is not ordering shingles for the roof just yet.

You can't put shingles on a foundation, and

you can't put frosting on dough.

It is a process. Even cleaning a room or eating a meal involves a process. So be intentional about this current piece or phase of the task or project, pour yourself into it fully, and do your best with this particular piece or phase. *Embrace the process.*

Not a bad idea to add this notion to your short list of truisms. Everyone should have one—a short list of truisms. This one can be "Everything is a process, including myself, but I can pour myself fully into this piece of the process, and I'm okay with it."

Try to have this basic stance: "I'm moving forward, I'm in a Renaissance, I'm exploring, strategizing, planning, learning, building, reflecting, preparing, and pouring myself fully into this piece of the process."

Ahhhh....

But this one piece could be the most important piece of this process, because it will set the tone for all that follows. And you never know what else in your life *will be set in motion* by doing extremely well *this current piece of the process.*

For example, let's say that you are looking for a new job, but you are not sure how to go about it, and the thought of changing jobs (or obtaining a job) is overwhelming to you. With "Incremental Resolution" in mind, you can carefully, intentionally submit a resume and cover letter to one position/company per week, starting in January, and then engage in a follow-up phone call one week later for each position for which you have applied. With this gradual, methodical process you can *incrementally be about the realization of your goal* of procuring a meaningful job. Keep it simple, and focus on one submission at a time. Spread it out. Pour yourself fully into this piece of the process. Embrace the process.

The net result of this way of operating is peace, and stability. Keep in mind that when we utilize our "Intentional Set Routine," spreading a project or large goal out over time is so much easier. With the above goal in mind, for instance, it is conceivable that you will have applied to and followed up with 24 meaningful positions which you have carefully chosen for yourself—all by July 1! Not a bad way to go about obtaining a job. And don't be surprised if even in the first month you are receiving email invitations for interviews.

Incremental Resolution. Little by little, poco a poco. If you can give yourself permission to *embrace the process*, and to pour yourself fully into *this piece of the process*, great things will happen, and you will become an architect of your present-tense.

> **It is generally more peaceful,**
> **culminating in a longer lifespan,**
> **and resulting in less anxiety**
> **if we can pace ourselves,**
> **break tasks up into baby steps,**
> **and embrace the process.**

It is okay to surrender to the process, embrace the process, and to be humble and submit to what you have planned for yourself. You can say 'Yes, Sensei, I will do what you are leading me to do. Wax on, wax off....'"

Renaissance

You may remember from European History class that the Renaissance was an incredible time of invention, exploration, a blossoming of thought and skill and knowledge and architectural pursuits. Music just took off during the Renaissance.

Well, this is how it can be for you and me right here, right now. Try to think of your present life as a *Renaissance,* and that everything is new, and you are writing your experience by living your experience. You are being fully invested in the moment.

You give yourself permission to look….

> **"through the lens of what can enhance
> me rather than hurt me,
> what can sharpen me rather than demoralize me,
> what can promote peace and wellness rather
> than destroy or depress me,
> and how to look at everyone in my life
> as my personal assistants,
> who are simply there to help me move forward in life."**

You have the attitude of someone who is moving forward, someone who is being intentional, someone who is an architect and operating within the infrastructure of an "Intentional Set Routine." You are a Renaissance person, and you are free to move about your life.

Try to have this basic stance: "I'm moving forward, I'm in a Renaissance, I'm exploring, strategizing, planning, learning, building, reflecting, preparing, and pouring myself fully into this piece of the process."

Pre-Renaissance Goals

With the above in mind, try to set aside an entire morning, perhaps on the weekend. It's nice to have a good night's sleep beforehand, and a healthy breakfast, so you are wide awake and alert. Set aside en entire morning.

During the first half of this morning, brainstorm with yourself and try to write down a handful of *Personal, Professional,* and *Health and Wellness* goals that you would like to be about, and like to accomplish over the remainder of the year. All you need is two or three goals in each category.

Now, the best time to engage in this activity is during December, so you can start off the new year in peace. But you can do this any time of the year. Just contemplate the remaining months and weeks in the year, and work with that.

I originally designed this as a healthy, more productive alternative to New Year's resolutions, which can often be like ropes of sand that disintegrate, as time moves on. These are abrupt resolutions that often are just free-floating ideas and which can sometimes be difficult to actually accomplish. But this is a better way to plan and strategize.

Try to view this "Pre-Renaissance" and as preparatory time for either a brand new year, or preparatory time for the remainder of the year, and preparation for newness. Ask yourself, "How far have I come, and where would I like to go?"

Going through a thoughtful, reflective process like this can help you to have a peaceful, smooth segue into the new year, or into the remainder of your year.

So, start with *Personal* goals for yourself. It can be anything that is important for you personally. It can be finishing a book (that was one of mine). Or it can be a relocation, or something that will help your relationship or marriage. It can be having your truck overhauled. It can be important dental work. What matters is that this is personal in nature, and very important to you. All you need is a handful, but you can have a few more than that, no problem.

Then brainstorm about the *Professional* goals that you would like to be about and to accomplish over the year, or over the remainder of the year. This can be obtaining a meaningful job, or starting or finishing a degree or certificate program. It can be a book you want to read to enhance yourself professionally, or a new language you want to learn in order to facilitate communication in your new job. It can be a new skill of some kind, or a new piece of understanding that will help you to move forward professionally. A professional goal can be anything that enhances us in terms of our work duties, our efficiency, our level of contribution, or even a goal which allows us to think about career options. All you need is a handful, but you can have a few more than that, no problem.

Then brainstorm about the *Health and Wellness* goals that you would like to be about and to accomplish over the year, or over the remainder of the year. This can be getting to a certain fitness level, getting down to a particular weight level, becoming buff and stronger, enhancing your dietary habits so that they are optimal and healthy, or even preparing for a 5k run or half-marathon or triathlon. It can be enhancing your spiritual life in some way, or learning to be much more consistent with good sleep habits. All you need is a handful, but you can have a few more than that, no problem.

Pre-Renaissance Strategic Gameplanning

When you believe that you are finished with your important *Personal, Professional* and *Health and Wellness* goals, you can use the second half of this block of time to strategize and write down a series of *strategic baby steps* that you can connect to each of your goals. When I personally did this the first time, I just used my phone notes, then I think I transferred things to a Word document. You can have your goals first, then take each category—start with your personal goals—and start thinking of some baby steps you can put in there under your first personal goal, using bullet points.

You can do the same with each of your personal goals, then your professional goals, and finally your health and wellness goals.

Now some of these baby steps will be ongoing, such as "exercising three times a week" as a baby step for a health and wellness goal of "Get to 185 pounds by December 1." Yes, that baby step is happening on an ongoing basis. Other baby steps might be time limiters, such as "Finish the layout and outline for this project by April 1" for a professional goal that involves completion of a large project. Or "Brainstorm with self about four career options" can be the first baby step for a larger goal of beginning training for a career.

This is "Strategic Gameplanning" and it can be challenging, so don't be afraid to involve your partner or someone else who knows you well, if you need help coming up with these baby steps.

Some of your goals might be short-term, and so you might have just a handful of baby steps. Other goals might be huge, and involve of necessity a lot more baby steps. But either way this "Strategic Gameplanning" allows you to **embrace the process, pace yourself, and be specific and intentional in every area of your life.**

Baby steps are peaceful, not scary. And you can easily incorporate your baby steps right into your "Intentional Set Routine." That baby step can become *yet another next right thing,* that you immerse yourself in, catch yourself doing something right in (check it off), and follow through with for the right reasons—this is important, this is healthy, this is in-line with wellness, this is a form of self-respect, this will help me move forward in life, etc.—*and NOT based on how you feel.*

It's just another next right thing (sounds like a song I might have to write). So, yes, this "Tripartite of Renaissance" (what I call it) builds on your "Intentional Set Routine," and the latter helps you to embrace the process in every area of your life—one baby step at a time, one day at a time. *Incremental Resolution.*

Some baby steps might be placed several months later, but they will be waiting for you when you get there. No big deal. I will give you an example. For this book, I had different aspects of what needed to be done laid out for myself with a series of baby steps. One of my baby steps was using two specific nights of the week for completing chapters. Another baby step was getting everything formatted and ready to transfer by a certain date. For music projects (yes, I am a singer-songwriter, and have been involved in music my whole life), my baby steps have been completing one song in Pro Tools at a time in my studio, being reasonable about the spacing of these baby steps.

So you see, you can use strategic baby steps for any goal that you are trying to accomplish. Baby steps help us to slow down, to pace ourselves, to be mindful and energized about *what is before us today.* And remember, this one piece of this particular process *might be the most important piece in the entire process, setting the tone for everything that follows.*

So do your best with each baby step, because each one is full of significance.

It's Both-And, Not Either-Or

So often we create false dichotomies for ourselves, and greatly limit ourselves from being productive and having a voice. We box ourselves in with our own limiting thoughts. But most often it is *Both-And* rather than *Either-Or.*

Even though a man believes that the sale of a house and an ongoing divorce process are both taking longer than he wanted or expected, this person can still move forward with his personal goals, professional goals, and health and wellness goals that are most important to him, WHILE these two processes are finishing up.

This man is personally responsible for only a few aspects of the sale of the house, and the divorce process, and these can easily be turned into baby steps, and treated much the same as any other next right thing in his week. It would be prudent for this individual to take some time to reflect on what he wants to accomplish in the new year, or remainder of the year, and to develop strategic baby steps for each of these goals, using this time as a Pre-Renaissance.

He can give himself credit for following through with important aspects, such as keeping the house in relatively good condition for people to view it, and responding to emails and attending meetings regarding the divorce, at times. *These two processes will have an end point,* and he is free to plan for meaningful personal, professional and health and wellness goals; THIS should be his true focus at this time.

Do not be limited by defeating thoughts and conclusions. Tell yourself the truth about your situation, have a voice in it, and be reasonable. Focus on what is before you, not on what is behind you, nor on what is extemporaneous and gradually fading away.

When you are in a Renaissance, everything is new. Life is full of hope, and full of wonder.

Summary

Having a set routine in place, and having a series of baby steps connected with your major personal goals, professional goals, and health and wellness goals will help you to not only have a peaceful segue into the new year (or remainder of the year), but will also help you to be far more "on track" with what's important to you, while embracing the process.

It is generally more peaceful, culminating in a longer lifespan, and resulting in less anxiety if we can pace ourselves, break tasks up into baby steps, and embrace the process. Picture yourself as being in a personal Renaissance, with everything new, and a life that is full of discovery and opportunity. Remember that you can view everyone in your life at present as your personal assistants, who are simply there to help you move forward in life. Remember that there is peace when we embrace the process. It helps us to pace ourselves, to avoid jumping ahead of ourselves, and to have a rewarding and wonderful experience in all areas of our lives.

---

89. Mother Theresa, Mother Theresa Quotes. (n.d.). Retrieved December 26, 2022 from BrainyQuote.com. https://www.brainyquote.com/quotes/mother theresa 108724

90. Mother Theresa. (n.d.). Retrieved December 26, 2022 from AZQuotes.com. https://www.azquotes.com/quote/863217

91. Mahatma Gandhi. (n.d.). Retrieved December 26, 2022 from AZQuotes.com. https://www.azquotes.com/quote/603660

THROW A ROCK IN A LAKE

When I was a boy, I often spent my free time either fishing or looking for frogs and tadpoles or other critters, walking around in nature, playing baseball and football, climbing trees, etc. I often threw rocks in lakes, and I often skipped flat stones off of the water, seeing how many times it could skip, and how far it could go before it finally dove into the water.

Perhaps you did that too when younger. Maybe you still do it. Good for you.

When my children were younger, I would teach them how to skip stones off of the water, thus passing on the tradition. Something I noticed even when young was that if I threw a large stone in the water, it created many ripples that went in all directions.

When you throw a rock in a lake, little ripples start spreading out from the point of impact. Those little ripples actually go a long ways, even though they get weaker, little by little.

> The point is, all it takes sometimes is one little tweak;
> one little change;
> starting one little thing;
> implementing one little action
> — *to completely revamp one's life for the good.*

Every action has a reverberating impact. It will automatically impact several other areas of our lives. You never know what you are setting in motion, simply by *doing extremely well one next right thing.*

It is important to START ONE NEW THING, to INTENTIONALLY PLACE IT IN OUR ROUTINE, and to ACTUALLY DO IT.

This involves energy and motivation and follow-through, which are foreign to the depressed mind, and basically incompatible with it. In fact, when we intentionally do something new, it can completely nullify feelings of low self-worth, low motivation, and low interest. It jolts the psyche like a high-powered battery charger jolts a dead battery.

Being intentional and starting something new is especially important for anyone experiencing a difficult transition or life adjustment, because transition times are bountiful seed beds for personal growth and change.

Take a moment and go through the following exercise. You may even want to write some things down on a piece of paper. It can be very meaningful:

What Do I Want to Start?

Possibilities:

Pick One:

When Will I Start This?:

Where Will I Write it Down? How Will I Hold Myself to it?:

It is best for your new idea/activity to be consistent with your personal values and goals in life. This way it will be very meaningful for you.

Personal Influence

We are always impacting people, whether we like or not. We rarely leave anyone in a neutral state. We are either enhancing people's lives in some way, or we are dragging them down in some way.

We must be mindful of the influence and impact that we are constantly having on other people around us. If we have children, we have to be mindful that we are constantly modeling for our children how to live, how to make difficult decisions, how to handle stressors and difficult times, how to communicate, how to cope, whether or not to self-medicate when times get rough, etc. They are absorbing everything they see and hear and experience, and all of this is being normalized for them.

We need to be intentional both with our actions, and with our modeling. Because this is all anyone else ever sees: what we actually do.

Be the Best YOU that You Can Be

Be the best YOU that you can be, and try to avoid comparing

yourself to anyone else. You do not need to be another person. You can admire someone's work ethic, or attitude, or their productivity, but when you start comparing yourself that person, you are getting in the weeds, and it will generally lead to anxiety. Comparing yourself to someone is a distortion of something good, in this case admiring or appreciating someone. You do not need to be someone else; you need to be comfortable in your own shoes, and be the best (fill in your name) that you can be—not the best so-and-so. Be simply the best *you*. This is the way of wellness. This is the way of peace.

Compete with *your* baseline; not with others.

So, think of your preferred career track and actual preferred position or role. BE THAT PERSON in the present tense. Ask yourself, "How would *that person* carry him/herself? How would *that person dress?* What kind of attitude and mindset would *that person* have? Endeavor to have the mindset and attitude of that role, and to arrange your current workspace or office similarly to what it will be once you are in that role—even if your current situation is a basement or a bedroom. This way of operating will help you to derive much more meaning from your current experience, and will help you to be much more intentional about everything you do. Think of yourself in that future role, and ask yourself, "How would *that person* handle this situation? How would *that person* communicate and interact with others? How would *that person* organize his/her time? How would *that person* emphasize self-care and work/life balance?" Be *that person*.

I encourage you to be an architect of your present tense, and to allow a Renaissance to take place in your life in which you choose what is important to you, you choose how you interact with people, and you choose the roles you wish to have in the present tense, and moving forward.

DAVID D. SULLIVAN

How We Define Ourselves

We all have to be very careful with how we define ourselves, and to avoid defining ourselves too narrowly. I will refer to the animated movie *Spirit* as a case-in-point of how someone, in this case a young stallion, can sometimes find oneself defining oneself based on present circumstances in life. If you have seen the movie *Spirit,* this will be very familiar to you. In this movie, this young stallion has everything going on for himself. He's young, he can run free in the wind, he has a mare that likes him, he has his family all around him. Things are looking up for this young stallion.

Then this horse gets captured by a group of men who are putting in a railroad over the mountains, and he gets thrown in with a whole bunch of other horses who have been captured. He gets turned into a slave horse, a work horse. And these men are not very nice. They are overworking these horses, forcing them to pull heavy machinery and logs, and the like. These horses are being mistreated, poorly fed, seldom watered, and some of them are getting sick, and some of them are dying.

After a while this stallion starts becoming depressed, and all he can see is his present set of circumstances. It's all bleak. He's just a slave horse, a work horse, getting weaker by the day. In time he forgets that he is a young stallion with a mare back home, and a family that misses him terribly. He forgets who he is, and all he can see are his circumstances. He starts to define himself by those horrible circumstances.

Then the Brian Adams song comes on (there are Brian Adams songs throughout this movie), and it's called "Remember Who You Are." That horse starts to remember that he is actually *not* a slave horse and *not* a work horse. He starts to remember that he is *actually a young stallion running in the wind, with a mare back home, and a family that misses him...*

And that horse breaks up out of there, and frees a lot of other horses as well, and causes a wheelbarrow full of trouble and mischief for that mean work crew. Yeah, he sets them back a ways. And he returns home to his mare and to his family, in peace, and in gratitude.

It's a great movie. You know, we do that too. We sometimes define ourselves by our circumstances, or our condition, or whatever, and we *forget who we are.*

Be so careful with how you define yourself. Each of us is much more than a particular diagnosis, or disability, or habit, or misstep or failure, or addiction, or overspending issue, incarceration, or, as in *Spirit*, a very unfortunate situation.

> **Allow yourself to see yourself as much more than the circumstances surrounding you.**
> **Your values, dreams, personal goals, professional goals, convictions, beliefs, passions, talents, insights, skills and interests are also a part of who you are,**
> **and these areas of your life need to have a voice; they need to speak!**

So, be intentional about these other areas of your life, and plan carefully activities and events that can broaden your experience, and increase the overall quality of your life.

You are more than your bad habit, more than your incorrect decision, more than your disability, more than your addiction, more than your upbringing, more than your job loss, more than your disease, and certainly more than your current situation.

Any new thing you start, or any instance of following through with what's important to you, will have a reverberating impact on every other area of your life, and *will have a ripple effect, and possibly set in motion other meaningful activities and endeavors.*

So yes, take some time and set up your "Pre-Renaissance" baby steps so that you can "be about" and give a voice to your creative endeavors and meaningful plans, thereby embracing the process. And don't forget to intentionally place creative time and musical time in your "Intentional Set Routine," if appropriate, with specific days and times, so that this creative aspect of your life does not bleed over into other important time-sensitive activities.

Be That Person

So, think of the person you would like to become. Maybe you want to be a better husband and father. Or wife and mother. Maybe you want to prepare for your new career, and perhaps you will be finished with training or schooling in a few months, or perhaps a year-and-a-half. Or, maybe you would like to enhance the way you carry yourself at work, and actually want to have a voice or be more respected.

Whatever person you are wanting to become, BE THAT PERSON. How would THAT person go about their day? How would that person plan? What kind of attitude would that person have? How would that person communicate with others? What kind of self-care habits would that person adopt? How would that person carry him/herself? How would THAT person make decisions? How would that guy move about and order his time? How would a typical day look like for that gal? How will basic surroundings and theme be different at that time? How determined will THAT person be?"

Be that person now, and you will be able to have a peaceful segue into your graduate program, or prepare for your career, or prepare for a new job or new location. Or even an upcoming new family situation or return to your family. Move and act and make decisions like *that person.*

If you are planning to be an executive leader, then act and move and plan like an executive leader. If you are planning to be a counselor or some other helping profession, then act and move and plan like that professional helper. How would THAT person plan a week, and how would THAT person act and dress, and spend a weekend? If you are preparing to be a nurse, or PA or any other allied-health profession, then act and move and plan like that medical person. How would THAT person do things? What kind of relationships and friendships would THAT person have?

> **Intentionally plan your week, your activities, your time, your interactions, your sleep/wake/meals/exercise in a way that**
>
> *approximates* **the** *person you are wanting to become.*
>
> **Institute whatever changes and adjustments that are necessary and appropriate for approximating those of THAT person you want to become.**
>
> **Be that person.**

The Significance of Today

It's good to have a daily approach to life. I just want to remind you that even though we are often contemplating the future, and forecasting, and even though I encourage readers to set up their "Intentional Set Routine" with one week at a time....

> **It's not really about three or four days, or even the week. All we have to work with is actually TODAY.**
>
> **Ahhhh, "but I can embrace the process and engage in baby steps TODAY."**

> So, surrender to the process, embrace the process,
> be humble and submit to what you
> have planned for yourself,
> and say 'Yes, Sensei, I will do what you are leading me to do.
> Wax on, wax off....'"

> All we *actually* have to work with
>
> is TODAY.

Think about it. Most of the incredible inventions and discoveries in history have come together in the course of a day. Yes, most of these were processes, for certain. But for the most part, throughout time *it has all come together to fruition and to climax IN THE COURSE OF A DAY.*

> Each day is incredibly significant,
> and, if lived well and authentically,
> has the potential to set in motion other well-lived days.

Try to be mindful of the importance of today, and try to use your time as efficiently and meaningfully as you can. Get the most out of a day, take something as far as you can take it, today. Resist the urge to overcrowd or overwhelm yourself, and remember to embrace the process. Do the best you can with *this piece of the process, today.*

Making one important change, or implementing one healthy activity will result in a ripple effect that will undoubtedly impact other areas in your life, and will set into motion other wonderful developments.

Any new thing you start, or any instance of following through with what's important to you will have a reverberating impact on every other area of your life. It will have a ripple effect, and possibly set in motion other meaningful activities and endeavors.

Watch the Ripples

When you throw a rock in the lake, and start something new—whether it be a new language, a new skill, a new healthy habit or routine, a new challenging activity of some kind, or even starting to actually have a voice—it will indeed have a reverberating impact on other areas of your life. Do not be surprised if your activity level and success level are on the increase in other parts of your life.

Success breeds success.

Movement engenders further movement.

So throw a rock in the lake.

Start something new.

Then watch the ripples . . .

OCD, PESKY TICS, SKIN-PICKING, HOARDING AND CUTTING

Obsessive-Compulsive Disorder (OCD) is a serious disorder impacting between 1% and 2% of the population. According to the DSM-5, the criteria of OCD are as follows:

- Presence of obsessions and/or compulsions
- Symptoms are recognized as excessive, unreasonable, and absurd
- Symptoms cause marked distress
- Intact reality testing
- Symptoms are present at least an hour a day

Obsessions are unwanted thoughts, images, urges and fears that greatly interfere with a person's life and functioning. *Compulsions* are outward physical actions or inward mental attempts to minimize the unwanted thoughts, images, urges and fears that are distressing.

Examples of obsessions: Fearing that you will contract a deadly disease or pass one on to others inadvertently, believing that someone will break into your home, worrying that you might cut yourself or stab someone else when handling a kitchen knife, stressing that your partner will never be your ideal partner, etc.

Examples of compulsions: Washing your hands 15 times so that you will not contaminate anyone, checking to see if the front door is locked several times and taking pictures of the lock, avoiding all knives or asking someone else to use a knife to cut up some vegetables rather than you, being over-clingy with partner and emphasizing partner's positive attributes, avoiding all schools and all young people, etc.

There are several subtypes of OCD:

- Contamination OCD
- Harm OCD
- Sexual Orientation OCD
- Pedophilia OCD
- Relationship OCD
- "Just Right" OCD
- Scrupulosity/Religious OCD
- Hit-and-Run OCD
- Real Events OCD

The OCD Cycle

A person has obsessive thoughts (such as fear of contaminating someone). These obsessive thoughts, urges, and images result in distress, anxiety, fear, and often physical symptoms. Then the person engages in compulsive behaviors and rituals to try and *alleviate* the distress, anxiety and fear (such as washing the hands 15 times—physical, or seeking reassurance from others—mental). But *the relief sought is only temporary and brief in nature,* and the compulsive behavior actually serves to *negatively reinforce* the entire cycle, so that it ends up starting all over gain very soon. It's a never-ending cycle of obsessions, distress/fear, compulsions, temporary relief, obsessions, distress/fear, compulsions, temporary relief, etc. Ad infinitum.

ERP Breaks the OCD Cycle

In ERP (Exposure Response Prevention) therapy, we seek to stop the OCD cycle in between the obsessive thinking, and the actual compulsive behavior.

In ERP, we learn to *live with the distress, discomfort, and fear,*

to coexist with it,

to tolerate it.

We learn to tolerate the discomfort, the distress, the anxiety, the fear. And as we do so, *habituation* happens. We find that little-by-little we are not feeling nearly as distressed and fearful, in the midst of the uncomfortable situation.

Habituation happens as we give ourselves opportunities to *live alongside* the fear and anxiety. ERP therapy is the top methodology for minimizing OCD symptoms, with a proven track record.

>Exposure Hierarchy

In ERP therapy, we try to design an *Exposure Hierarchy*, which is a simple list of potentially fear or anxiety-causing tasks or experiences. This list starts out with several easier, more manageable tasks that expose you gradually to distress and discomfort. As you have some successes with several easier exposures, you can then try an exposure that is a bit more distress-causing. The "toughest" tasks would be towards the top of this Exposure Hierarchy, or *Fear Ladder.* You are working your way up the hierarchy, little by little.

For instance, a person with *Contamination OCD* might have an Exposure Hierarchy that looks something like this:

Exposure and Related Distress Level

Eat item of food dropped on public restroom floor 10

Eat item of food dropped on personal kitchen floor 9

Touch public toilet seat, no hand wash 9

Sit with a small, full trashcan in your lap, for 7 minutes 9

Touch home toilet seat, no hand wash 8

Touch the bottom of tub or shower, no hand wash 7

Put hands in kitchen sink, no hand wash 5

Touch home bathroom door knob, no hand wash 4

Imagine touching toilet seat, no hand wash 2

As you can see, the easier exposures on on the bottom. As the person gets used to *living alongside the discomfort and fear,* they gain confidence. Little successes, and understanding that the exposure is *not nearly as bad as I thought it would be.*

This is good learning. This is habituating.

Then you can tackle the next exposure up on the list, and see how it goes. See how you feel while in the midst of that discomfort and strain. During and after each exposure, notice how you are feeling, notice what's around you, and try to be aware of any sensory input.

It's a good idea to write down what you have learned, after each exposure. This is important learning. You will notice that you are gradually making progress, and that your level of distress and fear gradually decrease, as you engage in these planned exposures.

Over time, you will notice that you don't have the same

thoughts and worries as previous. You will also notice that even when you do have such thoughts, it will not often lead to feelings of panic and crisis, as it did before.

These are good gains. And they happen as you learn to incrementally tolerate the discomfort and distress.

Here are just a few tips to keep in mind:

1. Practice prioritizing values over fears, leaning into anxiety, and doing the opposite of your urges related to safety, behaviors or compulsions.

2. Remember that "discomfort is not disaster."

3. While in the midst of an exposure exercise:

- As you start, write down what your stress/fear level is, 1-10.
- Do a little spot check every few minutes on what your basic anxiety level is, 1-10.
- Keep track of any urges you are having in the moment.
- Ask yourself, "What can I do for response prevention?" ("Thoughts are just thoughts, emotions are just emotions, and I am just a mere wave in the ocean").
- Ask yourself, "What thoughts am I having right now?"
- And be aware of when you are basically at 50% of your original distress and anxiety level.

Regarding fearful and distressing thoughts, think of these thoughts as little birds with wings, and remind yourself that these thoughts will soon fly away if you can just sit with it for a bit.

That's what birdies do.

Remember that there are two kinds of success, when engaging in these exposure exercises. If you find that your overall stress/

fear level has decreased during the exposure exercise, that is a success. But it's also a success to simply *sit with the distress, tolerating it, and smile and wave...*

The mere fact that you are sitting with it, and not trying to help yourself and give into what OCD is telling you to do— *this is a true success, even if your distress level stays the same throughout the time, and doesn't decrease.* So, don't be hard on yourself. Just sitting with it constitutes a success.

Remember that OCD is very mean, and very opportunistic. It picks on anything important to us. So, if you have a partner or are in a relationship, explain this to your partner. Explain that you are trying to recover from OCD, and at times it may appear that you are out of sync with yourself, but it's all part of the healing process. You are learning to help yourself, and you are making good progress. Explain this to your partner. And give your partner kudos for not giving you reassurance, when OCD is telling you to seek reassurance.

Your partner or family member can help you in this process of healing, if they have a basic understanding of the OCD cycle, and what you are needing from them.

OCD and Values

The OCD monster likes to pick on what's most important to us. We can start thinking of what could happen, or what might happen, and some of these thoughts are very scary indeed. Some OCD thoughts can violate a person's values, taking them hostage. Then in the midst of these distressing thoughts, you might feel ashamed or guilty, or that you must be a horrible person, because of what you are thinking. It is hideous.

For instance, OCD can take a person's earlier victimization and abuse and superimpose them onto the present, and try to convince a person that he/she will in turn be a predator towards children, even though this is totally against what the person believes. OCD always take us in a direction *away* from our actual values, and what is most important to us in life.

So, I say, let your values actually have a voice. Engage your fears, and face your distress. As you get used to living alongside uncertainty, discomfort and fear, you are keeping yourself from resorting to your compulsive behavior. You do not need to engage in these rituals and behaviors, because you are no longer trying to *fix* the distressing thought, or to *escape* from it.

Try to look at your compulsive behaviors and rituals as *coping mechanisms that have long since worn out their usefulness.* They are no longer needed, and they never actually helped anyway. Let them go.

Talk back to that OCD monster. Tell him, "I can beat you. You are evil, and controlling. But I'm going to keep starving you, as I learn to sit with my fears and distresses. I am no longer going to feed you. I want you to become very thin and emaciated. You're gonna dry up and blow away. Go on, git."

Now you can live consistently with your values, and allow them to shine forth.

As for how we view ourselves, and our own self-appraisal, be truthful, valid, and reasonable. This will help you to have a voice, and will safeguard you from conceit.

Pesky Tics

I know about tics. As a young person, I had my share of them. We do the darnedest things to try and alleviate our distress or fears. Some people engage in tic behavior in order to cope with a distressful situation, or what the person thinks might happen. It's a whole bunch of extra nervous energy, and the tic behavior comes in handy in such moments, as a temporary repositioning of the fear and distress into some interesting behavior. These tics can be blinking one's eyes in a certain way or rhythm, or dragging one's feet, or vocal sounds, or hand movements. And because these behavioral antics can be annoying or seem a bit strange to others, it is common for the person engaging in these tics to be verbally, emotionally or even physically abused and made fun of by others (who are not very nice or considerate).

This can be very emotionally damaging, and it can be very demoralizing. This tic behavior can be involuntary or semi-involuntary. Some people describe a brief period of time right before the tic behavior starts. We can call these "premonitory experiences" that give the person (often a child) a "heads up" or signal that the tic is about to happen. It can be a flush feeling or tingling. It is important for the person to identify this "premonitory experience" because it will help the person to reduce the tic behavior.

One the person is aware of this signal or "premonitory experience,'" the person can be taught a "competing response" in which to engage. And what I have just described is *Habit Reversal Therapy,* which is very effective for tic behavior, and other unwanted behaviors.

For example, if a child learns to tilt his head to the right after the "premonitory experience" of tingling happens, that child can instead tilt his head to the left when this initial sensation happens. This activity helps to reverse or extinguish the tic behavior. And then from there the child can practice this competing response on his own, in-between sessions.

Habit Reversal Therapy (HRT) is very effective, and is often just as effective as medications. The person learns to have confidence, and feels empowered to practice competing responses during the week. HRT helps a person to have more control of what what she does, and how she copes.

In recent studies, there were significant reductions in tic

severity in both adults and children with Tourette Syndrome (TS) and Chronic Tic Disorders (CTDs), with the use of Habit Reversal Therapy (HRT[92]).

The three main components of HRT are:

1. Awareness Training

2. Competing Response Training

3. Social Support Training

If you struggle with tic behavior, it's going to take some patience, a lot of support, and some honest-to-goodness determination to help yourself. You are learning to *replace* unwanted tic behavior with more healthy behavior.

For example, a competing response to hair-pulling might be to ball the hands into a fist and hold them rigidly against the body. For a person who repeatedly sticks out his tongue, the person can have a competing response of pursing his lips instead. It is important to select a competing response that is an action that other people cannot usually notice.

Trichotillomania (Hair-Pulling)

Trichotillomania, also known as hair-pulling disorder, is a disorder involving the recurrent, irresistible urge to pull out hair from your scalp, eyebrows, or some other part of your body. Individuals who struggle with this disorder usually try to stop this behavior. But this is difficult to do. When the person repeatedly pulls hair from the scalp, this can cause a whole range of problems, including bald spots, which can cause significant distress, and can interfere with one's life socially and professionally. And usually the person tries to hide what has been done.

From a Habit Reversal Therapy (HRT) perspective, you try to learn how to recognize *situations* in which you are likely to pull your hair, and to identify *patterns* in conditions that lead to hair-pulling. As I mentioned above, one helpful strategy is to clinch one's fist, and maybe hold the fist close to your side. You can also use a *decoupling* technique, and simply find something else to do with your hand, rather than pulling your hair.

This will take practice, but if you remain aware and keep at it, you can actually learn to stop the hair-pulling, having *replaced* it with another, less damaging activity. You are also learning to *live alongside* the strain, the urge, the pressure you experience. You teach yourself to tolerate the discomfort and tension. You are habituating to it, and learning that it's going to be all right, and hair-pulling is not necessary.

From a Cognitive Behavioral Therapy (CBT) perspective, you try to identify the distorted thoughts and ideas (self-talk) you are having. Remember that self-talk is what we tell ourselves about a situation, and what we believe about that situation. We can definitely get into the weeds on this one, and end up resorting to an unwanted or unhealthy ritual (hair-pulling) to obtain a temporary relief from the strain and stress.

So, tell yourself the truth about the situation, have a voice in the situation (valid), and be reasonable about the situation. This is a good way to correct your self-talk, and it will usually have a calming effect on an individual, because the brain understands the simple truth, authenticity, and reason. Write down your beliefs about hair-pulling, being absolutely transparent and honest about it. Then correct those beliefs to something true, valid and reasonable.

It is important to *interrupt the cycle* with hair-pulling. Right before a person engages in hair-pulling, there is usually an itch, a tingling, an urge, or boredom, or feelings of anxiety. Take note of how you feel in this stage, before the hair-pulling happens. When a person engages in hair-pulling, there is a temporary sense of relief, and this sense of relief serves as a *reward* to the brain. And the thing about rewards is, *we like them, and want to keep them coming.*

This reward-seeking is also a big part of addiction. We have to train ourselves that we do not have to receive a reward actually. The truth is, this hair-pulling is not good for us. If we have a voice in this thing, we can find something else to do with our hand that is actually useful or at least neutral. And the reasonable thing is that if we have a voice in these moments, we can easily engage in the alternate activity. Feeling good about ourselves, and feeling *well, becomes the new reward.* There are no down sides to catching yourself doing something right. It just feels good.

But in this case, the reward is more of a byproduct of helping yourself. It isn't an end in itself, which is often what happens with hair-pulling. When you engage in an alternate, *replacement* activity, this will not keep the Trichotillomania cycle going (as does hair-pulling), but IT WILL ACTUALLY BREAK THE CYCLE, SO THAT THE HAIR-PULLING DOESN'T HAVE TO TAKE PLACE.

Again, you are learning to live alongside the strain and urges, and to tolerate the uneasiness. It's going to be all right. You are learning to do other, more healthy things with your hand. You are helping yourself. You are moving forward, refusing to be a prisoner to an unhealthy habit.

Excoriation (Skin-Picking)

The strategies for Excoriation (Skin-Picking) are similar to those above, for Trichotillomania (Hair-Pulling). Both maladaptive coping strategies (I prefer to call them that, rather than disorders) involve the use of the *hands.*

So, HRT (Habit Reversal Therapy) also works very well for Excoriation. I suggest actually a two-pronged approach for Excoriation. The habit of picking at scabs, or otherwise picking at one's skin *is a maladaptive coping strategy*, in much the same way that hair-pulling is. Both of these behaviors involve the hands (manual) and slight physical pain (which can in the moment shift one's attention away from *emotional* pain). It is important to find an *alternative coping mechanism* that is healthy, pleasurable (instead of painful), creative, and which upholds your self-respect. Secondly, it is important to reward yourself with a special meal or special activity if you don't engage in the skin-picking for two or three days. The reason for this is simple: *rewarded behavior tends to increase.*

This particular maladaptive coping mechanism—skin-picking—can be very embarrassing for the individual, and can fill an individual with shame and self-rebuke. But, as with hair-puling, skin-picking also serves as a type of *reward*, albeit temporary in nature. Sure, there's a brief reward in this habit, as there is with hair-pulling.

It is therefore important to find a *competing, replacement activity* in which to engage—one which doesn't result in shame or embarrassment or beating yourself up mentally.

I suggest that you use your "Intentional Set Routine," and that you intentionally plan *alternative activities and coping mechanisms which involve your hands.* You can beat this thing! So, here are a few ideas of activities which involve the usage of your hands, but are not injurious to you:

1. A porous rock. You can find one of these on the Internet quite easily. These are great, because you can paint the rock with interesting colors (which involves the hands), and after the paint dries you an gradually start to chisel little pieces of paint out of the little craters in the rock (which also involves

your hands). This is a lot of fun, you get to be creative, and it is very therapeutic for you, as you carefully chisel paint out of little craters. It gives you a sense of accomplishment, and generally is a positive experience. And most of the porous rock kits actually come with either paint or a little chisel, or both.

2. <u>A yo-yo</u>. Yo-yos are fun, and they come in different shapes and colors. Again, this gives you something fun to do with your hands, and also increases your manual dexterity. You can even learn to do a few tricks with your yo-yo (they aren't just for kids). I particularly like the glow-in-the-dark type.

3. <u>Paint-by-Number</u>. These are great. You don't even have to be much of an artist to enjoy one of these. You can little-by-little paint all the 9's or 7's with one color at a time. What you end up with is often a thing of beauty that you can frame, and place on a wall, in which case it would be a testimony or evidence of the progress you are making. It is really cool to see the realistic landscape, etc., come to life gradually. You will have a sense of accomplishment if you engage in this activity.

4. <u>A squeeze or therapy ball</u>. These are great. And they come in all sorts of nifty colors. You have probably seen them in doctors' offices and basically all over the place. When you feel like engaging in skin-picking, just grab your squeeze ball instead, and spend some time with it. Imagine all your anxiety just being released right into the ball, and being all squished up into tiny little dissolvable fragments. This is good imagery. Again, it's an *alternative* or *replacement* to the maladaptive coping mechanism of skin-picking (or hair-pulling).

5. <u>A deck of cards</u>. Cards are amazing. It feels good to handle them, to shuffle them, to just look at them. Neat colors and shapes and often even royalty figures to boot! It's like stepping back in time. This can be a relaxing, fun activity when you are stressed, and feel like falling back into your maladaptive coping mechanism. Play some solitaire, or "Go Fish" or "War"

or whatever you feel like playing. Involve someone else if you want.

6. <u>A Rubik's Cube</u>. Emo Rubik's invention was originally used to teach young students about 3-D spatial concepts. Rubik at the time had no idea how popular his little game would be, worldwide. This is a great way to use your hands, to use your brain (definitely cognitively stimulating), and to just enjoy yourself. And they come in many different color combinations and styles.

These are just a handful of ideas and examples of alternative, healthy activities we can do with our hands. There are many other activities that you could probably think of, but this is a good start, and something to consider.

I should mention also that for anyone who is recovering from Carpal Tunnel surgery and the like, these manual activities can help to strengthen the hands, and to improve manual dexterity (while at the same time having a relaxing effect).

You can easily have a block of time in each day of the week, in which you intentionally engage in one of the above alternative activities. In addition to specific times, you can easily have something handy in which to engage when you feel pulled in the direction of picking your skin. Just take out that rock, or whatever you are using to help yourself. Little by little this alternative activity is taking the place of the unhealthy activity, replacing it, and extinguishing it. Pretty cool.

Hoarding

The Diagnostic and Statistical Manual of Mental Disorders - 5th Edition (DSM-5) defines Hoarding as such: "Persistent difficulty discarding or parting with possessions, regardless of their actual value."

There is also "a perceived need to save the items" as well as "distress associated with discarding them." This difficulty discarding things leads to pretty much *clutter on steroids,* and eventually entire areas of the home are no longer accessible or useable, because of the build-up of items. It can be fairly pronounced, in some cases.

There are many reasons that a person may hoard, such as "It was too good to pass it up" or "I spent money on it, so I should probably hang on to it" or "If I do not keep these pets, they will just be killed in a shelter or die in the street" or "I may need that some day" or "There is already enough stuff in the landfill—I don't want to add to it" or "If I can control this, I can control the rest of my life as well." And the list goes on.

And yes, this disorder can be extremely demoralizing, and can lead to deep depression, isolation, fear, and even disease and poor health. This is a serious disorder, but I already alluded above to a couple of possible notions that can *fuel* hoarding—an effort to save or secure self or animals, and an effort to have *some semblance of control in one's life.*

But again, in this case, the individual is falling into a *maladaptive coping mechanism that has long since worn out its usefulness.*

There are better, healthier ways to safeguard self and animals, and to be more in control of one's life. It's far better to come at both of these from a position of peace and strength, rather than desperation and fear.

Sometimes it's difficult to discard items because we think that they have utility or usefulness, or they have some aesthetic value, or there are special memories attached to the item, or we don't want to be wasteful, or we don't want to lose important information.

With hoarding, there are lots of distorted thoughts. So be

careful to correct your self-talk (what you are telling yourself, what you are believing) when you start to feel anxious or tense. Correct that self-talk to something true, valid and reasonable: "Okay, what's the truth here? How can I have a voice in this situation? And what's the reasonable thing here?"

It is good to have a visual on what you are actually believing about your items, so start writing down your thoughts and beliefs on paper, so you can easily see it and understand it. Then write your corrected self-talk right under it. For example:

"If I get rid of these items, I might inadvertently lose important money or items or something else that is inside of these items. I don't really feel safe without having these items around me." Of course, this kind of self-talk will usually lead to anxiety.

So then, write this right under your self-talk:

"The truth is, most of these items are not really needed, I've gotten along just fine without having to use these items, and a simple look at each item will suffice to ascertain if something of value is inside the item. I can have a voice in this situation, by actually picking up items and boxes, and beginning to have a sorting process in place. The reasonable thing is that I will probably have a sense of relief having a small success in clearing a portion of this room."

You have just *processed* the situation, and your brain, being an organic super computer, will understand and be okay with your new way of *relating* to the situation. You will become *more calm,* and you will be *out of the weeds* with your thinking, ready to keep going.

Remember *Incremental Resolution?* Well, talk about embracing the process. This is exactly what you will be doing to help yourself while you are starting to clear *one little section of the room.*

You do not need to clear the entire room all at once. No, just keep it simple. Pick one little section of the room, or one table, or one corner of the room, etc.

Find four boxes, and keep these boxes next to you somehow:

- Keep box
- Donate box
- Trash box
- Recycle box

Follow these two simple rules:

1. I must fill all of the boxes before I get a new box.

2. At the end of the day, take the Donate, Trash and Recycle boxes off the property. Let them go, and give them a new home.

It is best to identify a storage space in which to place "Keep" boxes, so that you can work on these later.

In this way, you are *incrementally, gradually* creating space in your home—breathing space, living space, peaceful space. Allow yourself to feel relieved and refreshed as you remove these boxes from your home, and take them to their appropriate new residences. Little by little you are becoming *free to move about my home.*

You are having a voice, in a big way.

Now, I am not suggesting that this process is easy. No, it won't be easy, but it will be refreshing, and it will be meaningful.

If you have not yet done so, read carefully the earlier chapter regarding the Second Little Cousin and the "Intentional Set Routine." This can really help you in this quest to create peace and more living space in your home. Implementing this important strategy can also help you to greatly reduce any depression you may have at this time. On a practical vein, you can use your "Intentional Set Routine" to place blocks of time in your week for clearing one small section of a room, for instance.

Cutting

People engage in cutting for various reasons. And sometimes young people will engage in cutting. I believe that the primary reason that people cut themselves is that sometimes *the slight physical pain associated with cutting takes the mind off of the excruciating emotional pain the person is experiencing.*

If only for a few moments, the person has some semblance of control in their life, and their attention is temporarily off of the emotional pain that is so damaging.

> **People will do the darnedest things**
>
> **just to have some *semblance of control* in their lives.**

But cutting is definitely a *maladaptive coping mechanism that has long since worn out its usefulness.*

There are better, healthier ways to cope with emotional pain, or abuse, or relationship turbulence. Certainly, if you begin to write about your concerns and thoughts (journal), this can help you to have insights, and to see patterns of thinking and patterns of behavior.

Cutting can lead to social isolation, family problems, and even suicidal ideation. It is fairly serious. I have screened many individuals at the ER who are unstable, and suicidal, and some of whom have cut themselves. This coping mechanism is not going to solve anything for you. It's only going to facilitate further self-loathing and further depression and further lack of motivation.

If you cut, see it for what it is: a maladaptive coping mechanism. And consider other ways to cope with anxiety, or emotional pain, or abuse, or relationship strain.

For anxiety, the best way to reduce it is to correct your self-talk (what you are telling yourself about a situation, and believing about it) to something true, valid and reasonable. If you need more information on anxiety, you can take another look at the chapter on the First Little Cousin, and it will help you tremendously.

If it is emotional pain brought on by verbal or emotional abuse, you need to *get out of this unsafe situation as soon as possible*, seek help, and find a safe place in which to live. Abuse is wrong, it needs to be reported, and you deserve to have assistance, peace, and safety. So, don't be afraid to speak up, and don't be afraid to reach out for help. This is an important decision, one which will safeguard you and empower you for the future.

If it is is emotional pain related to a problematic relationship, you need to communicate with that other person. You need to speak from the context of your personal values, start with how you are feeling, and then clearly state what that person is doing to *contribute* to how you feel.

You can write about your concerns with this relationship, and you can communicate with that person, most definitely. This is far better than cutting yourself. It's okay to *actually deal with the emotional pain, and give a voice to it.*

This is healthy, and this is in line with wellness. If you have some relationship turbulence going on at this time, I would recommend that you read the chapter "For Couples, and Those Who are Searching." This chapter will give you some healthy guidance related to navigating socially.

From an HRT (Habit Reversal Therapy) perspective, you can also decide on some alternative activities in which you can engage when anxious. For instance, you can have handy a paint-by-number piece of art, and pick one number, and paint all the little spaces with that number. This will get your mind off of what was bothering you, it will help to ground you in the present, and it will give you *a sense of control over your life,* if only for a moment. And it's not damaging you in any way.

Even a jigsaw puzzle or yo-yo or old-fashioned Clackers, which are sometimes called Knocker Balls, or in the Philippines "Lato-Lato." The latter is basically two hard acrylic or plastic balls on string, and you knock them together, making a clacking sound. These have been around for a long time. I used to love them as a kid. You have to be careful, but this can be very therapeutic, it can evoke positive emotions, while improving motor skills.

The point is, it's important to find a way to cope with your fear and anxiety that will not harm you. Try to find an alternative activity that you will enjoy, so you can engage in this activity instead of cutting yourself.

Doing this will help you to feel better about yourself, and will empower you and help you to have a voice in your life. It will give you a sense of control in your life. This confidence will carry over into other areas of your life, and you will learn to have a voice in general, as a way of life.

Summary

All of the above disorders can be very debilitating, and can greatly interfere with a person's life and basic functioning. Each of these disorders are directly related to anxiety, so you will find that as overall anxiety in your life dissipates, so will the above tendencies and ways of coping.

I believe that all of these habits and maladaptive coping mechanisms are not good for us, and they need to be replaced with either learning to live with the distress (with OCD), or replacing these habits with healthier, more productive alternative activities. We also need to correct our distorted self-talk right away to something true, valid and reasonable. This is always a healthy strategy in which to engage.

There is indeed hope for OCD, tic behavior, Trichotillomania, Excoriation, hoarding, and cutting. It takes time, but it is well worth the effort. In this chapter I have given you a basic introduction to these disorders, and basic ways that you can help yourself. But remember that you can make a choice to see a therapist who specializes in these disorders on your own, at any time. You may need this extra guidance afforded in the therapeutic relationship. But you will already have a good understanding as you begin that counseling experience.

But you may find that you don't need to see a therapist, and that you can actually help yourself, and guide yourself, using the principles found in this chapter, along with doing a little bit of research on your own perhaps.

No doubt, this chapter provides you with a good start, as you begin the process of recovery from these debilitating disorders.

So, try to be mindful in the moment, and remember that you always come to a "Y" in the road whenever you have the thought of using your particular maladaptive coping mechanism. You have a choice. There are other, more healthy coping mechanisms available to you at any given time.

You can indeed have a voice in this area of your life.

---

92. Neeladri Dutta and Andrea E. Cavanna, *Functional Neurology* 2013 Jan-Mar; 28(1): 7-12. Published online 2013 Jun 3. Accessed on PubMed Central on 10/30/2023.

TURNING THE PAGE

My therapeutic focus is helping individuals and couples to be architects of their present tense, and helping people to move forward in their lives, in a way that is meaningful to them. But sometimes painful, traumatic events in the past are negatively impinging upon the present, and are negatively impacting us in the present. This can take the form of disturbed sleep, nightmares, exacerbated anxiety, and interference with work and school.

So we will take a close look at a very difficult subject—painful memories—and how to have closure for them. You may be still reeling from the previous words or actions of another person that were very hurtful to you. It is possible to be robbed of sleep because of recurring nightmares, or to be afraid to go anywhere because of feeling unsafe or unsure of yourself or your surroundings. The painful experiences may have involved angry or belittling words, physical abuse, emotional abuse, verbal abuse, or even sexual abuse. But the experiences have had an abiding, debilitating impact on you.

It is just as important to guard one's thoughts with painful memories, as it is with other stressors and bothersome thoughts. Two important truisms should be kept in mind:

> You are no longer a victim. You are no longer on the receiving end of the abuse. Most likely that person is no longer in your life or proximity.

> You must not give that person power over you by continuing to fear and continuing to have a disrupted life.

The Power of Words

We should not kid ourselves. The angry, belittling, degrading, humiliating, hurtful words of others can truly injure us, sometimes more so than their actions or treatment of us. Words can heal, and words can tear down. And when we are on the receiving end of put-downs and shaming for a long period of time, we start to get used to it, and to be desensitized to it. We might even start believing what we have been told over and over. We can start to internalize what we are hearing repeatedly, so that it becomes a part of us, and a part of the way we view ourselves.

When this happens in childhood or youth, it can even impact the way we interact with other people, and the way we engage others in general. This often is the case as the person enters adulthood and tries to find their way in life.

But there comes a time when we must see it for what it is: untrue, unhealthy, inappropriate, sick words.

Abusive Actions

Whether it be physical, verbal, emotional, or sexual abuse, it is demoralizing, dehumanizing, objectifying, and deeply injurious. It is especially hurtful when it happens when we are young. It destroys trust, it ruins relationships, it breaks natural bonds, it isolates, and it disrupts one's childhood.

Some traumatic experiences are so painful, we are unable to handle them or deal with them at the time. It is too overwhelming, and we basically shut down emotionally. The brain is protective in nature, and it sometimes stores away painful experiences for a later time, when we are more capable of addressing the pain. It is not uncommon for an adult person to start remembering past trauma, in the form of intrusive thoughts or memories, or recurring nightmares. When this is happening, it is a signal to us that we are now ready to deal with the trauma, and to forever put it behind us.

This is not to suggest that we should forget. The passage of time and aging naturally fade the memory of past events. No, forgetting is not nearly as important as *having closure for the emotional pain connected with those events.*

The Importance of Closure

Through closure, we can indeed turn the page, and move safely into the next chapter in our lives; we can actually live without the debilitating, constant reliving of the events. There needs to be closure for the painful experiences of our lives, or we will continue to have to deal with "unfinished business."

And the brain, being the organic super computer that it is, will sometimes see this unfinished business as something that needs to be addressed or processed. And in a "quality control" sort of way, it will bring something to our attention that needs to be processed.

Sometimes something happens or someone says something that is remotely similar to something emotionally painful or traumatic that happened to us in the past, and just as water tends to find other water, and anxiety tends to find other anxiety, *trauma tends to find other trauma.* If it's similar enough, it can sometimes *bring it all back.* And that person is overwhelmed with all these painful memories, and cannot work or function, or sleep. It's a mess, and it's very scary.

We usually call that PTSD.

A Simple But Profound Form of Closure

There are many forms of closure actually. But I will share with you a simple and very effective form of closure that has helped many people.

There is firstly a writing phase, and then an experiential phase. There are three sections to this closure exercise: The Good, The Painful/Ugly (which is the main body of this letter), and the Declaration.

Take some paper, and write a letter to the person who caused the pain. In this letter you want to "let it all out," and to talk about the pain and the anguish. Talk about how this person impacted you negatively. Address the person as if you were saying these things directly to that person. Let it all out.

But I need to clarify that this letter is not for that person. This is for you. YOU are the one who needs to be convinced that it is safe and it is time to put the emotional pain connected with these events behind you forever. This is for you.

If you can, try to use your first paragraph to remember and write down anything good or helpful about that relationship or that person. This is a good place to start, if possible. Now, sometimes it is not possible, and there is absolutely nothing good about that person or their presence in your life. If this is the case, just skip this section, and move on to the next section.

Then take as many paragraphs as you need to describe how this person negatively impacted you, hurt you, victimized you, shamed you, or set a horrible example for you. Have a chronological approach, and start with the emotional pain that occurred *at that time.* Try to recount the earliest memories you have of the damaging impact of this person, and start addressing that person by their first name, or whatever you called that person. Talk about these early damaging words and actions (or lack thereof, i.e. neglect), and address that person. For example, "When you put me down and shamed me when I was 10, I felt abandoned, worthless, like I didn't matter to anyone, and I was devalidated and didn't have self-respect or a voice—because of YOU."

Then go to the next event you remember that was damaging, and speak to it. Still addressing that person, recount how this person's words or actions hurt or damaged you, and what impact it had on you at the time. Use a small paragraph for each instance, and continue to work chronologically.

Gradually write down all the painful/ugly aspects in the early instances, working your way towards the present. One paragraph at a time. As you are writing about past events, words, abuse, and neglect, talk about the emotional damage, the physical damage, the spiritual damage, the existential damage, the verbal damage, the shaming, etc.—in other words, describe the various kinds of harm that have occurred, and which you have endured. Whatever is appropriate.

Then gradually work your way towards the present, and eventually talk about how this has impacted you in the present in your interactions with other people, in the way you relate to yourself, and in the way you function in life. Still addressing this person, talk about how this previous maltreatment and abuse *are still negatively impacting you in the present.* Take as many paragraphs as you need. This can be a page, two pages, five pages, ten pages, or even twenty pages. But you need to get it all out: all the painful, all the ugly, all the damaging. Get it all out on paper.

No, this is not by any means an easy task. It will take some time, so pace yourself. It is not easy to recount past harm and pain, because you have to relive it in a way. But it is necessary, for two reasons: you need to see it for what it is—all the hurt, all the damage; and this will help you to actually *get past the pain, and be able to put it behind you.* Your brain will cooperate in this endeavor, and when you are done with both the written and the experiential portions of this closure exercise, your brain will start see this as *processed,* rather than as *unfinished business.*

One you are through with the painful/ugly section, then you are ready for the final paragraph, which is a paragraph of declaration. In this declaration paragraph, you want to cover at least the following aspects:

"I am no longer going to be under your power, I am no longer going to be under your control, I am putting you and the emotional pain connected with you and these events behind me forever. You are now history to me and you are removed from my life. I will still remember, because the brain is very powerful, and I need to be able to steer others away from monsters like you. But the emotional pain connected with you and with these events—I am putting this BEHIND ME FOREVER. I AM TURNING THE PAGE, I AM STARTING A NEW CHAPTER IN LIFE, AND I AM GOING FORWARD IN LIFE, AND PUTTING YOU BEHIND ME FOREVER!"

It doesn't have to be exactly like the above, but try to capture the essence and thrust of the above paragraph, and put your own personality and voice behind it. It's the most important section of this letter. This is your declaration. This is YOU TAKING YOUR LIFE BACK.

Then, either save it on your computer or, if hand-written, simply copy it for your records. You need to have a record of what you have processed, and what you have declared. Then take your letter, a lighter, and a small garden trowel. Then go to some place local like a woodlot or some place where you can be absolutely alone. You can take someone who cares with you if you want, for moral support, and to be a witness to what you declare. The best location is right in the middle of the woods with no one around. It's just you and the trees and the birdies and other wildlife. If you are a person of faith, then the God of your understanding hears you and, and if you believe in the existence of angels, then yes, they also are bearing witness to what you are doing and saying. Otherwise, rest assured that the birdies and trees and plants and wildlife around you will definitely bear witness to what you declare.

When you get to your chosen location, start reading your letter out loud. You can yell it out, scream it out, cry it out, but definitely be emphatic and as loud as you want to be. You are addressing that person who caused all of this emotional pain in the first place. So you can scream it out if you want. Yes, there will probably be a few tears, and some deep emotions. That is normal.

Start with the first paragraph—with anything good or healthy that came out of that interaction or relationship. This may not even be possible or appropriate.

Then start reading out loud each of your paragraphs that describe the emotional pain, abuse, damaging words, and lasting negative impact in your life. Go through these paragraphs one by one and yell or speak them them out *emphatically.*

When you get to the final paragraph of declaration, *be especially loud, especially emphatic, especially angry, and especially firm with your words:*

"You can no longer hurt me! I will no longer allow you to have power over me! I am no longer under your control! I refuse to be a victim! I am no longer a victim of your abuse and monstrosities! I am putting you and the emotional pain connected with you and these events BEHIND ME FOREVER! I still will remember, because the brain is very powerful. But the emotional pain connected with you and with these events—I am putting this behind me forever!! I AM TURNING THE PAGE, I AM STARTING A NEW CHAPTER IN LIFE, AND I AM GOING FORWARD IN LIFE, AND PUTTING YOU BEHIND ME FOREVER!

I AM NOW GOING TO BURN THIS EMOTIONAL DAMAGE YOU HAVE CAUSED, AND I WILL BURY IT IN THE GROUND, AND I WILL STOMP ON THIS DAMAGE. YOU WILL BE BEHIND ME FOREVER, AND YOUR HARM AND DAMAGE TO MY LIFE ARE GONE FOREVER! **I AM STARTING A NEW LIFE THAT DOES NOT INCLUDE YOU IN IT."**

Then crumple up your letter into a tight ball. With your garden trowel, dig a little hole in the ground, and place said letter in hole. Take your lighter and set it on fire, holding your hand over it to keep the wind from blowing it out. As far as possible, try to turn this letter into ashes, or at least so dark it cannot be read. Then with your trowel, cover up the hole again with soil, *then stomp on it several times emphatically.*

This is a very powerful and effective form of closure because it is very experiential. It engages all of your senses: sight, hearing, smelling, feeling, and yes even the fresh air helps you to taste better. While there is nothing magical about this form of closure, it is very useful.

You are now addressing the wrongfulness of the inappropriate words or behaviors. And you are declaring that this person can no longer hurt you, and that you are moving on in your life. And you are saying that this inappropriate treatment was not your fault in the slightest. And you are proclaiming that you are no longer going to be a victim.

So start writing. Have some closure in your life. Isn't it time?

Go ahead, turn the page . . .

Grief and Loss

Most of us have experienced some form of loss in our lives. It is devastating, even when we are expecting it. That loss can still hit us like a ton of bricks.

It is very important to allow yourself to emote when you are grieving. Don't hide your emotions, or pretend they are not there. Go ahead and cry if you feel like crying. Go ahead and yell if you feel like yelling.

And please do some writing. Yeah, do some journaling about how you are feeling, what you are thinking, what this person meant to you, how this person either enhanced you or hurt you (or both; often it's a mixed bag). When you write down your thoughts, you learn a lot. You process a lot. This is good for you. Keep writing. And remember....

Out of your brokenness

can flow healing for others.

There are stages or seasons to grieving. There is a grief process. Elizabeth Kübler-Ross came up with the five stages of grief in her monumental book *On Death and Dying (1969)*.

This is a wonderful book, and there are many very helpful books available on grief and loss. I will simply summarize these five stages of grief.

> **Denial:** This involves avoidance, confusion, excitement, and shock or fear.

> **Anger:** This involves frustration, irritability, and anxiety.

> **Bargaining:** This involves a struggle to find meaning, "What if" and "If only..." statements, bargaining with others or with God, and telling your story.

> **Depression:** This involves helplessness, hostility, and avoidance.

> **Acceptance:** This involves exploring opportunities, introducing new plans, and moving forward.

Keep in mind that while the grief process does usually include most or all of the above aspects, it can also jump around quite a bit. You can fluctuate between denial and bargaining for a while. Or you might feel that you have achieved some acceptance of the situation, then you find yourself going backwards to depression or even denial. Don't be too concerned if this happens. It is not easy to sustain a loss of any kind. Each person heals slightly differently, and the brain and the body have their own timing. Try not to rush the process, but rather embrace the process.

Keep writing, keep communication lines open, and keep availing yourself of helps and resources that can aid you in moving forward in peace.

Dealing with People Who Are Insensitive to Your Loss

Remember to be authentic, and to be in touch with your emotions. And it's okay to be sad, if that is authentic. You don't have to put on a happy face if indeed you are not chipper and happy. Most people are understanding, and they will most likely not expect you to be something you are not. Just in case someone tries to ask a lot of questions, or lead you into any other "landmine," try to ahead of time develop a little game plan for each possible landmine, and ask yourself "What is true in this situation, how can I have a voice in this situation, and what is reasonable in this situation?" This way you have already processed it and prepared for it, and it is much easier now to be authentic and honest, in the moment.

You don't have to be afraid of potential landmines. Remember that you are still in the midst of this loss, you are still processing it, the loss is still fresh, and that you are a bit emotionally numb at this time. It is okay for you to gently remind a family member or friend of this, if the family member or friend is wanting to delve into the situation or is asking a lot of questions about it.

Honoring the One You Have Lost

Try to live your life in such a way that you can honor the person you have lost. Try to make decisions and to plan in such a way that this person would be happy for you. Most likely you know that this person would want you to move forward in your life, to better yourself, to put your own unique mark on this world. So live to please and give honor to that person you love and miss. Resist the urge to mope around and feel sorry for yourself, or to shame or second-guess yourself. Take action, be intentional, keep writing, and by all means set up your "Intentional Set Routine" because this can help you revamp your life in a healthy and dramatic fashion.

This is giving that person you have lost a voice. Yes, when we have a voice and live our lives in such a way that is consistent with our values, our goals, our convictions and our passions in life, we not only help ourselves to move forward in life; we also honor and carry out the wishes of the person we have lost.

And by the way, this same approach also works for pets that we have laid to rest. These critters are like family to us, and they too would want us to be healthy and happy and to move peaceably forward in life. So honor them as well.

I speak to you a a person who has sustained many losses in life. It's like each loss takes a big 'ole bite out of us, leaving a gaping hole. And some losses are individuals who remain living, but are nonetheless gone from our lives. So it is important for us to think of creative ways to help ourselves to heal and grow. Music can be very therapeutic in this regard, as can sculpting, painting, drawing, learning, and writing.

Give yourself permission to branch out a bit, and to insert some artistic endeavor into your scheme of things—even if you don't consider yourself an artist of any kind. It can still be a very cathartic and helpful activity in which to engage.

Just enjoy yourself, and allow yourself to reflect what you are doing, and how you are feeling, thinking, and progressing, in what you create. Reflect what that person or animal still means to you. Create a monument to the remembrance of this person, this animal.

Summary

It is important to process past dynamics in writing about them. There are take-aways, and everything you can learn about a past experience will serve to enhance you, and help you to move forward in life. This important learning can help you to have boundaries and self-respect, to have a voice, and to chart a course for yourself this is consistent with your personal values and goals. Give yourself permission to engage in this reflection/learning process. Give yourself permission to "extract" anything useful or helpful from these experiences, *leaving only an exoskeleton of the experience, that can be blown away with the wind.*

ASSERTIVE COMMUNICATION AND BOUNDARIES

It is important to be able to communicate our thoughts and concerns in a manner that is tactful and to the point. Sometimes when we feel ourselves heating up and getting upset, it is best to take a step back, and to go to another room or area to collect our thoughts, and take some deep breaths to relax.

This is especially helpful when the conversation is elevating to the point of losing one's temper, or saying something inappropriate. Sometimes just a few moments to get a grip on the situation is very helpful. You can say something like, "Let's hold on a second, and take just a little break so we can collect our thoughts and calm down a little bit. Then we can come back and finish this conversation in a calm and adult fashion."

Most people wouldn't mind if something like that were said to them.

It's important to state what is on our mind without pouring gas on the fire. And sometimes it is a delicate situation, and using an "I" statement can really come in handy.

"I" Statements: The What

"I" statements are a way to tactfully and assertively

communicate our current emotional state, while at the same time pointing out specifically what the other person is doing that *contributes* to how we feel. Notice, I did not use the verb "causes," because nobody has the power to cause us to feel anything. This is in our top circle, and completely in our control (for the most part). But people can *contribute* to how we feel.

So here is the format for the "I" statement:

"I feel _____, when you _____; maybe we could . . ."

Notice it is starting with where we are, how we feel, and then specifically identifying what that person is doing or saying that *contributes* to how we feel. Then you can tag on a little suggestion at the end of it that is helpful. A little piggy-back suggestion that is proactive. Solution-focused.

"I" Statements: The Why

We use "I" statements because it is a way to take ownership for our own emotions. It is a way of being personally accountable for how we feel (since no one has the power to make us feel anything).

Most people (not all) will be less likely to take offense or to become angry, when we start with ourselves. We are not pointing the finger, we are not blaming, we are not cussing at the person, we are not speaking down to them condescendingly, and we are not pouring gas on the fire.

We use "I" statements because this allows us to specifically point out the negative/unhealthy words or actions of the other person, without pouring gas on the fire.

This is particularly helpful in any delicate situation, in a relationship, or even with a supervisor at work.

Keep in mind that it is still possible that the other person can be mad, upset, negative, unhealthy, inappropriate—even after we take ownership for how we feel, and attempt to be tactful. We cannot control the values, attitude, words, or actions of anyone else. But using "I" statements makes it a little bit less likely that the other person will be upset, and a little more likely that they will take us seriously.

"I" Statements: The How

Practicing "I" Statements

(Read the description, turn it into an "I" statement)

> Scenario #1: Your older uncle just walked into the room and told you, "You did it again! You put the dog food in a place where the mice can get into it! I've told you about that a million times! Are you dense?"

"I" statement:

> Scenario #2: Your boss once again has talked about you behind your back to other employees, and the word has gotten back to you. The content of what she has been saying is not very nice.

"I" statement:

> Scenario #3: Your significant other continues to basically ignore you when around the house, and is pretty much caught up in personal endeavors most of the time, impervious to your needs.

"I" statement:

> Scenario #4: Your coworker has a tendency to have a minimalist approach to work, and seems to be quite content with doing as little as possible, and letting other workers work harder.

"I" statement:

> Scenario #5: Your close friend whom you have known for many years has developed a habit of cutting you off and interrupting you whenever you are trying to express an important point, in public.

"I" statement:

General Boundaries

A general boundary is a limit that you place on yourself. It can be choosing to go to bed each night during a specific span before midnight. This is a limit you are placing on yourself. Or it can be the ability to say "No" when someone asks you to do something or help them with something, and you simply cannot pull yourself away at the moment, because you have something time-sensitive you have to get done. You can say, "Wow, I would love to help you, but I really need to get back to this thing. I have to get this done right away. Maybe next time give me a little heads up, and I might be able to help." That's a general boundary or limit that you are placing on yourself (it's also having a voice and being assertive).

Specific Boundaries

Specific boundaries need to be:

1. <u>Based on our values and preferences</u>. If your boundary is based on your values, it will be substantive, and will actually mean something. So make sure you know what your top ten values are in life, because they will help you to have boundaries in your life.

2. <u>Expressed</u>. A specific boundary needs to be *articulated;* it needs to be *spoken into existence.* It doesn't just happen. Have courage, have a voice, and tell that person what you really mean, what you really are convicted by, and where you stand. Stand up, and have a freakin' voice. Say what you mean. This is how you articulate a boundary into existence.

3. <u>Maintained</u>. If you do not take your own boundaries seriously, *no one else will.* And sometimes people will push the envelope, and test us, and try to minimize what we have said, or catch us forgetting what we said (these are forms of disrespect). It is not enough to speak a boundary into existence. We must *maintain* them as well.

You use specific boundaries if someone continues to insult you or discredit you, or if someone continues to relate to you in a way you have previously verbalized is hurtful or wrong. Specific boundaries are important whenever someone is gossiping about us, being insulting or condescending, or taking advantage of us, or continuing to speak disrespectfully to us (even in jest).

If you have tried to be tactful with someone—using "I" statements, reminding the person more than once about something—and the person still continues to act or speak in a way that violates your personal values and disrespects you, a specific boundary becomes necessary.

That person can even be a longtime friend, or a family member, or a coworker. Even these individuals can sometimes be inappropriate in how they speak to us, or act around us.

When this happens, a specific boundary becomes necessary.

Not everyone takes us seriously. Some people are just plain mean or inappropriate, running roughshod over the feelings and preferences of others. Some people actually enjoy disrespecting others, for whatever reason. So yes, sometimes it is important that we speak to the person in a firm voice, and let the person know with certainty that the behavior or words in question *must stop immediately.*

**Once this boundary is expressed,
and the person understands what you have communicated,
it is up to that person to decide whether or not to
recognize and abide by the boundary you have created.**

Please remember that when you create and maintain ____ville. You get to decide who is and who isn't allowed into ____ville. No one can push their way in, because you are the one who decides who is safe to trust, who is truly a good friend, and who actually cares about you genuinely. So, the main weapons of defense are not guns, but rather self-respect, self-validation, personal values, personal boundaries, and assertive communication.

You can say, "This right here (be very specific) needs to stop. I value our friendship, and I would like us to be able to continue on good terms. But this really needs to stop. You can still be yourself without doing/saying this" (again, be specific).

**You have just drawn a distinct line in the sand.
That is what a boundary is. A line in the sand.**

**You have declared "Thus far, and no farther, or
there will be serious repercussions."**

In other words, you are trying to determine if it is safe or appropriate for this person to continue to be in your inner circle of trust and close friendship.

Now, that person can have several different responses to your boundary formation:

1. That person can say, "Oh, wow, okay, I am so sorry. I didn't mean to hurt you. This friendship means a lot to me as well, and I will make an adjustment definitely. No worries. I will be more careful." This would be fabulous, and you have hereby strengthened that friendship, and placed it on a whole new level of respect and understanding.

2. That person can go off and give you the silent treatment, ignore you, and pout. If this happens, that person has thereby taken their foot and rubbed out that line you have drawn in the sand. They have essentially said, "I don't care about you, or your boundaries, or your silly values. Just grow up and don't be so sensitive." This is very disrespectful, and not very nice. You need to distance yourself from such a person, and that person has singlehandedly removed him/herself from your inner circle of trust.

3. That person can say, "No way, I'm not gonna stop saying that/doing that. Not gonna happen. I shouldn't have to change —you should accept me the way I am. Grow up! I don't have to change anything. You are wrong, this is ridiculous, I don't care what you say, I shouldn't have to change anything because I'm not doing anything wrong." A person can also use expletives along with this. Yes, again, it's completely inappropriate.

This person has made it clear that they don't care about you, or your boundary, or your values that it is based on.

This person has taken their foot and rubbed out that careful line you drew in the sand.

This is completely disrespectful, and shameful.

You need to distance yourself from this person.

**This is not a time for business as usual.
This person has definitely removed him/
herself from your inner circle of trust.**

We cannot control how that other person responds to us, when we speak a specific boundary into existence. It can be very hurtful when that person demonstrates that they don't care about us, or about our friendship with that person.

But remember that if you meet resistance after articulating a specific boundary, *do not cave in or give in to their antics.* CONTINUE TO REMAIN IN ____VILLE (insert your name), HAVE A VOICE, AND STAND YOUR GROUND.

It is not enough to speak a specific boundary into existence.

We must MAINTAIN that boundary as well.

**We must REDRAW that line in the sand, if it
has been rubbed out belligerently.**

**IF WE DO NOT TAKE OUR OWN BOUNDARIES SERIOUSLY,
NO ONE ELSE WILL.**

So, if the above happens, and that person has clearly demonstrated that they do not respect us or care about us, we need to *redraw that line in the sand, and re-articulate that boundary.*

You can say, for instance, "I am sorry that you have not taken me seriously, and that you have not cared enough about our friendship to have some ownership and decency. I HAVE NOT CHANGED MY STANCE. THESE WORDS/ACTIONS STILL NEED TO STOP, AND SINCE THEY ARE NOT STOPPING, IT IS CLEAR

TO ME THAT YOU DO NOT CARE ABOUT OUR FRIENDSHIP. THINGS WILL HAVE TO BE DIFFERENT NOW, FOR CERTAIN."

It is no longer prudent or appropriate to have a regular, ongoing relationship with that person. This person has actually removed him/herself from your inner circle of trust and close friendship. It doesn't mean that you hate that person; it *does* mean that this is not a time for business as usual. This is a BIG deal, and enough is enough.

That..........is a boundary. That..........is how you MAINTAIN a boundary.

Indeed, that person has actually *removed him/herself* out of your life, and out of your inner circle of trust. You need to now relate to that person *at an arm's length. No business as usual. You may have to block that person on social media, and no longer be chummy or casual with that person. This is having a voice, and this is having respect for your own personal boundaries, which are based on your values, and have substance.*

Now, this can be be a bit tricky when that person is either a family member or a coworker, or a roommate—someone that you have to be around frequently. But you can still be decent and respectful towards this person, more in a general or professional way. You can still move and act consistently with your personal values, which are always surrounding you. You can still remain in ____ville all the time, even when around that particular person. You can continue to have a voice, and continue to say what you mean and mean what you say (without pouring has on the fire). You can still be the best YOU you can be. No worries. *But you don't have to be chummy or casual with that person who has removed him/herself from your inner circle of trust. Hold your ground.*

Sometimes we must keep a semblance of relationship in place, for the sake of children, or for other circumstantial reasons. In those cases, we can still have self-respect and we can still maintain our boundaries. We don't have to continue to be chummy with someone who repeatedly disregards us, disrespects us, or takes advantage of us. If cutting off all communication and interaction with the person is not possible, or feasible, just do your best to live your values, and keep your boundaries in place.

And please remember that when you create and maintain ____ville, you get to decide who is and who isn't allowed into ____ville. No one can push their way in, because you are the one who decides who is safe to trust, who is truly a good friend, and who actually cares about you genuinely. So, again, the main weapons of defense are not guns, but rather self-respect, self-validation, personal values, personal boundaries, and assertive communication.

And don't worry what others think of you. Do what you know to be good, and true, and that which promotes wellness.

I believe this Chinese proverb says it best:

> **"If you're standing straight, don't worry if your shadow is crooked."**

Don't get caught up in what other people think and feel, or the decisions they make. Try to be comfortable in your own shoes, and to live in harmony with your own personal values and goals in life. This is the way of peace; the way of wellness.

It is important to keep in mind that it is possible to be compassionate towards others, while at the same time having healthy self-respect and dignity. Compassion and self-respect are NOT mutually exclusive. We can and should have both, in order to have balance and wellness in our lives.

Consider the Audience

When someone asks a Reader's Digest question, we don't need to give a Britannica response. Considering one's audience/recipient is key, and having an accurate conception of the actual request is essential. Make sure you have a conception of who your audience is, even if it is an individual. What kind of individual is it? It is a child? Is it a child in an adult's body? Is it a professional person? Is it a student?

Also understand what the actual question or request is. If you do not fully understand what that person is asking or saying, have a voice and ask for clarification. Then proceed, and pick your words carefully, watch your tone of voice, and be careful with your volume (top circle). Say what you mean, and mean what you say.

If you are giving a presentation of some kind to either a small group or to a large audience, make sure you have a good understanding of what the make-up of that audience is. Are these a bunch of students or colleagues who are eager to learn about something specific? Then give them all you have, and let your words and thoughts shine forth. Is this a mixed group of people with different backgrounds and knowledge bases? You will need to explain as you go, use simple words, and pretend you are speaking to bunch of elementary students. I say this, because some adults are actually operating on that level in how they perceive things.

Take your audience into consideration. Use visuals, use illustrations, so that the recipients can have *anchor points* that connect them to the substance of what you are trying to communicate.

Perpetual Caretaker

Sometimes a person, as a child or adolescent, has to "take care" of their parents, or be a go-between or mediator between parents, or even be a "counselor" to a parent, when that parent doesn't have the decency or propriety to seek professional help. They just let it all out on the young person. Technically, we usually refer to this as the *parentification* of the child. It's not at all healthy.

And that young person grows up as a *caretaker,* feeling like they need to constantly take care of everyone around them, and feeling guilty if someone is not doing well. This care taking role can easily follow a person into adult life. The person ends up being a caretaker of adult siblings, and also a caretaker of a partner in a relationship. This is very unhealthy for this person, but also quite damaging for the relationship.

I have seen the above progression many times, as clients have told their stories, and have related their backgrounds.

So, if you were pushed into a caretaker role of being a parent to your parents, in the present you can see this for what it is, and decide to *shed this caretaker role,* since it has long since worn out its usefulness. Give yourself permission to let go of this caretaker role, because it wasn't healthy back then, and it's still not healthy now. And it's no longer necessary. Let it go.

Try to go about your life and your work from a position of peace and strength, with your values intact. You can be kind and helpful to others *for the right reasons,* because kindness or helpfulness is one of your values, and you are deciding to be value-driven. Yes, you can still be a good parent, be a good adult son or daughter, be a helpful but wise coworker, and be a source of peace and support and honesty for your partner. This is the way of wellness.

You can cease to be a perpetual caretaker, and do what you do because it is good and right and wholesome, and consistent with who you are.

If you are a nurse or other medical worker, and your former

care taking role from earlier life has been superimposed upon your current medical role, you can shed that perpetual caretaker aspect from your role, and go about your work in peace and strength, because you *want* to, not because you *have* to.

Perpetual care taking leads to burnout, and is not healthy for us. Let it go.

In closing, I simply want to say, "I feel wonderful, when you implement that which works. Maybe we can keep a good thing going, and bring a little assertiveness into our communication with others."

Any lines in the sand that are needed?

FOR COUPLES
(AND THOSE WHO ARE SEARCHING)

Be the Right Person

Whether you are married, engaged, in a relationship, or dating, one thing is for sure: none of us were trained to be a partner in a relationship. We basically have to learn as we go.

Secondly, it is important to understand that when two people come together in a romantic relationship, it's basically two worlds colliding. There are different values, different worldviews, different goals and preferences, different dreams, and so on. This is why it takes time to truly get to know someone, and to ascertain if indeed there is compatibility in all areas. We must also understand that there will be at times disagreements, confusion, and misunderstandings. After all, the two of you are not clones of each other; that would be rather boring.

Thirdly, and most importantly, please understand that it is more important to BE the right person than to *look* for the right person. In other words, we must be comfortable in our own shoes, and we must have a good understanding of who we are, why we are, and where we are going. If we can have some basic understanding and stability in this regard, it will set us up to be successful in a relationship.

Don't Undermine Yourself

For many years I have worked with couples in premarital counseling, during engagement, in early marriage, in middle marriage, during crisis, including midlife crisis, during periods of unfaithfulness, and also helping couples who are in the midst of separation and divorce.

No, it has not been easy. Nor is it easy for the individuals in relationships with turbulence, difficult adjustments, and the like.

And so, what I tell you now I tell you from my heart, and with full conviction. Please hear what I say.

There are many kinds of intimacy and bonding. There is musical intimacy, literary intimacy, culinary intimacy, cultural intimacy, spiritual intimacy, recreational intimacy, the arts intimacy, and even historical intimacy. There are many ways in which to bond with the one for whom you care, and many ways to achieve mutual understanding and appreciation.

The problem is, many people nowadays rush straight into the physical or sexual intimacy, bypassing so many other ways to bond, and *they shortchange themselves in the process.*

When there is physical or sexual intimacy happening, there is such an emotional pull and attachment that is created, that it casts a heavy taint or influence onto everything else. It may appear for the time that the person is deeply in love with their partner, and inextricably bonded to that person forever.

But many times the couple has not taken the opportunity to truly know each other in other ways and in other settings. Typically, it is the woman who is on the short end of the stick, and is left puzzled, confused, possibly violated, and uncertain when all of a sudden their partner shows signs of either aggression or substance abuse or flirtatious behavior, or any manner of concerning behavior.

> **If the couple had taken the time to grow
> the relationship gradually,
> and to know each other in a variety of ways,
> prior to sexual intimacy,
> they would have had much greater understanding
> of the values, tendencies, behavioral patterns,
> and priorities of each other.**

And just in case you think this writer is just an old-fashioned stick-in-the-mud who has not caught up to modern times, let me say this. I have seen many many train wrecks in relationships because the couple did not take the time to actually know each other in a variety of ways, prior to engaging in sexual intimacy. *This is a practical consideration.* This is a matter of import. And I hope seriously that you will take it to heart, whether you are just in the dating stage, or engaged, or already married. You owe it to yourself and to your partner to develop various forms of intimacy and knowing. *Broaden that relationship.*

It is best for sexual intimacy to be reserved as a capstone or culmination of all the other forms of intimacy for a couple. Unfortunately, when sexual relations are engaged in prematurely, or in a context that is absent of other important ways to have intimacy, it can actually be injurious and harmful.

It is very important for a couple to consider premarital counseling with either a trained therapist or a local clergy person that they respect and trust. These professionals are able to help the couple discuss the various areas of the relationship, and to understand the seriousness of what they are considering.

So, if you are not yet married, please consider premarital counseling. It can help you avoid many pitfalls in life and in the relationship.

A Little Hiatus

If you are just starting out with college, or a brand new career, or you just recently got out of an abusive or otherwise negative relationship, I would encourage you to consider a hiatus away from the social scene for a while, to heal, to collect your thoughts, to know yourself better and what you want in life, and to be able to eventually come at a relationship from a position of *peace and strength,* rather than desperation, neediness, or mere loneliness.

Try to consider this as "ME" time, personal development time, "getting my ducks in a row time," healing and recalibrating time.

And don't feel guilty about it; don't shame yourself. This is good for you, and in-line with wellness. Take a little break, and develop yourself.

"This is Me"

So I ask you to please participate with me in this important exercise. Grab a blank piece of paper, and at the top of that paper, centered, put the title, "This is Me."

Then, do about two or three "returns." There are three rows in this "This is Me" worksheet. In the top row, moving left to right across the page, there will be three aspects. On the far left, write the word "**Values**" with a line under it. Then put about 10 bullet points underneath it. You most likely already have these. Just simply input your top 10 values, or non-negotiables (what's most important to you in life). These values will be guiding the entire process, which is cool.

Moving 2-3 tabs to the right, right in the center of that row and center of the page, write the word "**Relationship**" with a line under it, and three to five bullet points underneath it. I say three to five—*whatever it takes to fully express where you stand on that particular area,* that's what you write about, whether it's five or twenty-five. This one is MACRO, big-picture, general. Ask yourself this question:

> **"What aspects of an important relationship are most important to me?"**

So, dynamics, preferences, what kind of relationship are you looking for/wanting?

It's best to spread this "This is Me" worksheet out over at least a week to ten days, so that you can come back to it, and add thoughts to it, scribble all over it, etc. You need to reflect on each of these areas, and take your time with it. This worksheet will be a lot more meaningful and useful of a tool if you do it this way. Spread it out a bit. Reflect.

Then moving to the far right of the top row and page, write the word "**Partner**" with a line under it, and three to five bullet points underneath it. For this one, you ask the question:

> **"What characteristics of my ideal partner are most important to me?"**

So, this one is MICRO, specific. In other words, what kind of person are you looking for/wanting in your life? Be very specific. Pretend that you are ruler of the world for a moment, and you can speak this person into existence. What would this person's appearance be like? You can talk about that. How would this person communicate? How would this person carry him/herself in public? What about response time? Anything important to you—this is what matters. After all, this is a "This is *Me*" worksheet, not some other person. So be very specific, and be dead honest about this worksheet. And try to summarize your thoughts in bullet form—whether it's five or eighty-five. About three to five words per bullet.

Then do 2-3 "returns" for the second row. This second row has only one area or aspect in it, and it's right in the middle of that row. Simply write the phrase "**Three Year Preferred Scenario**" with a line under it, and *no bullet points.* For this one, ask yourself some questions:

What do I see myself doing three years from now?

What's the general direction I see my life going over the next three years?

What does life look like, at that time?

What would I like it to look like?

What kind of person am I with?

What is going on day to day?

What kind of work am I doing?

Where am I living?

Take your time with this, spread it out, and come back to it, adding thoughts as you reflect. Then try to summarize your thoughts as best you can in *three to five sentences,* and put them right there.

Then do 2-3 "returns" to the third row. There are five aspects or areas in this third row, and the context of this third row is *a very important relationship that is rapidly moving forward.* That is the context.

On the far left of this third row, write the word "**Finances**" with a line under it, and three to five bullet points beneath it. For this one, you ask yourself these questions:

What's most important to me, when it comes to finances?
(That's a good place to start)

What will *spending* look like in this relationship, in this household?

Do I see us having a realistic budget in place?

If so, what are some aspects I see in that budget?

What will *saving* look like in this relationship, in this household?
(Saving for the future, saving for emergencies, saving for trips)

Is this a *joint endeavor*, with common funds, common expenses, common planning?

Or is this myself doing my fiscal/financial thing over here on an island, and my partner is over there on another island doing their fiscal/financial thing, and we smile and wave?

Will I use pronouns such as "we" and "our" when it comes to finances, or will it be "my funds" and "his/her funds"?

Important questions, important area, for certain. Do your best to summarize your thoughts as best you can, in bullet form, whether is ten or a hundred-and-ten. And by the way, it's perfectly all right to go on to another page, or onto the back side of the page. It's just a worksheet and rough draft. You can scribble all over it.

Then do just 1-2 tabs to the right. Then write the words

"**Inlaws/Family**" with a line under it, and three to five bullet points beneath it. For this area, ask yourself these questions:

Is it important to me for my family to be involved and engaged in this relationship?
(Write a few thoughts about that)

What do I consider to be *appropriate* involvement and interaction between my family and this relationship?

What do I consider to be *appropriate* involvement and interaction between my partner's family and this relationship?
(Key word is *appropriate*)

What do I consider to be *inappropriate* involvement or *interference* between my family and this relationship?

What do I consider to be *inappropriate* involvement or *interference* between my partner's family and this relationship, And what would that look like? How would I know if that were happening?

Is this relationship my top priority and commitment in life, and everything else, including my family of origin, take a back seat to it?

Or is my family of origin my main priority and commitment in life, and everything else, including this relationship, takes a back seat to it?

Or is my job or my career, or some other area in life my main priority and commitment in life, and everything else, including this relationship and my family of origin,

take a back seat it to it?

Important questions, no doubt. And very important area. Do your best to summarize your thoughts as best you can, in bullet form, whether it's 12 or 112.

And by the way....each of these areas are *make or break areas.* **These are some of the main reasons that couples break up and divorce. You need to be on the same page in each of these five areas,** or else there will be huge red flags sticking up all over the place, and there will undoubtedly be turbulence in the relationship.

Okay, then do 1-2 tabs to the right, and write the word "**Children**" with a line under it, and three to five bullet points beneath it. For this area, you want to ask yourself some questions:

Do I want to have children/more children?
(Good place to start)

How many do I want?

When do I want them?

How will these children be raised?
What do I have in mind in terms of interaction, discipline, modeling?
(Yes, our children are constantly absorbing and normalizing how we communicate with partner and with them, how we handle stressors, whether or not we self-medicate with substances, and whether or not we have a balance between firmness and kindness, distinguishing between the *person* and the objectionable behavior)

Will there be any house rules in place, that everybody agrees to and abides by?
If so, what do I see as some of these house rules?

What are my thoughts about phone usage and ages, and dating, and social media, etc.?

Important questions. Important area. You definitely need to be on the same page with this one. Do your best to summarize where you stand on this area, in bullet form, whether it's 15 or 65.

Then do 1-2 tabs to the right, and write the word "**Communication**" with a line under it, and several bullet points beneath it. You will probably have to put some extra bullet points on this one, of necessity. Then ask yourself these questions:

What forms of communication am I most comfortable with?
Do I prefer face-to-face? Am I okay with video chat or texting?
Do I have any pet peeves that I *cringe* at?

What about *close communication*, as in a "Debriefing Session"?
Is this important to me?
(If so, write something about it, if not, move on)

What are my thoughts about *response time*?

What do I consider to be *appropriate* communication and interaction between myself and other people out there, some of whom may or may not have a romantic interest in me?

What do I consider to be *appropriate* communication and interaction between my partner and other people out there, some of whom may or may not have a romantic interest in my partner?

(Key word *appropriate*)

What do I consider to be *inappropriate* communication and interaction between myself and other people out there, some of whom may or may not have a romantic interest in me?

What do I consider to be *inappropriate* communication and interaction between my partner and other people out there, some of whom may or may not have a romantic interest in my partner? And what would that look like? How would I know if that were happening?

(Key word *inappropriate*)

Very important questions, and very important area. I work with a lot of couples. I love working with couples, though it can be challenging. *Communication* issues is probably the main reason that couples seek counseling. Yes, you need to be on the same page with this one. But before you have substantive conversations together, you first need to know where *you* stand on this and other areas. So reflect, and take your time. Summarize your thoughts as best you can in bullet form. You may need to go onto the back side of your paper, or onto another page, with this one.

And for the last category to the far right of this third row and page, write the word "**Lifestyle**" with a line under it, and several bullet points beneath it. You will need a LOT of bullet points for this area, as it is very broad in scope.

So, ask yourself these questions:

What will the general ambience or atmosphere
of this home, this relationship, be like?
What would I like it to be like?

What will *recreation* look like in this home, this relationship?
What will day trips, weekend trips,
hikes, adventures, look like?
What would I like to see happening?

What will *entertainment* look like in this
home, this relationship?
What kinds of movies will we watch?
What music will we listen to?
What will "fun" look like?
What would I like it to look like?

Is the "Spiritual/Religious/Metaphysical, *Om*" part of life
important to me?
And if so, how do I see this manifesting
itself in daily and weekly living?
(If not, just go on to the next question)

Will there be any recreational weed or
alcohol or any other substance use
going on in this household, in this relationship?
What are my thoughts about that?
What would I like to see happening?

Am I interested in broadening this relationship,
and learning about my partner on a variety of levels,
and experiencing a variety of bonding experiences?

If so, am I interested in *musical bonding*,
And planning a variety of experiences—
a string quartet in the park,
a symphony orchestra,
an R & B concert?

DAVID D. SULLIVAN

A rock concert?
A spiritual or religious concert?
(Write down your thoughts about planning a
variety of experiences involving different kinds
of intimacy, and listening experiences)

Am I interested in *recreational bonding*,
and planning a variety of experiences
and a variety of sports activities,
and a variety of attended sports events?

Am I interested in *spiritual bonding*,
and planning a variety of shared experiences,
with a variety of worship experiences or styles?
(If applicable, think of indoor and outdoor
activities and experiences)

Am I interested in developing *culinary bonding*,
with a variety of planned dining experiences,
and a variety of planned shared cooking experiences?
(If applicable, think of different genres of food,
and some that you have never tried)

Am I interested in *historical bonding*,
and planning a variety of experiences
at various interesting places, such as
museums, old battlefield exhibits,
and preserved and restored buildings and artifacts?

Am I interested in *the arts* intimacy,
and visiting together a variety of art exhibits,
and art shows in parks,
or
Simply having fun engaging in shared
painting experiences, sculpting experiences, and the like.

And of course, what are my thoughts about *physical intimacy*?
What are my preferences regarding

**forms of physical intimacy?
What about frequency of activities?
What are my preferences regarding oral activities?**
(Yes, this is an important part of a relationship.
So you need to *spell it out,*
and be very specific about what you
actually want. Be dead honest.)

As you can see, this *Lifestyle* area is very broad and comprehensive. I have included some of the more salient features of lifestyle, but it's certainly not exhaustive. Feel free to add whatever other questions or statements to this, so that it is more personalized, or more complete (as you wish).

So, a few added points about this "This is Me" worksheet.

When you are done reflecting and writing about your preferences in each of these areas on this sheet, try to type it up in a word processing document, so you can save a decent-looking copy of this with your important papers. You can also take a photo of it and save it in your favorites. Because this worksheet will be a *very important and very useful social navigating tool* that will guide you, protect you, and facilitate careful discussions with the one you love.

Indeed, this will be a very important statement of *where you stand* on a variety of areas.

Now, there is a *flow* to this "This is Me" sheet. I consider that top row to be a *rule-out row.* You can know quite a bit about a person even after two or three dates. You will be able to know somewhat about their basic appearance, about how they communicate in general, how this person carries him/herself in public, whether or not this person has good eye contact with you, etc. You already know what you have in mind, in terms of a partner, and you also know what you have in mind regarding a relationship in general. And your values are guiding this entire process.

So, if you start feeling uneasy simply by being around this person, check your values, and see if any of them are being compromised simply by being around this person. In this case, this should be considered as a red flag, and as significant. Take note of it. You can easily *bow out gracefully* from this situation, without causing any serious hurt feelings. Be honest with yourself.

Naturally the conversations will go onto various topics, and you will get a general idea of what this person is wanting in a relationship. You are also gaining lots of insight about who this person *is,* and how this person *carries him/herself.* Again, if it's red lights you can *bow out gracefully* from this situation/relationship, without causing any serious hurt feelings. Be honest with yourself.

But there might be green lights all through these early interactions. No compromise happening, and this seems to be the *kind* of person for whom you are looking, they seem to want something similar in a relationship to what you want, and you feel safe and respected when around this person. Green lights.

So then naturally (sometimes) the conversation will go onto the area of the near future, and what each of you are wanting for the near future. But even if it doesn't, you can easily ask, "Hey, by the way, what do you see yourself doing three years from now?" Then let that person respond. See if what that person says is at least similar to what you yourself are wanting for the next few years. It might be fine, or maybe this person says they want to be in Zaire for the next five years on a Red Cross trip, and you want to remain state-side. It might be a deal-breaker, or maybe not. Depends on whether or not you are comfortable with a long-distance relationship. Just be honest. Be dead honest about it.

So, if all lights are green, and this is becoming a serious relationship, you definitely need to start discussing these five important areas on the third row of the "This is Me" sheet. It will be easy for you to engage in these careful discussions, because you have already spent time in reflection on these areas, and you don't have to start from scratch.

You need to be on the same page with each of these five areas. You may have to *lead the dance,* and initiate a discussion regarding one of these areas.

Now, keep in mind that there is *considerable wiggle room* for each of you, in these five areas. You both can make *adjustments* here and there, as needed, so that you come closer together in your understanding.

Yes, each relationship is a *dance,* with give and take.

Sometimes it's a fast dance.

Sometimes it's a slow dance.

Sometimes it's an interrupted dance.

And sometimes you feel *like you're dancing all by yourself.*

•

But it's still a dance...

So you can make adjustments, but in doing so, *never compromise your values, or your personal goals, or your convictions and beliefs, or your passions.*

That usually doesn't result in peace or wellness. No, don't compromise who you are just to make peace in the relationship. Have a voice, be authentic, and transparent and honest with your partner. You deserve that from yourself, and your partner deserves this honesty as well.

I used to do perform a lot of weddings (and also a lot of funerals, unfortunately). When I worked with a couple for two or three sessions right before their wedding, the contents of this "This is Me" sheet is what I would share with them, so that they could ascertain *if they had basic compatibility in the relationship.*

So, **this is a way for you to do *premarital counseling* on your own.** It is a social navigating tool, so try to get it done as soon as you can. It will help you know yourself a lot better, and will help you to avoid the many pitfalls that are out there.

And if you are married or already in a longterm relationship, you can still benefit from going through the above process. This will help you to know yourself even better, and will help the two of you to have meaningful and robust discussions on areas of import. It could even help you salvage your relationship, if it is currently going south on you. It can help you get on the same page.

Naturally, it is ideal to have these types of conversations before the relationship proceeds to engagement or marriage. That is the ideal, and it can really help you make decisions about your future and your potential partner in a manner that is consistent with your values, preferences, personal goals, and personal views.

It's all about *expectations.* You both have them, and this "This is Me" worksheet will help you to discuss them.

When Unfaithfulness Happens

Through the years I have worked with couples at every stage of their experience, from pre-marital counseling all the way to separation and divorce or death of a spouse, and the healing process afterwards. When unfaithfulness occurs, it is deeply hurtful to both individuals. Let me explain.

Unfaithfulness hurts the innocent spouse because it is a deep and powerful violation of one's heart and soul. It touches that person on the level of values, which is deep. It is indescribably painful, and catastrophic in terms of upheaval, abandonment, possible self-blaming, and possible comparisons to the persons with whom the guilty partner has been in contact or been involved.

Words cannot express the pain and anguish that come to a person when the one they love turns their attention, affection or priorities to someone else.

Infidelity and unfaithfulness can occur in a variety of ways. It can range from casual conversations that turn into flirtation, to texting and sexting another individual, to viewing porn online, to going to strip clubs, to an outright affair or one night stand or ongoing sexual liaisons with another. *But though there are many flavors of infidelity, they are all devastating in their impact.*

It should be noted that unfaithfulness also very much hurts the one who engages in it. Most often there is self-loathing, a violation of one's own values, feelings of guilt and shame, and knowing forever that the person you love and have committed your life to has been hurt in a most devastating manner.

It is undeniable. Infidelity hurts the one who engages in it, and it hurts the one who has been back at home the whole time. It also hurts any children that are involved, extended families of both partners, close friends of both partners, any congregation or social network of which both partners are a part, etc.

To the One Who Has Engaged in Infidelity

It is vital that you understand that just because *you* are over it, this is not synonymous with your *partner* being over it. Your partner might still be reeling with an onslaught of emotional pain, misgivings, doubt, second-guessing, deep feelings of abandonment and rejection, and feelings of low self-worth and self-doubt.

Firstly, expect for there to be good days and bad days. There can even be long stretches of relative peace and harmony, followed by abrupt days or weeks of despair, anger, frustration, questioning, intense caustic language, etc. Especially for a woman, this can be especially damaging on several levels.

It is worth noting here that for the most part, men tend to derive their identity from that which they do, in other words, their work. For the most part, women tend to derive their identity from their relationships, and most importantly their marital relationship and their role as mother. This is not to say that women are not deeply involved in their careers. This has absolutely nothing to do with one's career track. Obviously, in today's scheme of things, there are indeed exceptions to what I have just said. But I think my words are still relatively true in most cases.

The reason I state this is because most often, in a heterosexual relationship, it is the man who engages in infidelity, and the woman who is on the receiving end of pain. Obviously anybody can be unfaithful at any time. But from my experience, this is most often the scenario. In a heterosexual relationship, it is very important for the man to understand that *infidelity strikes at the very core of a woman,* because she places so much import and significance *on the relationship. Her identity is tied up in it. When infidelity occurs, it is often an existential crisis of the severest type, for the woman.*

Men need to wrap their heads around this.

Second, it is important to look at the situation and the relationship *through the innocent partner's eyes.* Try to see things from her or his perspective. This will help you to be in the moment, to empathize, and it will mitigate against your tendency to react negatively when your partner is angry or frustrated, or is not terribly careful with words.

The pain and the abandonment need to be released at times, when it gets to be unbearable.

Third, try to have authentic remorse, repentance, and humility during this time. This stance of humility will help your partner to heal, and it will help you to be more likely to have an attitude of building trust in the relationship.

Fourth, if your partner starts to ask questions about *the other person,* and your activities with that other person, try to answer your partner's questions as best you can. No, it's not comfortable, and it's not easy. But this concise explanation and description will help your partner to heal. And if your partner starts to *compare* his/herself to that other person, *quickly reassure your partner that he/she is the apple of your eye, the only person that you love and have feelings for, and the only person that you have attraction for.* Give your partner lots of reassurance that he/she *is good enough.*...because your partner will undoubtedly be thinking otherwise. *Over-articulate* in this area. Lots of love, lots of reassurance.

Fifth, if pornography has been present, and is causing trouble in the relationship, please remember this: Women can sometimes personalize/internalize issues surrounding porn activities in their partner, and become emotionally hurt/damaged if they compare themselves, or feel inferior or undesired. I have seen porn activities cause significant damage in relationships, and sometimes the tendency is for the one who is engaging in it to *minimize* the importance of it, because *"it's not a real person, and not real infidelity."* Yeah right. Well, I have news for you. *It sure feels real* to your partner. And it's very damaging to your partner, and to the relationship.

The same goes for "emotional affairs" and activities or liaisons that didn't actually involve physical aspects. This can still be extremely hurtful to your partner, and very damaging to the relationship. Try not to minimize what has happened, but *have a voice* in it, see it for what it is, be humble, have true remorse, look through your partner's eyes, and be an agent of healing in your partner's life.

Sixth, if you have jealousy or controlling behavior, understand this. Jealousy involves an *uncertain* thought process. It can be very helpful to pause, write down what you are telling yourself about the situation, and correct your self-talk to something true, valid ("How can I have a *voice* in this situation") and reasonable. *Your controlling behavior is a by-product or result of your distorted thought process.* If you are truthful and valid and reasonable with how you relate to this situation, you can then *choose* what your next actions or behaviors will be. In so doing, you will come into the situation or the conversation *from a position of peace and strength,* and *not* from a position of *frantically trying to grasp on to some ledge of safety while free-falling in your thought process* (which is what controlling behavior really is).

Seventh,

Every time you follow through with something you say you will do,

it is like making a deposit in the Bank of Trust for your partner.

That is how you rebuild trust in the relationship. All your partner sees, and all anyone actually sees, is *what you do.* So let your actions and your follow through's speak for you.

If you say you will be at a certain location, *be there.* If you say that you will pick up your son or daughter at a certain time, *do it.* If you say that you will check in with your partner at certain intervals, *make sure you set your alarm for five minutes ahead of time.*

You will be creating a track record of truth, reliability, trust, and dependability. These ongoing deposits in the Bank of Trust will continue to add up. Your partner could eventually acknowledge this track record of trust. This can help you to facilitate healing.

You can easily have three lists to which you have easy access (use your phone notes):

1. Evidences of my partner's care
2. Catch myself doing something right; follow-throughs, instances of correcting self-talk
3. Insights that I have

Be the best husband, the best partner, the best father (or mother), the best person you can be. Live in your top circle, and let your actions back up your words. Don't let anything or anyone stand in your way or deter you from doing your very best in these important roles. Hold you head up high—above the turbulent waters—and have *staying power.*

And if your partner is giving you the cold shoulder, dissing you, and appears to be closed to the idea of reconciliation—*just continue to be the very best partner you can be. Continue to be proactive with planning conversations, be in the moment and answer all questions honestly, be present and a part of things as you are allowed to be.*

Keep doing the next right thing, regardless of what your partner is saying or doing. Whenever possible, shine a big light on what you are doing to improve yourself, and to move forward in life. Your partner will not know about your progress unless you talk about it. Your actions and staying power and follow-throughs will speak loudly. But you must also talk about your progress.

I must be straight with you. There are no guarantees.

Sometimes the other partner has experienced too much emotional pain, and comes to the conclusion that there can be no reconciliation or future for the relationship. But please continue to be the best partner you can be, even in the midst of this incredible uncertainty. Resist the urge to make assumptions.

Be patient, be an agent of healing, embrace the process....

To the One Who Has Been Hurt

Please allow yourself to emote, to feel, to communicate, and to think. It might be helpful to write down your thoughts in a journal. If you have questions or concerns, share them with your partner right away, and don't let all of that angst be kept inside to rot, fester, and turn into toxic resentment on the one hand, or debilitating depression on the other.

It might be helpful to talk to a trusted counselor or a clergy person, so that you do not give in to the tendency to blame yourself, or compare yourself. Often it is much easier to process what we are experiencing when we have an objective, outside voice responding to what we are saying. That trained professional can help you to see patterns, pitfalls, and help you to be productive even in the midst of uncertainty.

Resist the urge to compare yourself to that other person. This isn't about you, and it isn't about that other person. It's about your partner, who had a lapse in judgment, good sense, faithfulness, and morality. See it for what it is, AND PLEASE DO NOT BLAME YOURSELF FOR WHAT HAS HAPPENED. This is false guilt, and not helpful, nor necessary.

Do not start to *compare yourself to that other person.* This is the tendency in many cases, but it is not good for you, and again, this isn't really about you. There's nothing wrong with you. Sure, we can all make improvements, but comparing yourself to that other person is *damaging to you.* It will cause you to feel like you are *not good enough.* Resist the urge to compare yourself to that other person. This is not helpful, but damaging.

When your partner is being truthful and humble, let your partner know that you appreciate it. When your partner is blaming you, or is minimizing his or her actions, call your partner out on it, and let your partner know you see right through the subterfuge and mental gymnastics.

Healing from an *instance* or *history* of unfaithfulness takes time. So do not worry if you have three fairly good days followed by two horrible days. This should be expected.

And to you also I say, *Be the best wife, the best partner, the best mother (or father), the best person you can be.* Live in your top circle, and let your actions back up your words. Don't let anything or anyone stand in your way or deter you from doing your very best in these important roles.

Talk to someone when you are down, keep communication lines open. Do not isolate.

To Both of You

I recommend that both of you take part in the Affair Recovery Bootcamp. This is a seven-day experience of readings, videos, writing, processing, and conversations. This is an excellent program, it is absolutely free, and it has helped many many couples to have better understanding, and to have healing in their relationships. There are tasks and assignments for the partner who has engaged in infidelity, and there are tasks and assignments for the partner who has not. This is a very helpful week-long Boot Camp whenever there is unfaithfulness in a relationship, and I highly recommend it. Here is the link to this important bootcamp:

https://www.affairrecovery.com/surviving-infidelity/first-steps-bootcamp

There is another resource that can be very helpful when there has been electronic involvement, such as visiting porn sites or communicating with someone in an inappropriate fashion electronically. This resource is called Covenant Eyes, and in this scenario, the partner who has been unfaithful gives his or her partner the ability and the permission to be aware of the sites and activity on all of his or her devices. An emailed report is generated on a regular basis for the other partner to view. This can be absolutely huge and very helpful for transparency, and for the rebuilding of trust in the relationship. This is an accountability piece, and it is very important. Here is the link to this resource:

https://www.covenanteyes.com/

Yes, it is possible for there to be healing in a relationship when there has been unfaithfulness. It takes time and dedication. It is very helpful to re-examine one's original marital vows, or, if there is not a marriage in place, the original commitments that were made. Remind yourself of what you once committed and promised your partner. Be honest with yourself, and ask yourself if you can recommit to those vows or commitments to your partner at this time.

Both partners should go through this process, and should consider this along with the context of the "This is Me" worksheet, which contains your values, preferences, preferred scenario for the future, and stance on the major areas of a relationship.

This will help you decide if continuing the relationship is a good idea or not. Sometimes there is healing and reconciliation when unfaithfulness occurs, and sometimes there is not healing and reconciliation.

As always, it is important to have self-respect, integrity, and honesty in the relationship.

Be safe, and be true to your values.

Debriefing Session

Communication is such a vital part of a meaningful relationship. When it is happening, there is usually peace in the relationship. When it is either not happening or is very strained or volatile, the relationship can be anything BUT peaceful.

This is where the "Debriefing Session" comes in. Yes, it is possible for two people to talk right past each other. It is also possible for assumptions to take place, for resentments to be held, and for misunderstandings to be common.

Debriefing sessions are common in the military, in law enforcement, and in the business world. So let me explain what I mean about a "Debriefing Session" for relationships. It's a little different. This should be at a time that is private, free from distraction and noise, and consistent. If you have little ones, make sure that they are either already in bed, or at least in their own rooms. Some people find it easier to have a "Debriefing Session" on the weekend.

Sit right next to your partner in a relaxed setting. This is a cozy, informal setting, and you can even have popcorn if you want. The popcorn actually helps, and it sets the tone. Sit next to each other on either a love seat or a sofa. It is an atmosphere of acceptance and love. But it is very focused. Please turn your phones off for this. This is dedicated time for the two of you. Once-a-week is about right, in terms of frequency.

So let's say you are starting this "Debriefing Session." Try to start things off with an affirmation. Say something that you appreciate about your partner, maybe something he/she did or followed through with, or said, or how that person is dressed—it can be anything, but it needs to be authentic and honest. You are catching your partner doing something right, and that feels good for you, and feels good for your partner. This is very healthy.

Then you can talk about your day, and stressors you had, and how you handled those stressors (just the highlights). Then you can talk about a concern or insight that you have about the relationship.

But you are doing all of this with a calm voice. You are picking your words carefully, you are watching your tone of voice, and being mindful of your volume, and you are not pouring gas on the fire (no need to). AND you can take your time, because *you have a captive audience.*

So, here is a principle of this "Debriefing Session." ONLY ONE PERSON TALKS AT A TIME. WHOEVER HAS THE PEN, HAS THE FLOOR. THE OTHER PERSON'S JOB IS TO *ACTUALLY LISTEN*, AND RESIST THE URGE TO JUMP IN THERE, AND INTERRUPT.

So you have a captive audience. Take your time, pace yourself. And when you are done, pass the pen to your partner. Now it's your turn to listen. The pen is an important visual aid that will help both of you to be mindful and respectful, in the moment.

And hopefully your partner will reciprocate, and give you a nice affirmation. That would be nice. And both of you will know ahead of time that this is how this thing starts. With an affirmation.

Your partner can then talk about their day, and stressors they encountered, and how they handled those stressors (highlights). Your partner can also talk about the relationship, and a concern or insight he/she has about the relationship. Your partner can also *respond* to what you just said. But your partner is doing all of this with a calm voice. Your partner is picking his/her words carefully, watching his/her tone of voice, being mindful of his/her volume, and not pouring gas on the fire (no need to). And your partner can take his/her time, because your partner *also has a captive audience.*

When done, your partner can pass the pen back to you. And at this point, when you first get that pen back, it's a good idea for you to summarize just the main points of what your partner just said. You can say something like, "Honey, I just want to make sure I am hearing you correctly." Then you can summarize the main aspects of what your partner just said —just the highlights. And if you are on the right track, your partner can nod his/her head in agreement.

Then you can carefully *respond* to what your partner just said.

So, a few important dynamics are happening here. Number one, the two of you *are actually hearing each other.* You are each giving to the other the gift of hearing, which is a valuable gift. You are each facilitating the other actually having a voice in the relationship, and you are validating each other. This is wonderful.

Secondly, *you are dealing with issues in real time,* before anything has the potential to be swept under the rug, or fall through the cracks, or to be internalized so that it becomes toxic resentment. None of that is happening, because you are dealing with issues in real time, and you are getting things out there on the table. This "Debriefing Session" is a little microcosm of the relationship. It's a *dance within a dance.* And you are practicing careful communication.

And thirdly, *there's no wait time!* You don't have to wait for two hours or two days to get a response from your partner. You're going to get an *immediate* response, and so will your partner. This is fantastic.

Now, this "Debriefing Session" can go on for 20 minutes, 40 minutes, and hour—I would say that an hour is just right. You can get a lot done in an hour. And time tends to move right along in a "Debriefing Session." I think it's because both of you are fully engaged, and totally caught up in what each other is saying.

More important than the duration of this meeting is the *frequency* of it. Try to schedule one "Debriefing Session" every week, with a recurring day and time. This is best.

Now, there are some pretty nifty outflows to this "Debriefing Session." Firstly, you will find yourself being a little more careful communicator and responder in other areas of your life. The careful communicating happening in the "Debriefing Session" will *spill over* into the other areas of your life, and you will find yourself being a more active listener, and a more careful responder with your own words and tone.

Secondly, you might have something on your mind—maybe a concern or an insight about the relationship that is a bit sensitive in nature—and you know that there is a "Debriefing Session" coming up in just a couple days. You can hang on to that concern or insight until then, and bring it up then, in the "Debriefing Session," where you can be more careful with it, take your time with it, and the two of you can wrap your heads around it safely and efficiently.

> **In a "Debriefing Session" you can shine a
> big 'ole light on your progress,
> your struggles, your concerns, your triumphs,
> your love for your partner,
> your passions, your longings, your dreams.**
>
> **You can *lay bare your very soul* in a "Debriefing Session,"
> and give your partner a glimpse of *who you are*.**

You can even talk about your earlier marital vows, or earlier commitments you made to your partner, *and express what these vows and commitments mean to you NOW, in the present tense.* This can be very powerful, and can facilitate healing in a relationship. It can also help to place the relationship in the present, and can give you a huge voice in the here and now.

You can even devote an entire "Debriefing Session" to a specific topic, or an upcoming trip, or an upcoming relocation, or anything you want. It's the perfect time and place and format for really wrapping your heads around something of import. You can even set up a large (or small) dry erase board, so the two of you can have a nice visual on what you are saying, deciding, and planning. And this can also be used for writing two columns—aspects on which you agree, and aspects on which you do not agree. Then the two of you can concentrate on the areas of dissonance, and each agree to make some little adjustments in order to bring some congruence and peace into the situation. Remember, there is some wiggle room, so model for your partner how to make a simple adjustment. Just don't violate your values in the process.

So, the "Debriefing Session" is a practical, ongoing, meeting of hearts and minds.

Now, most women absolutely love "Debriefing Sessions." There are probably exceptions. But this is something that we guys need to understand about our ladies. Men, for the most part, like to *fix things,* and *find quick solutions,* and then move on. Most women are not at all wanting this in us, however. What they really truly want from us is for us to:

> ***Come along side them,***
> ***Support and Attend,***
> ***and Listen carefully.***

They want a Collaboration,
not a quick fix.

They want security and safety,
and love, and caring
in the relationship.

You can make suggestions, sure.
They do not mind this.
But put a premium on listening,
and supporting.

And you will get plenty of practice do just that in the regular, ongoing, "Debriefing Session." It is wonderful, and that's why most ladies absolutely *love* "Debriefing Sessions." They are actually *heard*.

I work with a lot of couples, and many people have told me that for the very first time they actually felt like their partner *heard them*, in a "Debriefing Session."

Here is a summary of the "Debriefing Session":

Debriefing Session

- Consistent time each week
- Casual, seated right next to each other (popcorn)
- Warm, accepting setting
- No pressure
- Whoever has the pen has the floor
- The other person's job is to actually listen, not interrupt
- Start with an honest, authentic affirmation, something you appreciate about what your partner has done, or followed through with, or said, or how they dressed today
- Then talk about your day, and stressors you encountered in your day, and how you handled those stressors

- Then talk about concerns you have in the relationship, but you are being tactful yet firm, not raising your voice or throwing gas on the fire
- You have a captive audience, so you can take your time
- When you are done, pass the pen to your partner, and now it is your turn to actually listen

* Nothing stated in a "Debriefing Session" is meant as an attack. It is rather meant to bring health, healing, and wellness to the relationship.

* We cannot do a thing about the past, except learn from it.

* We can have ownership for past mistakes, and humility. This goes a long ways toward helping your partner feel safe and comfortable.

* You can also give your partner tangible ways you are engaging in self-improvement, in the present tense.

* A debriefing session helps both of you to be transparent.

* Give your partner a window into your innermost convictions, resolutions, and efforts. Let your partner *feel* your priorities.

Collaboration: *It's a Dance*

One of the most important things to remember about any meaningful relationship, is that *it's a dance.* Try to think of it that way. It's a dance, and there is give-and-take. I mentioned this up above, but I want to reiterate it now.

Try to have a *collaboration* in working with your partner. Work together, plan together, enjoy the journey together, strategize together, but a budget together *together.* Don't place something in that budget unless both of you are in agreement. And don't spend anything or pay for anything that is not in your budget unless *both of you* are fine with it.

So often one partner will isolate (or both), and each partner will be trying to chart a course forward in isolation. This can be very frustrating, and can lead to friction in the relationship. So, work together, plan together, have a lively dance.

Have a collaboration, and have each other's backs. For instance, talk about how each of you would like to spend time with friends. Guide each other into safety and propriety. You each can have a voice. As long as one of you feels uncomfortable about something, or some person, that should be a deal-breaker, and a good enough reason *not* to engage in it. This is having a united front, and this preserves the respect and dignity of both of you. You both can creatively find alternative activities with which you both feel comfortable. This is not raining on your partner's parade. It is being honest, and having the back of your partner. You can safeguard each other, love each other, promote the peace of each other.

It's a collaboration.

ROCD and What to Do about It

ROCD, or Relationship OCD can be present sometimes in a relationship. A person can be insecure in their relationships in general, and particularly in their intimate relationship. You might find yourself worrying about your partner's overall loyalty, or doubting your own personal feelings for that person. All of this can be somewhat normal in a relationship. But sometimes these worries and insecurities can get out of hand, and cause turbulence in the relationship.

These insecurities and fears can start to take over your life, and can start turning into obsessions that culminate in compulsive behavior or mental acts. This can take the form of having to constantly seek reassurance from your partner, or checking your feelings when you are with your partner. This is when you know that your fears and insecurities have turned into

ROCD.

ROCD can be debilitating mentally and emotionally. It can impair our functioning and our work. For instance, a person can spend all morning texting their partner to check on their whereabouts, which can result in getting behind at work. Or a person can obsess about whether or not what they have in their relationship is actually true love, constantly comparing one's feelings to the ones they see portrayed in fiction. You can start comparing yourself to that person you see in that movie, etc., and you can start feeling like you are not good enough, which can lead to anxiety and depression.

It is important to remember that the more you engage in these obsessive thoughts, the more you will be engaging in compulsive behaviors that are detrimental to your relationship. It's a vicious cycle.

Your partner may be giving you reassurance, but this doesn't seem to help you. You are caught in a vicious loop, and other questions start arising. You might start thinking about different outcomes or actual events, and you are off in Conjectureville.

So, the moment you *start* to have insecurities, fears, and anxious thoughts, *immediately take a step back, take some deep breaths, and ask yourself, "What is the truth about this situation? How can I have a voice in this situation, and what does that look like? (Valid), and what is the reasonable thing about this situation?"*

Take a few moments to *process* what you are actually telling yourself about the situation at hand, and what you are believing about it. Be truthful about it, have a voice in it, and be reasonable about it, and this will always have a calming effect on us. It will get you out of the weeds with thinking, and your fears and insecurities do not have to result in compulsive behaviors as coping mechanisms.

If you do not know what the truth is, *ASK*. Go ahead and have a sit-down with your partner, and *ask* specific questions that are of concern to you. *Engage* your partner, and let your partner *respond.* Allow your partner to explain and clarify, and to shed some light on your concern and fear. This collaboration will ease the pressure on you to engage in unhealthy compulsive behaviors and second-guesses.

The truth is, even if you find yourself presently in the midst of doubt, fear, and insecurity, *you do not have to put feet on these fears, and start wasting valuable time with checking behavior or comparing your relationship to other ideal scenarios.*

You can instead tell yourself the truth about the situation, have a voice in that situation (start communicating, when you both have time), and you can be reasonable. When you are living in ____ville, you learn to have a voice all the time, and you will see those emotional and mental pitfalls coming, even before they get to you. You will be able to avoid disruptive and distorted thinking, because you are aware of your surroundings, and you are aware of your own thought process.

If you try to put into practice what I have suggested above, and you still find yourself struggling with debilitating fears and insecurities about your relationship, with resulting problematic compulsive behaviors, I recommend that you try to make an appointment with a therapist who specializes in OCD, so you can have some further guidance in this area. This can be very helpful.

Also, please read the earlier chapter on OCD, if you believe that you may be experiencing some of the symptoms of Relationship OCD. That chapter can give you a methodology that helps you to *live alongside* the fear, distress and uncertainty; to tolerate it.

Becoming *Present Tense*

It is always helpful for a couple to be *present tense* with each other, and not to hold the past against each other. This is not to say that healing is not needed in a relationship sometimes. You can indeed work through that healing process together. I have explained above how partners can help themselves in this regard, and help the relationship. Certainly, if healing and rebuilding are needed, *be about them.*

But once you both work through the angst and the pain and the sad or damaging history, *try to move forward.*

Try to now start building *new history* together. Start writing a new chapter together, with shared experiences, shared adventure, shared day trips and getaways. Continue to have the weekly consistent "Debriefing Session," and keep the communication lines open with each other. You can even take your original marital vows, or original commitments, and together discuss and declare what these vows and commitments mean to you *now, in the present tense, in the hear and now, in this brand new chapter of your life together.*

And you both need to agree that neither of you will start throwing the past in the other's face, if the urge comes along. You both need to agree to keep that crap/garbage/pain/sad history *behind you.*

Each of you can think about the past, learn from the past, and *extract whatever you can learn from that past memory—that past hurt—extract and learn and be sharpened by as much as you can from that previous hurtful experience, leaving only an exoskeleton of that previous hurtful experience, that can easily be blown away with the wind. Just let it go, let it be blown away with the wind.*

You both know that we cannot do a *thing* about the past, except learn from it. And by this time you have both learned a lot.

So, apply that wisdom and those insights to this present new chapter, and start writing together a *renewed love story*.

Another Word to Those Not Yet Married

Long before marriage, try to see your partner in a variety of settings. Pay careful attention to how your partner handles him/herself in public. Notice how your partner communicates to others in general. Observe how your partner treats you and how your partner relates to you when around other people. And try to ascertain if your partner stares at others, or spends a lot of time on his/her phone when in your company.

Please remember that the patterns of behavior and communication that you see now do not go away when you get married; they only *increase.*

If you are thinking "Oh, I can change my partner over time, no problem. It'll be just fine" you might want to rethink that. While we do have an influence over our partners, we cannot do a thing about their priorities, inclinations, patterns, communication style, substance use, or general lifestyle.

If you are not yet married, and your partner has a tendency to have anger outbursts, or to yell at you or call you names, or to be flirtatious with others, or to ignore you, or to be more into self than you, *these tendencies will only increase with time.* Please complete the "This is Me" worksheet, so that you can have a good idea of *where you stand* in a variety of important areas. Be careful, and choose wisely.

Advice to Women Being Abused

If you are currently in a relationship, and your partner is verbally, emotionally, physically, or sexually abusing you, *you need to get out of that relationship immediately.*

Talk to someone in privacy about it. Have some self-respect, talk to a trusted counselor or a member of the clergy, and get some help. If it is actually unsafe for you to leave, there are safe houses and women's shelters that are private and secure at which you can temporarily stay, get some sleep, get some food, and get some healing.

And you can also get an order of protection going ASAP. Express *fear* and *specifics* on the forms, when applying for that order. It will be taken more seriously.

Please do not stay another moment in a relationship in which you are being victimized and abused. ***You are valuable, you have a future, and you deserve much better than that.***

Here are two places you can call anytime to get immediate help:

National Domestic Abuse Hotline
800-799-SAFE (7233)

Women in Distress
954-761-1133

Yes, men can also be victims of abuse. These phone numbers can also be used by men.

Please be careful and take your time when you are getting to know someone and are in a relationship. Be observant, and resist the urge to minimize problematic traits of your partner.

Be good to yourself. And most certainly, if you are currently in an unsafe situation, contact someone who cares as soon as possible. And *seek safety.*

Attachment Styles and Dating

I think it is prudent to have a *Secure* attachment style. John

Bowlby came up with this in his important book in the 1950s. But you don't have to read a book on attachment styles in order to help yourself move in a healthy manner. Just aim for the *good stuff*, and thanks, John Bowlby:

10 Signs of Secure Attachment in Adult Relationships

Able to regulate emotions and feelings in a relationship
Strong goal-oriented behavior when on your own
Great at bonding, opening up to, & trusting others
Knowing what you're about in life and what purpose you want to fulfill
Can communicate your needs effectively
Feeling like you have an impact on the world around you
Comfortable with closeness & mutual dependency
Actively seek emotional support from your partner and also give emotional support to your partner
Comfortable being alone and use that time to explore
Strong capacity to reflect on how you are being in a relationship[93]

A Word about Youngins'

If you are currently going through a difficult breakup or divorce, remember:

1. You are modeling for them that sometimes relationships don't quite work out, and we learn from it.

2. Be sure to let them know that you are not trying to replace their mother/father, and that she/he will always be their mother/father.

3. Let them know that you are just trying to find your way in life, and to get to know people.

4. Tell them "Feel free to ask me questions and tell me things that are important to you."

5. Reassure them that this breakup or divorce is certainly not their fault (because kids sometimes think that).

And remember that our youngins are constantly absorbing and normalizing *everything we do.* They soak up our attitude, our priorities, how we handle stressors, whether or not we self-medicate with substances, how we communicate to their other parent (or anyone), whether or not we spend quality time with them, our worldview, our political preferences, our hobbies, our passions, how we spend our free time, whether or not we sneak a peek at a cute lady or guy when their other parent is not looking, our spiritual ideas, and the list goes on and on.

We are ALWAYS setting the tone for our children, whether we know it or not, and whether we like it or not. So we might as well live our lives in such a way that is consistent with our values, our personal goals, our convictions and beliefs, and our passions in life. We might as well model for them how to handle tough situations, and how to manage one's time. We might as well teach them about a good work ethic, and about personal accountability.

And by all means, be intentional about spending regular quality time with your kids. Give them the gift of hearing. Just be in the moment with them, and let them tell their stories. They will talk about all kinds of things, but just be there in the moment with them. Catch them doing something right, if it is appropriate. Always distinguish between the *person* and the *objectionable behavior,* when correcting them or guiding them. You can address the problem attitude or behavior, while at the same time *loving that child to pieces.*

This is embracing the important balance in parenting between *firmness* and *unconditional love.* And you help that youngin to actually have a voice in life, and to deep down believe like they *actually matter.* This will impact your kids in a big way as they grow older, and eventually enter the adult world. They will be more likely to have a voice at that time, to feel like they actually matter, and to believe that they can actually exert an influence on their surroundings. They will also be much more likely to have some basic personal accountability, because you modeled this for them, when they were young.

And lastly, children today live in a world that is constantly changing and morphing. Their entire world is in chaos, and nothing appears to be sound. Parents are the one thing in their world that *doesn't move when they push against it.* Parents can be that presence of stability in their lives that they can bounce ideas off of, and they can use as an *anchoring point* in their fragile world.

So, don't be afraid to be a *parent* for your children. Yes, you can still be a parent and be firm even while loving them, spending quality time with them, and enjoying life with them. It's an important balance.

And by all means, try to have a *united front* with your partner, when it comes to your children. Have each other's backs, and back each other up when talking with your kids. As you know, kids will sometimes play one parent off the other. They can and will be manipulative, and they are ardent students of human behavior. So please have a united front in all your dealings with your youngins. Use the pronoun "WE" rather than I, when possible.

These youngins need to know that both parents are on the same page, that you both truly care, and that you both will stand your ground and back each other up, when they are trying to play one of you off the other.

Practical Helps

When in a relationship, and you find yourself starting to

become upset about something, try to hang on till a little later in the day, when both of you are more relaxed, and in a better frame of mind, and then come together to talk about it. You can also hang on to the topic/issue and bring it up in a few days at the next "Debriefing Session," when you can give it careful attention, and discuss it in a safe environment.

Also, if the two of you are are talking and both of you are becoming louder and more upset as the seconds go by, you can both agree to have a *red card* on top of the refrigerator. And when you are sensing that things are beginning to get a little out of hand, you can hold up that red card, and this will send a strong signal to your partner that you *want to have a pause in the conversation, so you both can go to a different part of the home and calm down, take some deep breaths, and collect your thoughts.* Then you can come back in 15 minutes and resume that conversation, when both of you are a lot calmer. We can accomplish more, and think more clearly, and speak more appropriately, *when we are calm.*

So both of you can agree to having a red card that either of you can use, when necessary. And you both can agree to honor the red card, if the other holds it up.

Reciprocation is an Extra

I just want to gently remind you that *reciprocation is an extra,* and that you need to be careful with your expectations in your relationship. You need to discuss these with your partner. The "This is Me" sheet will greatly help you to do this—to identify your expectations in a variety of areas. These areas, and this reflection, become fodder for robust and meaningful discussion with your partner.

But even if you are decent, and kind, and courteous, and helpful to your partner, there is no guarantee that your partner will return the decency, the kindness, the courtesy, or the helpfulness to you. It's a messed-up world, and you and I cannot even begin to control what another person—let alone our partners—think or feel about us, or how they respond to us, or *if they reciprocate our love and kindness back to us.*

No, we cannot control any of that. But we can have a voice in life, and we can put one foot in front of the other, and we indeed can model for our partners how to live, and we can set the tone for our partners as to how to relate to someone they love.

We can do that.

And if by chance your partner does reciprocate, and loves you, and cherishes you, and has your back, and dances along with you, *consider it extra.*

You can then sing along with the passing-by fella in the *VeggieTales* episode *Lord of the Beans:*

> *"Oh, I'm a luck fella*
> *I'm a lucky boy*
> *I've got a new umbrella*
> *And it's me pride and joy!"*

---

93. Cited from the site, https://www.attachmentproject.com/blog/secure-attachment/. Accessed September 27, 2023.

SUBSTANCES IMPACT MENTAL HEALTH

As I write this important chapter, I just want to say that I am in recovery myself, and I have a polysubstance abuse history. But my main go-to substances were weed and alcohol. So I do not think that I am better than anyone else, and I come at this subject with humility, having learned tough lessons in life, and having experienced firsthand the detrimental impact of substances.

I am also a substance abuse counselor, and have been for quite a while. I enjoy *giving back* to others, and my aim is to help, not hinder.

Values Revisited

We have discussed previously the foundational nature of values; how deeply rooted they are in our being, and how important they are. They really should inform every decision we make in life, and be allowed to impact our every-day existence.

Nothing or no one can take your values away from you, or change them. The only person who can touch your values is you. This is where substances come into the picture. With substance abuse and especially physiological or psychological dependence, after a while the substance of choice becomes *the overwhelming value around which everything else revolves.* It's just a matter of time. Whatever good values we may have had at one time, they get put on the shelf, and the value of feeding our addiction takes the forefront of our thinking and our planning. In truth, substances are basically the only thing that can remove our values or make them of no effect.

The Impact of Substances

Ongoing substance abuse can affect the brain's health both short-term and long-term, especially if pre-existing mental health issues are present. In fact, those who have a chemical dependence are almost twice as likely to have anxiety and mood disorders already. Paranoia, hallucinations, depression and other debilitating conditions can develop on top of these illnesses. Often, people suffering from substance use disorders will develop mental health issues that compound with a pre-existing condition, making daily life even more difficult to navigate.

These changes in mental health will produce behaviors that are consistent with substance use disorders. Family and friends will often report:

• Secretive or suspicious behavior

• Changes in their social environment, sometimes distancing themselves from those they were close to, while spending time with new, separate groups

• Bouts of hyperactivity, irritability, and anger

• Lowered performance and attendance at work or school

• Decreased motivation and interest in things they once loved

• Suspicious and paranoid thoughts towards close friends and family

• Risk-taking behavior and frequent instances of getting into trouble

These changes affect the patient's ability to maintain relationships, succeed at work or school, socialize, learn new skills, and to contribute positively to society in general. This isolation can subsequently lead to feelings of shame or defeat, and present a barrier to a patient seeking treatment for their drug or alcohol misuse. (Pathwayhealthcare.com)

A Word about *Herb*

Cannabis has been around for a long time. Weed has always gotten a free ride socially, since the 1960s. Weed hasn't been nearly as scrutinized or looked down upon by society as alcohol has. But herb can be just as detrimental to one's life, albeit in a slightly different way.

For one thing, the human brain continues to develop into the mid-twenties. When a young person is regularly using Cannabis in childhood, in their teens, and into their early 20s, THC is so powerful, it can actually negatively impact the *actual development of the brain.* Not a good thing at all. And that young person must now try to find their way in life with a brain that has been hijacked, and is under a cognitive cloud. Yay.

Important research went into the study "U.S. Surgeon General's Advisory: Marijuana Use and the Developing Brain" in 2019. Very important findings were reached in this study[94]. First of all, Marijuana use during pregnancy can definitely harm the developing fetus. THC can negatively impact fetal brain development. Marijuana use during pregnancy can result in adverse outcomes, such as lower birth weight, and apparently this is the case regardless of maternal age, race, ethnicity, education, and tobacco use.

And even after birth, THC has been found in breast milk up to six days past the last usage. THC can affect the newborn's brain development and result in hyperactivity, and poor cognitive function.

Again, the human brain continues to develop from before birth into the mid-20s, and it is definitely vulnerable to the effects of addictive substances. Specifically, marijuana use can result in deficits in memory and attention in teens, even after a month of abstinence. For teens, there are declines in IQ tests, and school performance, which can put in jeopardy social achievement and professional development. With THC, there are also documented increased rates of school absence, dropout, as well as suicide attempts.

In addition, the risk for psychotic disorders, such as schizophrenia, increases with frequency of use, potency of the marijuana product, and as the age of first use decreases. Teens who abuse marijuana also are much more likely to misuse opioids.[95]

So, if you are trying to move forward in life, THC is not going to help you. It's going to drag you down big time. It also has four times the amount of tar as cigarettes, so if you are going to use it, try not to smoke it—it's absolutely horrible for the lungs. THC decreases critical thinking, slows down reaction time, hampers memory and retention, and there are areas of the brain that no longer have any electrical activity after just two years of regular use (I have seen the PET scans).

Both alcohol and Cannabis can exacerbate mental health symptoms, and negatively impact productivity, cognition, response time, memory, critical thinking, and motivation.

As if this wasn't bad enough, daily marijuana users are about one-third more likely to develop *coronary artery disease,* compared with people who have never used the drug, researchers say. The investigators found that Cannabis use was associated with higher levels of a type of blood fat called triglycerides and LDL ("bad") cholesterols, as well as higher body mass index. THC in blood vessels may produce *inflammation* and the buildup of *plaque,* which can lead to heart disease, the researchers suggested[96].

I have seen many train wrecks, and many clients have told their stories of how weed has negatively impacted them in a variety of ways. Indeed, it has impacted me very much in my own life. I have helped many people to put the herb behind them, and these folks have experienced a new life of peace, productivity, and cognitive awareness.

So my guidance to you would be, try to put this stuff behind you, if you are actually trying to move forward in life. Everything I just stated is easily substantiated by simple research. You must make up your own mind. Do your own vetting, have a voice, and don't just fall in line with every passing fad or pastime or new drug. The truth is available if we are open to it. The problem is, most people do not want to hear it. They just want their thrill, their high, their stupor, their malaise. They just want instant gratification. But this is actually not a good mindset, nor a good way to live.

It is far more healthy, more in-line with wellness, if we can find alternative, *healthier* ways to cope, to improve our sleep, to ease anxiety. *Actual* coping strategies really do help us to cope, to sleep better, and to be far less anxious. Those strategies are found throughout this book. And as for gratification, it's good to *wait for it,* for it will come, if we are living consistently with our values, our personal goals, our convictions and beliefs, and our passions.

True gratification that is satisfying comes from an honest day's work,

a well-laid plan,

a robust follow-through,

and an authentic idea and expression.

The Jellinek Chart

If you are abusing alcohol or a particular drug, including Cannabis, you need to be aware of the basic progression that substance-abuse takes. The Jellinek chart helps us to have a visual on this incredible progression. More correctly stated, it is a *downward* progression, or decline.

The Jellinek curve was created by E.M. Jellinek, and later Dr. Max M. Glatt added the slope upward in recovery. At the end of this section, I will give you a website where you can find the actual Jellinek chart. For those who wish to be in recovery, it is useful to print this Jellinek chart and to keep it handy where you can frequently view it.

At this time I will summarize this chart, and explain it as best I can.

In the **Progression stage**, there is an increase in alcohol tolerance, and the onset of memory blackouts. Please keep in mind that this chart was designed primarily in the context of alcohol. But the same exact progression happens with any substance.

In this stage there is secret drinking or using to compensate for increased tolerance. Accordingly, there is increased dependence on the particular substance of abuse. There is increased thinking and planning and scheming related to that substance of choice. There is also a decreased ability to stop using the substance of choice, and the compulsive need to keep going after one use.

In the **Crucial stage,** drinking or using is bolstered with excuses. There is a system of defense to justify drinking behavior or using behavior. There is grandiose and aggressive behavior sometimes, culminating in becoming a big spender to purchase friendship and convince self that all is well. There can at times be belligerence, the picking of fights, and increased aggressive behavior. Efforts to control usage fail repeatedly.

In this stage, family and friends are avoided, and there is a general deterioration of meaningful relationships. There can be work and financial troubles, and a reduction in job performance caused by abnormal use of the substance of choice. There can be a neglect of financial responsibilities.

Also in this stage, there can be unreasonable resentments and deep hostility against everything that makes the alcoholic or addict face up to the actual problem. In this stage there can be geographical escapes; a move to get away from the problems created by excessive drinking or usage. There can also be early morning drinking or early morning using, starting the day with the substance of choice, and continuing to use or drink around the clock in order to keep a certain amount of the substance in the blood stream at all times. There is physical deterioration, and marked physical and psychological breakdown such as cirrhosis, brain damage, and neurosis. There is also the onset of lengthy intoxications, and uncontrolled drinking and usage for days, weeks, and sometimes months.

When I say that addiction and alcoholism are monsters, it is definitely an understatement. They completely take over a person's life.

In the **Chronic stage,** there is moral deterioration, and the code of ethics that the person has breaks down. The alcoholic and addict will beg, barter, or steel in order to get their substance of choice. At this stage there is impaired thinking, and indefinable fears of impending danger not related to reality. With alcohol, there can be trembling and shaking brought on by prolonged use. There is an inability to initiate action, and a lack of coordination caused by prolonged usage of the substance of choice.

At this stage there can be vague spiritual desires, in other words a turning to God as a last resort to keep a drink down or one more usage of the substance of choice without getting sick. All alibis are exhausted in this stage, and no more excuses can be found on which to blame the alcohol or substance usage. At this point the person completely admits defeat, and there is a realization that the person has no control at all over the addiction or alcoholism. There is a vicious circle of drinking in order to get well, and no longer getting high or drunk. There is a desperate effort simply to maintain a *semblance of functionality.*

If an individual continues down this downward spiral, it ultimately leads to insanity, loss of everything meaningful to the person, utter demise, and premature death.

Thankfully, a person does not have to continue down this road to despair and demise. The person can actually begin a life of recovery. **Recovery is life.** And in recovery, *the person begins to rediscover his or her values, relationships, motivation, appetite, health, and overall wellness.*

In recovery, there is an *honest desire for help.* There is a cessation of usage. There is an understanding and acceptance of the fact that alcoholism and addiction are illnesses, and not character defects. In recovery the person learns that they are not alone on this trek, and that there are also other people who are trying to start life over. There is an appreciation of possibilities of a new way of life.

In recovery, there can be reconnection with one's primary

care physician, and basic examination and lab work. The person might start attending individual and group therapy, in order to learn coping skills for recovery. There is better nourishment, and more realistic thinking. Also the desire to escape vanishes, and the person learns how to deal with *life on life's terms,* without resorting to *the filter of a substance that merely masks life's problems.*

In recovery there is a new adjustment to family needs, and appreciation of friends and family and work associates. New interests develop, and there is the rebirth of ideals and personal plans for the future. In recovery there is the return of emotional stability, and a incredible improvement in the financial status of the individual. More attention is given to personal appearance, and the person is much more aware of their tendency to rationalize or minimize their usage or drinking.

In short, the person is now able to have true ownership, and true accountability. Their brain and body are healing.

Yes, the projected course of usage for all substances, including Cannabis—which has always had a free ride socially—the projected course is downward with increasing inability to control one's desires and choices, and the deterioration of one's relationships and commitments.

In recovery, the very opposite is the case. *There is an upward movement in one's life, a rediscovery of one's values and personal goals, and increased awareness of ways to manage life's stressors without resorting to substances.*

For more information on the Jellinek curve, and to see an actual visual of the progression, here is a website that will give you this important visual:

https://hopeshedslight.org/pdf/ProgressionAddict_jellinek_chart.pdf

How to Build a Recovery Program

There are three main aspects of a quality recovery program: **support, accountability, and coping strategies or education.** This powerful trio helps a person to move forward in life, free of substances.

If a person is still in the midst of increasingly serious usage or drinking, they may need to have a medically-supervised detox experience. This is especially important if the substance of choice is alcohol or benzodiazepines, such as Xanax, Klonopin and Ativan. With alcohol and Benzos, a person can have major complications and life-threatening withdrawal symptoms. So medically-supervised detox is the best way to go. The staff can help the person remain calm and stable while they are going through withdrawal.

Ideally, this detox experience should be immediately followed by a residential rehab experience in a quality structured program. As for length of program, 90 days is best, but 28 days will also suffice. In residential rehab, the person learns coping skills, learns that addiction and alcoholism are illnesses, learns that there are many other people who are dealing with substances, and the brain starts to heal so that they can start thinking clearly about life. There really is no substitute for this very valuable experience. Although it can be very inconvenient at the time, and the person may have to leave family and work in order to attend residential rehab, it is actually the best decision to make, in terms of recovery.

Again, recovery is life. It must become the primary motive and primary priority in the person's life, or it will not work. If a person can place a **first priority on recovery**, *everything else will fall in place as it should.*

If, for whatever reason, you are not able to check in to a protracted rehab program, you can still *approximate* this experience by setting up for yourself an IOP or *Intensive Outpatient Program* in which you will attend 3-5 block classes per week, for several weeks. A person is often able to continue working even while being involved in an IOP program. This can be very helpful. There is much accountability and support, and good learning takes place. There are IOP programs all over the place, if you are interested in one of these.

As for **support,** a person should start attending a regular a support group for recovery immediately following return to home, or if no rehab, right away. This can be AA, NA, *Celebrate Recovery*, *Smart Recovery,* or any other substance recovery group. There are face-to-face meetings, and there are online meetings. Face-to-face is best, because you learn from other people, and there are people in the same room who can catch you when you are trying to minimize your usage or drinking. They can also support you when you are having a difficult day, and when you have low morale and low self-worth. But sometimes an online group can be appropriate, if you live in the middle of nowhere, or you are crunched for time. There are 12 step-based groups such as AA and NA, and there are non-12 step-based groups. But support is very very important in recovery.

As for **accountability,** the person in recovery really needs to find a person who has good recovery going on to be a sponsor or accountability partner. Or it can be a recovery coach. This is very important, because you need someone that you can call 24/7/365 whenever you are having an urge to use or drink, and feeling unsafe. There can also be weekly check-in times. A good sponsor will help you in your time of need. Just do whatever your sponsor says, and everything will be fine. Accountability is extremely important in recovery. You will also get some accountability in the recovery groups that you attend.

Coping skills and education can be initially learned in the rehab experience. They can also be learned in substance-abuse counseling with a qualified substance abuse counselor. In therapy, the individual will learn that they must change up their people, places, and things. In other words, they must start hanging out with a different group of people who are not actively using or drinking.

In therapy the individual also learns how to handle urges to drink or use. If the person can get busy doing something, those urges do not last very long usually. The important thing to understand is that even after many years in recovery, those thoughts of using or drinking can occur at any time. Absolutely anything can be a reason to use or drink, positive or negative. Yes, therapy is an important component of a good recovery program, and should not be skipped. You can also get focused education and coping strategies in an IOP program. And as an adjunct to what you are doing by way of education, you can also start reading a good recovery book, such as the AA or NA Big Book, or some other helpful book.

Important Principles in Recovery

1. **People, Places, Things**. You will need to find friends and people you hang with who either *do not drink or use,* or who are in good recovery themselves. This is your best bet. Yes, it is possible to still hang out with folks who are still drinking and using, but you will have to have a voice and tell these friends not to offer you anything, and not to drink or use around you. Some people are willing to cooperate with this request, and others are not too interested. But help yourself, and put some boundaries in place in your life. Try to find some new friends who are in recovery, and don't use or drink. It will be a lot easier for you, and you won't be surrounded with temptations. Mix it up. Same thing with places and things. Stop hanging out at that place you used to get plastered at. Don't put yourself in situations that will pose a danger to you, and a relapse risk.

As for things, if you have any roach clips or pipes or bongs or whiskey shot glasses, or drink mixers, GET RID OF THIS STUFF RIGHT AWAY! If this kind of thing is still laying around, it is one more way for your substance of choice to pull you back in.

Remember that alcohol and all substances are cunning, baffling, powerful, and *extremely opportunistic.*

So go ahead and "shine a big 'ole light on the situation" by telling your close friends that you are trying be in recovery, and asking them not to offer you any substances. When we communicate our wishes and shine a light on our situation, we are far less likely to engage in sneaky, secretive thinking or planning (or fall into a trap).

Think ahead, and whenever you are planning on being a part of an event in which there will be drinking or using, and it's difficult to get out of it, *intentionally think about how you will handle the situation.*

Although this is not ideal, there are near-beers and virgin mixed drinks as alternatives to alcohol. Most people don't mind at all if you are not drinking or using. You can be a designated driver, and thereby be quite popular.

2. **Hungry, Angry, Lonely, Tired, Bored**. Avoid these! Make sure you have set up your "Intentional Set Routine" and are operating within it. Then you will have a regular time for sleep, wake, meals and exercise. You will be much more on top of things. Because being hungry or tired can pose a relapse risk. And if being around a certain person or situation promotes anger or frustration in you, take a look at your values, and see if any of them are being compromised (that's usually what's happening). Stop hanging around that person or that situation, as best you can. Because being angry can pose a relapse risk. And if you are bored stiff, *find something meaningful to be about.* Get a job. Start training for a career.

Find a fun hobby or a fun experience, such as joining a sober canoe trip down a river, or something similar. This is great, because you get to be around other people who are also trying to enjoy life without substances. And you can also take back some territory and reclaim it, if perhaps you used to use that particular river for drunk tube floats with friends. Being bored can pose a relapse risk.

3. **<u>When that thought comes around, get busy doing something that is clearly under your control</u>**. This is important. These thoughts, these urges, these cravings can come around any 'ole time they want to. It can be three months from now, or 13 years from now. You can be watching a football game, and all-of-a-sudden there's a commercial with Snoop Dogg sitting on the beach with a Corona in his hand. These urges to drink or use can come around any time. So when they do, just get busy doing something that is clearly under your control. Top circle. Just open your "Intentional Set Routine" and it will tell you what to do. No guesswork. Just get busy, and that thought—that urge will go away. It won't stay around. You will thereby be extinguishing that thought, and it probably won't come around very often. *It's only when we entertain that thought, when we give that thought the time of day,* that this thought can become problematic. And that thought can develop feet that walk to the corner store, or to the local dispensary, or can call someone up and make a connection. Now you're in troubled waters. So, don't give that thought—that urge the time of day, and don't entertain that thought. And it will go away. Get busy doing something that is under your control.

4. **It's a Disease**. Try not to think about your usage or drinking as a *character defect*. There is no need to shame yourself. Rather, think of your problem as *a disease*. That's what it is. It's taken time for medical boards in states to come around to this truth, but they are doing so, ever-so-gradually (thankfully).

You don't shame someone who has Diabetes or heart disease, do you? You don't look down on someone who is recovering from major back surgery, right? So neither should you shame yourself, or look down on yourself, simply because you have a disease that involves substances, and the overwhelming urge to use them. It may have started out once upon a time as a *choice,* or act of the will. But after a while that substance of choice takes over. You no longer are using or drinking because you want to, but rather because you feel you need to. It has become your go-to thing. And you are no longer using or drinking to get high or drunk necessarily, but *to just basically function and be normal.* It is a *disease.* Accept it. And now you are starting your recovery from this horrible, life-destroying disease.

5. **"Cunning, Baffling, and Powerful"** *and Opportunistic*. I added to what the Big Book says. Yes, it's true. Alcohol, and all substances, are cunning, baffling, powerful, and I like to add on the adjective *Opportunistic, because anything, good or bad, can be a reason to drink or use.* Your favorite team won, time to celebrate—pass me a cold one or two. Or pass me that pipe and that lighter. Time to light up. Your favorite team lost, time to drown your sorrows in your go-to substance—pass me that bottle. Pass me that bag over there, and a fresh needle. Be very careful. *Anything* can be a reason to drink or use. Be on your guard. We're dealing with substances that are very tricky, and extremely cunning. They will indeed take advantage of our loneliness, despair, transitions, and even our triumphs.

6. **Relapse is Not a Failure.** In fact, some would say that relapse is just a normal part of the recovery process. I don't know if I would go *that* far, but slips and falls do at times happen, when we are trying to maintain sobriety. If that happens, don't beat yourself up or shame yourself. This will only make if more difficult. Consider this as a *learning opportunity* that can actually help you to make better decisions for yourself, and

to actually have a voice and to be intentional about your life. Get right back up, throw away any alcohol or any remainder of substances still lying around. Get right back on the road of recovery. It's not a failure, *it is a learning opportunity.* Be careful with this one.

7. **Don't Set Yourself Up**. The Good Book says it this way: "Make no provision for the flesh" (Romans 13:14). In other words, *don't set yourself up* for disaster. Alcohol, weed, and all substances are *cunning, baffling, powerful,* and *opportunistic.* We start scheming, and planning, and no one knows except us. It's our little secret. Remember that where your focus is, *that is the direction you will travel.* So, try to help yourself, not hurt yourself. If you are going away for the weekend, and you start to make plans to maybe grab something on the way to your hotel room, PAUSE, stop yourself, and catch yourself in what you are planning. *Then make an intentional, concerted effort to make other plans that will steer you away from that opportunistic plan, and towards recovery, which is life.* Turn the table on yourself, and creatively plan an exciting, meaningful weekend for yourself that *doesn't* involve substances, and doesn't need to. Instead of setting yourself up for disaster and relapse, set yourself up for sobriety and wellness. Be an architect.

8. **No One is Exempt**. I used to work with physicians and PAs and dentists all over northern Ohio who were is various stages of change, and various stages of professional demise with their particular professional boards. Certainly these medical professionals ought to know better, right? Well, this is something we need to understand about substances, and about ourselves. *No one is exempt.* When it comes to addiction, alcoholism, and substance abuse, anyone at any time can fall victim to opportunistic, squirrelly thoughts. We all, every one of us, can fall prey to passing thoughts to drink or use, and engage in self-medicating when the going gets tough. *Even if we know better.* Sometimes our good sense and moral fiber get

thrown right out the window, and we seek to escape the rigors and stressors and headaches of our lives, and drown ourselves in a substance of some kind. No one is exempt. All the more reason to be on our guard, to allow our values, personal goals, convictions and beliefs, and our passions in life *guide us away from danger, and toward safety and wellness.* If you have a partner or close friend who truly cares about you and has your back, talk to this person when you are having urges to drink or use. Allow that person to lead you away from these self-defeating thoughts. Be teachable, and humble. This is the way of wellness.

Increasing Endorphins Naturally

Exercise

Exercise is one of the most important and healthy ways you can increase your body's production of both serotonin and endorphins. A clinical review published in the November 2007 issue of the "Journal of Psychiatry and Neuroscience" explains that exercise may increase tryptophan availability in your brain, leading to increased serotonin production. Aerobic exercise also increases your brain's production of endorphins. You don't need to engage in heavy physical activity—even activities like hiking in nature can promote the release of endorphins, according to *mayoclinic.com*.

Breathe

Most people breathe unconsciously without fully appreciating the benefits of deep, abdominal breathing. Yet taking deep breaths that stem from your abdominal region not only helps you feel more relaxed, it may also increase your body's production of serotonin, endorphins and dopamine, another neurotransmitter that helps with mood regulation, according to Jeffrey Rossman, Ph.D, in an article for *rodale.com*. Rossman suggests a specific breathing technique known as *resident breathing*, which synchronizes your heartbeat with your breath rate and encourages the production of these neurotransmitters. As a vocalist, I know the value of abdominal breathing. When we breathe correctly, we should see our tummies move in and out.

Meditate

Meditation is another beneficial, natural way to increase your body's production of endorphins and serotonin, according to a journal article by Robert Nash, MD, published in 1996 in the "Journal of Orthomolecular Medicine." Meditation and other forms of deep relaxation help stimulate the action of your hypothalamus and your pituitary gland, the parts of your brain responsible for producing these and other important neurotransmitters.

Nutrition

Eating certain foods can stimulate the release of serotonin and endorphins. People with low levels of serotonin and endorphins often experience cravings for simple carbohydrates like bread, pasta or sugary foods, according to Henry Simmons, M.D., author of "The Chemistry of Joy." These foods cause a spike in your body's production of endorphins and serotonin, yet also result in their rapid depletion (remember the "surges" we talked about earlier?). Emmons suggests enjoying foods with a high vitamin content, like green and yellow leafy vegetables and high-fiber cereals, and reducing processed, sugary, calorie-rich foods, to support your body's production of serotonin and endorphins. (*healthyliving.azcentral.com*)

Conclusion

So, if you are in the midst of significant substance or alcohol usage, and it is becoming increasingly difficult to stop usage or drinking, it probably is time to consider getting help, and starting a quality recovery program.

It might be good to contact a local substance-abuse counselor either in private practice or at an agency, and begin the process of education and recovery. Again, The best way to begin recovery is with a medically-supervised detox, followed by inpatient rehab for a minimum of 28 days. If this is absolutely impossible, then you can begin individual and group substance-abuse counseling immediately, and even consider an Intensive Outpatient Program (IOP) therapy scenario. Taking these simple steps could possibly save your life.

There is indeed hope for anyone who is in the midst of substantial substance abuse or dependence. Sometimes the hardest thing is to ask for help, and yet it is the single most important step to take.

So take the step. Simply ask for help. Ask for help from someone who is trained, and preferably in recovery themselves. Ask for help, and begin your success story.

Indeed,

Recovery

Is

Life

94. "U.S. Surgeon General's Advisory: Marijuana Use and the Developing Brain." August 29, 2019. https://www.hhs.gov/surgeongeneral/reports-and-publications/addiction-and-substance-misuse/advisory-on-marijuana-use-and-developingbrain/index.html#:~:text=The%20human%20brain%20continues%20to,decision%2Dmaking%2C%20and%20%20motivation.

95. Jones, C.M., & McCance-Katz, E.F. (2019). Relationship Between Recency and Frequency of Youth Cannabis Use on Other Substance Use. Journal of Adolescent Health, 64(3), 411-413. doi:10-1016/j.jadohealth.2018.09.017.

96. Dr. Ishan Paranjpe, Stanford University. As cited in Daily Marijuana Use Increases Heart Risks. Newsmax Health, February 28, 2023.

BEYOND TENTATIVENESS

How We Lose Our Voice

There are many ways to lose one's voice. Often this happens in childhood or youth, when the young person had parents who didn't spend much quality time with them, and never validated the young person or caught them doing something right. Sometimes it can be the exact opposite. The parents constantly catch the young person doing something wrong, and shame the young person. What happens is the young person in this scenario never actually develops a voice, doesn't know who they actually are, and believes that they are exactly what their parents have made them out to be—a worthless, voiceless, waste of a human being.

This is how it feels to the young person, and this is how they have been *molded* into becoming who they are. As I've said previously, our children constantly are absorbing and normalizing *everything we say, do, and how we handle stressors, how we communicate with them and with their other parent (and with others), whether or not we self-medicate with substances, what we believe and hold as truth, our hobbies and how we spend our free time, and whether or not we spend quality time with them, and actually care about them.*

All of this is absorbed by the young person, and is internalized.

It becomes a part of them, and normalized. It becomes the lens through which they view all of life, and their world.

And when parents haven't been parents, but instead have been monsters and shamers, *that young person starts life out actually voiceless, fearful for the future, and in desperate need of love, attention, comfort, validation*—is it any wonder that so many young people experiment with various substances, and hang around unsavory peers who also have messed-up, dysfunctional home lives?

Abraham Maslow's first three "needs" for human beings are physiological, safety, and *love and belonging.* People—including young people—will gravitate towards *anyone or anything that provides for physiological and safety needs, and their need to belong—to be loved.*

So, if you are a parent, please facilitate physiological wellness, provide a safe place in which to grow, and exhibit much unconditional love and acceptance for your children, while guiding them according to your personal values and sense of right and wrong. Be firm, but by all means *love your child*—distinguishing between the *person* of that child, and the *questionable behavior* of that child. Enjoy life with that child, and allow that child to tell his/her stories. Children have many stories, if they are allowed to share them.

Self-Validation: Having a Voice

When we enter early adulthood, we come to a "Y" in the road. We have some decisions to make. We can copy and carry over some of the dynamics, principles, ways of relating, etc., from our upbringing, and paste them onto our present. Sometimes this is healthy, expected, and in-line with wellness. And sometimes it's not. Sometimes we have to pick and choose the aspects of our upbringing that are noble and useful, and leave the others behind. But regardless of what we do, we need to make some important decisions for ourselves.

Indeed, we get to choose our values (what's most important to us), our worldview (how we see the world), our convictions and beliefs (it's not usually best to just throw all of these away from our upbringing, unless they are not what we wanting to believe, or wanting to hold deeply within us). But try to do what appears to be *right* and *healthy.* We get to choose how we will live our lives—how we will communicate, how we will carry ourselves, how we will interact with others, how we spend our time, what we plan for ourselves, whether or not we use recreational weed (currently legal in 39 states and climbing), or alcohol or any other substance. Hopefully we will do our own vetting, our own research, be honest with ourselves, not just do what everyone around us is doing, have a voice, and move forward *carefully,* not haphazardly.

The point is, *we get to choose everything for ourselves.* This is both scary, and refreshing. But we should engage in this process, because it is good for us.

But for someone who has not had a very healthy upbringing, but rather one of demeaning and shaming, or abuse or neglect, this transition to "freedom" and to adulthood can be fraught with *fear and tentativeness.* It can also be a danger zone in which the person throws away everything from the past, and allows the false dichotomy of a pendulum swing to take the person to the far off distant galaxies in the opposite direction of how they were raised—regardless of how damaging or toxic this chosen lifestyle and direction may be.

I have had *many* clients in both groups, some with a great deal of tentativeness, afraid to attempt anything, or to make any definite move.

And some with a "no care" attitude and "anything goes" mentality,

plunging haphazardly forward, with no thought of potential outcomes.

Debilitating fear, inability to make sound decisions, and tentative difficulty managing emotions and interactions with others.

Or,

Reckless over-articulation of freedom, and drowning oneself in this or that substance, or this or that lifestyle—as long as it's *way different than how I was raised. Time for some instant gratification.*

I suggest that both of these conditions or approaches are not ideal, and that both can lead to depression, uncertainty, self-shaming, regrets, having no meaning, and feeling no sense of worth....*malaise, stagnation.*

Now to a better way....

Having a voice is the better way. So, you had a crummy, dysfunctional, messed-up, confusing, chaotic, injurious, invalidating upbringing. Okay, join the club. So did I. Absolutely horrendous in so many ways. BUT THIS DOES NOT HAVE TO DESTROY YOU OR STIFLE YOU OR KEEP YOU DOWN OR TAKE AWAY YOUR VOICE FOREVER....YOU CAN STILL HAVE A VOICE RIGHT HERE, RIGHT NOW.

That's right. If you haven't been validated much previously, SELF-VALIDATE; CATCH YOURSELF DOING SOMETHING RIGHT. You can *choose* to have a voice in the here and now, regardless of what has happened to you, and regardless of whatever mistakes you have made. Your ill-treatment, victimization, failures, addictions, moral lapses, former crime....*these need not define you. Don't let them define you. There is so much more to you! You have talents, skills, insights, dreams, at times courage, at times sensitive compassion, at times….a little hope for the future.*

Yes, build on *that*. Learn to self-validate. Learn to have a voice, to put one foot in front of the other, to *incrementally move forward in your life.* You can do so.

Examples and Guidance

Young Adult Having a Voice After Dating/Assault/Rape.

You have been taken advantage of, victimized. It hurts, it stings emotionally. You feel violated. You have mixed emotions of shame, anger, worthlessness, at times blaming yourself for what happened. First of all, you need to give yourself time to heal, to emote, to write about what you are feeling and thinking (yes, this is actually helpful). You need to process what has happened, though it can be difficult, and you may have to just lie down for a bit, and come back to it later. But journaling and writing can help you process your pain, and to *connect the dots and collect your thoughts.* This is good for you, because you will have insights all over the place. Keep track of those. Don't be afraid to talk to a caring therapist, as this can be very helpful. Remember, *out of your brokenness flows healing for others.*

> **You can have a voice** by allowing this horrible experience to sharpen you, enhance you, make you stronger, wiser, and help you to have boundaries in your life. This experience can even be a *catalyst* for growth, and *strategically moving forward in life.* It may even help you put together a new career track that has never crossed your mind before. And you may need to get an order of protection in place, and start putting some careful boundaries in place in your life. Be good to yourself, and safeguard yourself. This is consistent with wellness.

Young Adult Having a Voice After an Upbringing of Shame,

Denigration, and Devaluation.

You have been shamed and ridiculed a lot in your upbringing. Your parents and other adults in your life have not had a very positive impact on you, but rather have had a silencing and devaluing impact on you. As you look back, the times when these "adults" actually spent quality time with you, or caught you doing something right, were few and far between. It was mostly negative or neglectful, or abusive, or all three. First of all, I want to remind you that this treatment was inappropriate, and harmful to you in many ways. But this treatment was *not your fault.* Yeah, I know, none of us is perfect, and we all have our moments. We all, when young gave our parents fits at times, and made life difficult for them. *But there is no excuse for a parent to shame or silence or denigrate or neglect or abuse a young person. Absolutely no excuse.* So, don't excuse it, and don't blame yourself for how you were raised. This is *on them.* Having said that, I also need to tell you that *there is absolutely nothing standing in your way to have a meaningful, productive, exciting future.* Nothing at all. Now, there may be obstacles, such as extreme financial difficulty, temporary legal trouble, burnt bridges, drug or alcohol issues, or some family members that you pissed off. Okay, so it is what it is. Go forward anyway. Go forward, in spite of your background, and in spite of the obstacles that may be in front of you.

The patterns of attitude, ways of responding, and fear-based closing down in the past were coping mechanisms that have *long since worn out their usefulness.* Your life situation is much different now, and you now have the opportunity to actually have a voice, to remain fully in the moment, and to validate yourself.

> **You can have a voice** by taking a single weekend, setting aside big blocks of time on both days, and brainstorming with yourself about *what really matters to you, and what you would*

like to accomplish. Use the principles in this book to develop a *strategic gameplan* for yourself, using baby steps as a way to *incrementally* tackle one baby step at a time. You may need to go to college or trade school. Just do it. In the USA, there are many ways to finance one's education and training. Nothing is standing in your way. Learn to self-validate, and to catch yourself doing something right. Set up your "Intentional Set Routine" so that you can be on top of things, and have good self-care in place. Remain in ____ville, have a voice, with your values surrounding you, and nothing but blue sky ahead of you. And allow the "personal assistants" in your life to help you move forward in life. Resist the urge to use substances as coping mechanisms (they're not), and resist the urge to adopt a "who cares" attitude. Be careful picking the people you hang around. Make sure they will have a healthy influence on you. Refuse to be a prisoner of your past. Choose to be an architect of your present tense.

Adult Having a Voice After Experiencing a Protracted Period of Incarceration.

You've been locked up for what seems like forever. It was long enough anyway. Regardless of your guilt or innocence, this experience has taken a toll on you emotionally, physically, existentially, and cognitively. It has been demoralizing, and potentially silencing. And now you are either free once again, or are just about to get out. It can be very scary, and you can have a great deal of tentativeness and hesitancy, as you start to think about and plan for the future. Your head plays tricks on you. You start thinking, "What will folks think about me? How long will these charges or convictions remain on my record? Is it pointless to try to move forward in my life under this crap load of negativity?"

When you have these thoughts, don't think that it's weird. Start writing down your questions, and start keeping track of your uncertainties. Turn these questions and uncertainties into *action steps.* Make some simple plans for yourself. If you need a driver's license, ask yourself, "What baby steps can I plan for myself, so that I can eventually get my license back?" If you need a job, turn your job-seeking into a part-time job of sorts, and devote a large block of time in each day to *be about* it, and inundate your area of town with resumes and applications. It's a numbers thing. The more you apply, the more likely it is you will get an interview. If you have basic deficits happening in your life, in terms of housing, food, insurance, SSI, survival—contact your local community mental health (CMH), and ask for an intake appointment for "case management." You will probably qualify for Medicaid, and this will most likely pay for your services. A good case manager can help you put in place adequate housing, and help you to apply for Medicaid or Section 8 or a Bridge card with DHHS.

> **You can have a voice** by taking advantage of these services and opportunities all around you. Allow your "personal assistants" to help you to move forward in life. Find yourself a stable job (yes, there are companies who will hire individuals with past legal trouble, just be patient). Shine a light on *what you are doing to help yourself* in the here and now. With every resume or application you submit, include a brief cover letter that contains your experience, your passion, your desire to work hard, and your desire to better yourself. If you are excited and hopeful about the future, *that employer will be more likely to also be excited for you, and want you to be a part of their organization.* You can even take one class at a time while working, and gradually, incrementally make progress in a degree program that is meaningful for you. This is living in ____ville; this is having a voice.

Adult Having a Voice After Experiencing Extremely Difficult Transitions, Such as Divorce, Loss of Career, Loss of Loved

One, Loss of Parental Rights.

Transitions. Losses. They can take a toll on us. They can throw us into a valley of depression, or a whirlwind of anxiety. As for losses, they can strip away our dignity and our purpose in life, leaving only a vacant shell of a person. I understand. I've often wondered how many layers of an onion can be peeled away, until there is nothing left to peel. It can be personally and existentially a pit into which we have been thrown. A pit of demise. But, as I've said before, *transitions can be incredible seedbeds for creativity and personal growth.* And even losses can shape us and mold us into the person we actually need to become. It is consistent with wellness to engage in some writing about what you are feeling and thinking, and about what you are *learning.* This is important learning. I can safely say that some of the best songs I have written in my life have flowed out of some of the most deep and dark valleys I've experienced, and some of the most excruciatingly painful losses I've sustained. Do some journaling, and connect some dots. You will be amazed at what you learn from yourself.

> **You can have a voice** by giving yourself permission to reach out to others who are hurting, and also to those who are encouraging. Resist the urge to isolate. Immediately set up your "Intentional Set Routine" and remember to follow through with what you do *for the right reason—this is healthy for me, this is important for me, this is in-line with wellness, this is a form of self-respect, this will help me keep my job (or be on time, or be productive)—do it for those reasons, and NOT based on how you feel.* This will help mitigate against the depression in your life, and you will start to have some motivation. Remember that regular exercise increases Dopamine wonderfully well. Adopt the role of Architect, and begin a Renaissance in your life. You get to choose who you talk to, the activities in which you engage, the work that you do, the hobbies you enjoy, and the day trips you plan. Begin writing your new chapter, and

don't guilt yourself for doing so. It's the right thing to do. Set a tone of health, healing, success, and authentic living for those you have left behind, laid to rest, or those who are watching. Go ahead—exert an influence on your surroundings.

Young Adult Having a Voice After an Upbringing of Parentification, Caretaking, or Being a Counselor or Mediator for Parents.

Sometimes our parents do not act like actual parents, but rather have dysfunctional or creatively hurtful ways to bring a young person *into the midst of their personal or relational pain.* Or these parents can turn a young person into the *scapegoat* of a family—a sort of dumping ground for all ills, all hurts, all blame, all shame, and all unhappiness in the home. Sometimes the young person can be turned into a counselor for a parent, or a mediator between two embattled parents. Or the young person can be relied on extensively as a caretaker of other siblings, when the parent has substance issues, or deep depression, or is always gone, or just doesn't care about being a parent.

All of these unhealthy roles mentioned above are *deleterious, damaging, unhealthy, inappropriate and completely unfair.* If you can relate to any of these aspects, you know firsthand just how damaging these roles can be, when foisted on us at a young age. As I have said before, children absorb and normalize *everything* their parents do and say, and how they live. If we start out being a caretaker as a young person, chances are we will keep that unfortunate and damaging role going *even into our adult years* (if we are not careful). If you experienced parentification as a young person, see it for for it is—very unhealthy and inappropriate. Now, as an adult, you can shed this caretaking role, put it behind you, and liberate yourself from this unbelievably damaging role.

> **You can have a voice** by not allowing yourself to be driven

and desperately drawn to *take care of coworkers, family, friends, strangers, partner, everyone and their grandma.* You can *choose* to live in ____ville, to have a voice, and to retain your basic sensitivity and compassion for people. You can *choose* the individuals you want to help, and you can spread out your helpfulness. If you have a family, concentrate on your family. If you have a partner, have a collaboration, and decide *together* whom you want to help. Now you can come at your *helping* from a position of strength and peace, rather than desperation and drivenness. Go ahead, shed that debilitating caretaker role.

Individual Having a Voice After a Protracted Period of Addiction or Substance Dependence or Compulsive Gambling or Pornography or Overspending.

You have been in the thralls of a particular substance or of gambling, porn, or overspending, or something else. The hardest step in recovery is actually admitting that we need help, and being open to help. Once you have given yourself permission to receive help, you can begin to *build your recovery program.* Yes, it will take full recovery for you to be able to go on with your life free from that substance of choice, or the need to gamble, or the need to view porn, or the need to overspend.

I advise you to read carefully the full chapter on substances and recovery, as there are important principles therein. But remember that the three main components of recovery are *support, accountability, and education.* You can obtain both support and some degree of accountability by regularly attending a recovery group for your particular area of need. There are recovery groups for just about everything you can imagine. And these groups are everywhere. I suggest in-person groups, because they are usually more meaningful, and there is a higher degree of both support and accountability.

I suggest that you quickly obtain a sponsor, accountability coach, or recovery coach. The facilitator of the meeting you attend can suggest someone. This is an important component in your recovery experience. You can keep in touch with this accountability partner, have regular check-ins, and also call this person when you are not doing well. You also need education, and you can get that through reading, through meeting regularly with a substance abuse counselor or general counselor, or attending an IOP group nearby (these are excellent). For gambling, porn and overspending, there are groups to attend, there is literature to read, and yes, a good counselor can help you put your life back together.

> **You can have a voice** by *choosing each day to be in recovery.* Yes, it is a daily decision. Make your goal to *avoid that first drink or usage, that first gambling activity, that first caving in to an opportunity to engage in porn, that first overspending activity.* Make that your primary goal each morning when you wake up. Make that your focus. Keep it simple. Surround yourself with sober friends and family, and supportive individuals. Set up your "Intentional Set Routine" so you can keep busy engaging in that which is important to you, and avoid becoming *hungry, angry, lonely, tired, bored.* Be fully engaged in your work, and fully engaged in your leisure. Be fully engaged in your relationships with people. *Learn now to live life on life's terms, without the filter of a substance, a filter of a gambling compulsion, a filter of pornography, or a filter of overspending* between you and life. View these past habits as *coping mechanisms that have long since worn out their usefulness.* Start living in ____ville, have a voice, and chart a course that is important and meaningful for you. Recovery is life, and it's going get better and better without that strangling go-to habit dragging you down. Move forward, putting a first priority on recovery.

Individual Having a Voice After Sustaining a Major Physical Disability, Loss of Usage of a Limb, Loss of Mobility, or Loss of Ability to Engage in a Particular Skill.

You feel like the ground has been pulled out from under you. You feel you have no foundation. The thought probably crosses your mind now and again that there is no point to go on. Life is pretty much over. You will never be a complete person again. But hold on. Be careful. While I express my condolences for the "loss" you have sustained, I want to help you and encourage you. Please don't define yourself by this particular injury or loss of ability. *There is so much more to you than this particular loss or setback.* Get in touch with your values, your actual personal goals, your dreams, your passions in life. Let these guide you. Remember your personality, your sense of humor, your insights, your accomplishments thus far. Allow everything in the past three sentences to define you now. *This is who you are.*

Cooperate with whatever "personal assistants" are in your life —physical therapist, rehab personnel, primary care physician, specialists, partner (if applicable), family, friends, counselor. Keep your appointments. Let these assistants help you move forward.

And start writing. In your journaling include an aspect of insights and progress, and also ideas that you have about possible career tracks that might be interesting for you. You might even consider a career or sideline as a life coach, or as a music therapist, or as a practitioner who helps people gradually learn to play their instrument again, after an injury or setback in life. This can even be a role as occupational therapist. Yes, out of your brokenness can flow healing for others. You can be a source of hope and healing for others, if you have a mind to.

If you are having to learn to use your hands again, consider activities such as bouncing a ball, using a yo-yo, or peeling potatoes and carrots in order to facilitate improvements in manual dexterity. Start slowly, with something simple, such as a squeeze ball, and work your way up. Incremental resolution.

> **You can have a voice** by *remembering who you are, thinking of possibilities, and setting up some action steps for yourself.* If you are wanting to further yourself with a degree or certificate program, embrace the process and turn your quest into a series of strategic baby steps. Consider taking one class at a time, to finish a baccalaureate degree in your chosen field, while you work. Remember that anything in the IT field, or allied health field, business and marketing field, or helping professions *is in high demand, with a great outlook for future growth.* Do not make the assumption that you cannot work or contribute in a meaningful way, simply because of your disability or limitation. Assumptions are usually wrong.

You can use one week as a Renaissance Week in which you have a block of time in the morning, and a block of time in the afternoon applying for relevant jobs, and engaging in follow-up calls. Remain in _____ville, have a voice, and *be the person* you are wanting to become. How would *that* person go about the day?

<u>Individual Having a Voice After a Protracted Period of Being Battered, Verbally and Emotionally Abused, Controlled, Shamed, Silenced, and Devalidated by One's Partner (who ought to be in jail actually)</u>.

First of all, are you safe? Are you in a safe place? Have you removed yourself from the place where this predator lives? If you haven't yet removed yourself, or you are afraid to remove yourself for fear of being harmed, go to a private part of the home, and call 911. Start to take action. Allow the authorities to come and help you to leave the home *safely.* They can take you to a family member's house, or a friend's house, or to a women's shelter that is secure, and in a different part of town. Begin the process of getting your life back. The staff at the shelter will assist you in getting an order of protection in place, and you should also complete a police report, and allow the state to press charges against this monster, if they choose to do so. Put your safety and wellbeing first.

Once you have taken the steps to be safe and secure, as listed above, you are now ready to start planning your new life. This new life will be filled with safety, awareness, boundaries, self-respect, opportunities, progress, and a meaningful future.

If you have any drug or alcohol issues, make sure you start to put a first priority on sobriety, and get some support, accountability, and education in place for yourself. The last thing you need is for substances to drag you down, or to set you up for a repeat performance because of unsavory connections and influences. Mistreatment and abuse are more likely to happen in the context of substance abuse and unsafe associates. Your new life needs to be substance-free. And now you can begin to meet *life on life's terms.*

> **You can have a voice** by considering this *me* time. This is personal development time. This is *not* a time for rushing right back into another relationship. Take a break from the drama, and have a *hiatus of health.* Think of what you would truly like to "be about" and accomplish in your life. Think of this time as a new chapter that you are writing. What do you want your life to look like? What do you see yourself doing professionally? What career resonates with you? Aim for that. Plan for that. Get some action steps in place for yourself. Do some research, make some calls, find out what it will take for you to *begin to move forward in your life.* This would be a good time to complete the "This is Me" worksheet (see the couples chapter). This worksheet will help you understand who you are and why you are, a little better. It will help you to think about what you would like life to look like three years from now. It will also help you to socially navigate safely and carefully. Remain in _____ville, have a voice, with your values surrounding you, and some meaningful plans in front of you. Go forward, *sharpened*

and *enhanced* by your former experiences.

•

**You can think about the past,
learn from the past,
and** *extract whatever you can learn from that past memory
—that past hurt—
extract and learn and be sharpened by as much as you
can from that previous hurtful experience . . .*

*leaving only an exoskeleton of that previous hurtful experience,
that can easily be blown away with the wind.*

Just let it go, let it be blown away with the wind.

Creating a Renaissance

Reframing

This is where your personal Renaissance begins. It all starts with reframing. This is the lens through which you view your world, your situation. When you look through the lens of Renaissance, you see first of all a blank page, a new chapter. You see newness and discovery. Having learned from what is behind you, you are poised to move forward. Everything is new, and everything is possible. *And you view every person in your life as your personal assistant, who is simply there to help you move forward in life.* You become aware of how these individuals are sharpening you and enhancing you. Even the people you don't like. They are also your personal assistants. Be aware of them, and appreciate them. Some of these folks don't even know that they are helping you. But they are.

You then become an *architect* and you set up your "Intentional Set Routine" infrastructure, using preferably a full-size paper schedule book. This works best. On the weekend, you set up the coming week, starting with your *self-care foundation* of sleep, wake, meals and exercise. You are learning to be consistent with these basics. Any aspect important to you goes into your schedule book for the coming week. This SR Infrastructure has wheels on it, because it's attached to time. And you are an architect riding on the back of it. Allow yourself to operate within this dynamic infrastructure of an "Intentional Set Routine." All of your important tasks and goals for the week go in there. You are on top of things, and you are checking things off and catching yourself doing something right. It feels good. You have this attitude:

> *"I'm in a Renaissance, I'm moving forward,*
> *I be jammin', I be goin' places.*
> *I'm ready to roll. Look out. Out da way, go on, git!"*

This is your stance. Now you are ready to engage.

Engaging

Start to explore, and to research. Look carefully into that which excites you and ignites you about the future. Start exploring what a typical day looks like in several key career tracks. Compare market demand for those career tracks. Have a close look at salary ranges for your top career tracks. This is a good time to engage in the "Weighted Factorial Analysis," which will give you the ability to be very personal and subjective about your choices, while at the same being able to be objective in your analysis.

Out of this exploration and analysis can come an intentional *determining* of what you actually want to do. You can narrow your search down to *one option, the best option, the option that captures at once your interest and passion, the option that is congruent with who you are.* You've already vetted the possibilities, and you have *determined* that this is the best option, the best path to follow.

This is an important process. And engaging in this process is so much healthier and happier than being pushed into something by parents or loved ones or well-meaning friends or teachers. Always remember this:

> ***It's hard to move forward when we're pulled.***

So, Engage. Choose. Determine. Now you are ready to put some meat on the bones.

Embracing

Now you get to *forecast.* You get to *plan.* But please remember that *everything is a process,* and that it is best if we can

> ***Embrace the Process.***

Incremental Resolution. This is the way of peace. The way of wellness. No doubt. Slow down, pace yourself, be in the moment openly and freely. *You can think more clearly when you are calm, and you can move more intentionally when you pour yourself into one next right thing at a time.*

Set aside an entire morning, perhaps on the weekend. Make sure you have had a quality sleep, and a wholesome breakfast. Write down a handful of personal, professional, and health and wellness goals that you would *like to be about,* and like to accomplish, over the remainder of the year. Then think of some *strategic baby steps* that you can attach to each of your important goals. Remember that some of these baby steps can be ongoing, such as exercise, and some of them can be time-limiters, such as, "Be done with this aspect of this project by June 1."

When we plan and forecast in this manner, we can embrace the process in all the major areas of our lives. This will result in more productivity, peace, efficiency, and will *keep you jammin' in your personal Renaissance.*

You have a plan now. A realistic, well-thought-out plan that is actually doable. And you are poised for *peace,* because you are embracing the process with baby steps. You are now ready to *become.*

Becoming

You have narrowed your search down to something specific that you would like to do. You've done some proper vetting and comparing. You have your sights on a career path or project or something new and exciting, and are ready to roll.

So, BE THAT PERSON. How would *that person* go about the day? How would *that person* plan and set up his/her "Intentional Set Routine"? How would *that person* be proactive, and make calls to universities and companies? How would *that person* dress, eat, exercise, communicate with others, and plan his/her day? *Be that person.*

It is what you make it. *Nothing is standing in your way.* You may think that there are obstacles in front of you, blocking your way. These may be financial in nature, or familial. Maybe it's your own self-defeating self-appraisal that is dragging you down. Maybe you are hearing a rerun of demeaning words and put-downs from your upbringing ringing in your ears. Maybe it's a logistical hurdle, and you don't know how to take care of kids, work at your job, and also move forward with a degree or certificate or training program at the same time.

All of these are not actually obstacles.
They are opportunities.
That are waiting for you to take action.
They are permeable, manageable, and you

> *can see right through them*
> *to your preferred future.*

•

> *They are simply stepping stones.*

So, place an action step in your "Intentional Set Routine" for this week, to make a call to a local university (or online university) to talk about your career questions and plans.

Complete the FAFSA online, and pick the schools or programs you want your information to be sent to.

Allow that school of choice to present to you their financial aid package. This package will most likely include some grants, and some student loans. You can also *take one or two classes at a time, thereby embracing the process, and little-by-little, poco-a-poco, complete your degree or certificate program.* I have seen many individuals do just that, because they either have a lot going on in their lives, or because they prefer to pay as they go, and not to incur debt.

Engage in your preferred professional scenario in a way that is appropriate for you. A full load usually requires a person to just focus on their classes. A part-time load allows you to work part-time while you take classes. Taking one or two classes at a time allows you to pretty much continue to work full-time, if you need to do so.

Or your quest may be about a new job that you would like to obtain. So, turn your quest into a part-time job of sorts, and *inundate your area with resumes and applications, until somebody contacts you for an interview.*

It's a numbers thing. So keep at it. Or it may be some other goal that is important to you. Do something with it. Turn your ideas into action steps. You've already spent some time ascertaining what your main personal, professional, and health and wellness goals are. Now you can actually BECOME the person you have in mind. You can *even now* BE THAT PERSON.

Networking

We are all in community. Even those of us who are basically hermits need some human interaction at times, to stay sane. So, don't isolate as you engage your future and take action. *You actually need people.*

Don't be afraid to ask questions, to contact mentors and people of wisdom. These individuals will guide you on your way, just as others guided them on their way earlier on.

Collaboration is key. It's important for couples, for certain. But it's also important for individuals, as we try to move forward in life. Collaborate with others, and try to have someone else's back. It is of value to move in this manner. You are not alone in your quest, in your journey. There are people who care in your life, if you are open to allowing them to care. And if there is no such person in your life that you can think of, *find a quality friend, someone who actually cares about you.* You don't need a lot of these individuals necessarily. Sometimes just a handful of true friends or family members can be sufficient, to help us on our way.

We are sharpened and enhanced by others.

> **We need to allow our personal assistants to move us along.**

They will do so, if we are looking for the ways in which they are sharpening us, enhancing us, teaching us, modeling for us, setting the tone for us, moving us forward.

No Longer Afraid

There are many ways to fall into tentativeness. Many avenues to brokenness, silence, stagnation, devalidation. But there is only one way out of this fear, and that is by HAVING A VOICE. We learn to self-validate—to catch ourselves doing something right. We learn to catch others doing something right also, and the value of a well-placed affirmation.

If you have implemented the strategies I have shared with you in this book, then by this time you are either contemplating a Renaissance, or you are in the midst of one. If you haven't yet thrown a rock in a lake, and attempted or started something new and meaningful, *do so now.*

All we have to work with is right here, right now.
But there is much significance in a day,
and in an intentional moment.

There is much that can be done, planned, orchestrated, and set into motion. Today is what you have. Embrace the day. Get the most out of this day. Try to smile today. Notice the positive impact of your personal assistants today.

You are no longer stifled by fear, devaluation, or self-sabotage. You are living and remaining in ____ville (if you haven't done so already, please put your name there). You actually have a voice. Your values are surrounding you and guiding you. ____ville is a safe place, a place of peace. Your plans and dreams are safe there. You can move about freely there. You can say what you mean, and mean what you say, without pouring gas on the fire, in ____ville.

You are free to move about the occupational landscape, free to move about the social landscape, and free to move courageously forward with your Pre-Renaissance goals and baby steps. Tell yourself the truth about your present life. It is absolutely full of wonder and possibility.

You know what to do if anxiety comes around. Immediately correct that self-talk to something true, valid (have a voice in that situation), and reasonable. This will have a calming effect, and will get you out of the weeds. If your anxiety appears to be automatic, more emotional, and part of OCD, you need to *sit with the fear, the distress, the uncertainty,* and by so doing you will *habituate* to the uncertainty, and will no longer feed your OCD monster. You will beat it. Or you might have to get back to that top circle, and get busy doing something that is clearly under your control. Or you might have to let go of a couple aspects of your "over-busy" crammed life, and *simplify.* Use these strategies, because anxiety can truly interfere with your plans.

You know what to do with depression and lack of motivation. It primarily has to do with immersing yourself in every next right thing, catching yourself doing something right, and *following through for the right reasons, and not based on how you feel.* Remember that *feelings follow function.* You can set the tone for yourself, and put one foot in front of the other. This is *Behavioral Activation.* This is what helps with depression.

You also know how to improve your sleep. It primarily has to do with having closure on the day, tying up some loose ends, and especially *avoiding taking any unfinished business with you to bed.* Use your "Personal Inventory." And think of your happy place. Remember that sleep in the number one factor with mental health. And yes, you need eight or nine hours.

**When you help yourself,
and when you put into practice a strategy that is useful,
you are having a voice in a big way.
This kind of living will bring you up out
of tentativeness and fear.**

Grabbing Life by the Horns, Peacefully

So here we are in the final section of the final chapter of this book. As I write this, I ask myself, "What can I share at this time that is appropriate, and will help the reader move forward in life *peacefully?*"

What Having a Voice is *Not*

>**Having a Voice is Not *Drivenness***

I know about drivenness. I used to be very driven, and prone to burnout. A little over 20 years ago, I had to spend two nights in the hospital because of severe, debilitating anxiety. This was brought on by *drivenness.* That's when I learned just how powerful and debilitating anxiety can be, and that's when I realized that *having too full of a plate* was a significant factor with anxiety. I had to simplify. I had to start embracing the process. I had to start practicing the *fine art of saying "No."*

Having a voice is far different than *that.* When you have a voice, and live in ____ville, you can pace yourself, enjoy the journey, and actually be more productive. Having a voice leads to *peace,* wellbeing, and efficiency. It helps you to do what you do because it's important to you, not because you *have* to. Having a voice involves *calmness,* not pressure. Think of Keanu Reaves (Neo) at the end of first *Matrix* movie. The agents are shooting bullets at him, and Neo is able to stop and freeze the bullets in mid-air. He is able to *slow things down,* and *embrace the process.* He thus gains perspective and clarity. There is peace. He then engages his world.

That is how it is when we have a voice, and live in ____ville. I'm not suggesting that you go off and put yourself in front of flying bullets (it's just a movie). But I am suggesting that you too can slow things down, you too can embrace the process, and you too can gain perspective and clarity. You can have peace, and engage your world.

What Having a Voice Is

>Having a Voice is *Intentional*

Do what you do because it is important to you, and meaningful for you. Operate within an "Intentional Set Routine" and have a place and time for everything that is important for you in the week. Pour yourself into each next right thing, check it off and catch yourself doing something right, and follow through with each next right thing for the *right reasons:* "This is im

portant for me, this is healthy for me, this is a form of self-respect," etc.

Every time you make a choice for yourself, or decide on a direction that is consistent with your values and personal goals, your have a voice.

**Intentionality is the opposite of self-sabotage.
It will lead you safely away from self-sabotage and defeat.**

Self-sabotage has to do with fear. When you have a voice, you can give yourself permission to *be about* that which is important to you, even if it's a little different or scary. You don't have to miss out on anything significant. You are being intentional.

Perhaps you have been handed a "script" by your family of origin, and they have pushed you into this script for many years. It was dysfunctional, unhealthy, and toxic back then, and it is still toxic now in the present. *Shed that script,* because it is not truthful, valid, or reasonable. And write your own script for your life that is based on your values, personal goals, preferences, passions, and three-year preferred scenario. You can have a voice, and you can be intentional about what you do. This will bring you out of the tentativeness and fear you have been under for so many years.

Being intentional will help you to exert an influence on your environment. It will help you to start something new. It will help you set the tone for yourself and for everyone around you. It will also help you to eliminate any depression that is in your life. *Now, that is having a voice!*

>Having a Voice is *Incremental*

I will say it again, *everything is a process.* And we are all in process. So, embrace the process. This is *Incremental Resolution.* Be okay with that. Slow down, you're moving too fast (sounds like a song—it is—Simon & Garfunkel). Pace yourself. Listen to the birds singing their cheerful songs. Hear the music in the trees. Watch the grass and grain and trees swaying in the wind.

When you have a voice, and remain in ____ville, you can indeed slow down. You can put one foot in front of the other, and move forward *incrementally.* Hopefully you have already set up your Pre-Renaissance goals and strategic baby steps. This will help you to embrace the process in every area of your life. We can actually accomplish more when we are calm and when we are embracing the process. We have more clarity when we are calm.

When you operate incrementally, you will understand that even mundane tasks and duties are full of meaning and value. You won't mind being about them, because you are still moving forward in your life, in the process.

When it comes to one of your baby steps that you have placed in your "intentional Set Routine," you can also pour yourself into that next right thing, and have an appreciation for the rich meaning and value of the moment. And of course, you never know, *but this one piece of the process right here just might be the most important piece of the entire process. And you never know what you are setting into motion, simply by doing extremely well this…one…next…right…thing.*

Embracing the process and being incremental will help you to gradually make significant progress in your major goals. It will help you to enjoy the journey, and to appreciate the people and blessing in your life. It will also help you to be far more productive, because you are *more in* the moment with what you do. *Now, that is having a voice!*

>Having a Voice is In-Line with Self-Care and Wellness

When you are living in ____ville and having a voice, you are much more aware of the basics. You are very much aware of your sleep habits, eating habits, exercise regularity, and personal time to reflect. You have these important components before you always, because they are in your "Intentional Set Routine" for each week. You are thereby much more likely to be consistent with these important aspects of self-care.

I'm sure you agree that our physical health impacts our mental health, and vice versa. You can do well in both areas. I try to exercise three times per week. That is my plan, and that is my routine. It happens consistently, only because I keep at it. That exercise is staring at me in the face in my schedule book. I know how important it is. It's not very scary. And because I'm living in Davidville and having a voice, each next right thing matters to me. It has meaning. And so yes, I will engage in regular exercise *for the right reasons.* And you can do so as well.

Of course, there are so many benefits to exercising. But having a voice also helps us emotionally and mentally. It truly feels good to have a voice, and to get things done, and to embrace the process and enjoy the journey.

When you grab life by the horns peacefully and have a

voice, you will experience improvements in self-appraisal, mood, ability to handle stressors, ability to communicate appropriately, and ability to relax when it is time to relax.

There are incredible benefits to having a voice. This way of living promotes wellness, because it's not haphazard or *fly by the seat of your pants.* When we are in a Renaissance and having a voice, life is more consistent, more predictable, and more substantive and interesting. And the body and brain absolutely love consistency and routine. They thrive with these, and this results in wellness. *Now, that is having a voice!*

>Having a Voice is Both-And; *it Facilitates the Success of Others*

In this dog-eat-dog world of *Me, Self, Pride, and Intense Competition,* it is easy to get swept up in the myopic drama and protracted fray. But when we have a voice, and remain in ____ville, we are liberated to *be all we can be,* while at the same time safeguarding the dignity and ideas of others.

> **Being *me* does not cancel out *you*.**
> **I can still facilitate your success,**
> **while creating my own.**

We can sharpen each other. We can enhance each other. You can have a voice, and I can have a voice. We don't have to interfere with each other's voices.

And most likely, if I can help you move forward in life, and facilitate your success, I will also be blessed and enhanced. You can call it Karma, but I prefer to call it *natural reciprocity.*

Yes, you can move forward in your life, and you can take a whole bunch of people with you, because of your example, and because of your habit of catching them doing something right.

You are constantly setting the tone for everyone around you.

That's a good thing, that is, if you are having a voice and living in ____ville. If you are not doing this, you could possibly have an undesired impact on others *inadvertently*. It's better, and more in-line with wellness, if we remain in ____ville and have a voice. We will be much more aware of how others are doing, and we will be in a much better place to actually help them.

And helping others does not in the slightest way detract from who we are, or where we're going. It has the opposite effect. It propels us forward.

Naturally, you still need to have self-respect and general and specific boundaries in place, when needed. Because while moving forward we sometimes need to set some limits on ourselves. And we sometimes need to put some specific boundaries in place, because sometimes people are not very nice.

But this does not keep you from having a both-and approach to living. You can facilitate the success of others, and promote their peace and wellness. All while remaining in ____ville, and *choosing* your actions and words carefully. *Now, that is having a voice!*

A Summary of Wellness

It is all about balance and wellness. If we are endeavoring to do our best with diet, exercise, sleep, water intake, sunlight etc., this will help us to be happier and more productive.

We should aim for a nice healthy, gradual dopamine increase with lasting impact, associated with regular aerobic, cardiovascular exercise, and other wholesome activities. This is being good to ourselves.

It is in line with wellness to identify your passions in life, and to try to find a place for them in your routine, as this will add meaning and substance to your life.

Doing things for the right reasons is always best, and is in line with wellness.

It is healthy for us and in-line with wellness to allow our values to inform and impact our daily living and decision-making. Life will be more peaceful for us if we do this, and we will be more in-sync with who we are.

Allow your values to guide you and protect you and inform you, as you begin the process of exploring career options. This will lead to peace, and will keep chaos away from you.

It is in line with wellness to allow our passions to inform what we do and plan.

> **It is generally more peaceful,**
> **culminating in a longer lifespan,**
> **and resulting in less anxiety**
> **if we can pace ourselves,**
> **break tasks up into baby steps,**
> **and embrace the process.**

It is consistent with wellness to engage in some writing about what you are feeling and thinking, and about what you are *learning*.

Incremental Resolution. This is the way of peace. The way of wellness. No doubt. Slow down, pace yourself, be in the moment openly and freely.

The body and brain absolutely love consistency and routine. They thrive with these, and this results in wellness.

It's better, and more in-line with wellness, if we remain in ____ville and have a voice.

Be simply the best *you*. This is the way of wellness. This is the way of peace.

Don't get caught up in what other people think and feel, or the decisions they make. Try to be comfortable in your own shoes, and to live in harmony with your own personal values and goals in life. This is the way of peace; the way of wellness.

You can be kind and helpful to others *for the right reasons,* because kindness or helpfulness is one of your values, and you are deciding to be value-driven. Yes, you can still be a good parent, be a good adult son or daughter, be a helpful but wise coworker, and be a source of peace and support and honesty for your partner. This is the way of wellness.

If you have a partner or close friend who truly cares about you and has your back, talk to this person when you are having urges to drink or use. Allow that person to lead you away from these self-defeating thoughts. Be teachable, and humble. This is the way of wellness.

Be good to yourself, and safeguard yourself. This is consistent with wellness.

It's better, and more in-line with wellness, if we remain in ____ville and have a voice. We will be much more aware of how others are doing, and we will be in a much better place to actually help them.

Whenever you speak the truth, you have a voice. Whenever you share an opinion, you have a voice. Whenever you are intentional about a task, and you follow through with that task, you have a voice. Whenever you allow your personal values to inform your daily life and decision-making, you have a voice. Whenever you speak a boundary into existence or maintain a boundary, you have a voice. And whenever you have self-respect, are reasonable with yourself, or catch yourself doing something right, you have a voice. All of these activities will mitigate against tentativeness, will foster self-validation, and will help you to have a voice and to be an architect of your present tense.

Intentionality is the opposite of tentativeness, so it naturally mitigates against it, and helps a person to actually have a voice.

Intentionality and having a voice are exactly opposite to tentativeness, fear, and "settling."

So I hope you will make the decision to be in a Renaissance, to live in ____ville, and to have a voice in life. This intentional movement will be for you a

Metamorphosis,
like a butterfly spreading out
it's brand new, wet wings,
and airing them out,
then taking flight for the first time.
This is how you will feel as
you move forward,
and shed the script that others
have written for you.

It's time to start writing your own life script.

It's time to begin a Renaissance.

It's time to grab life by the horns, peacefully.

It's time to throw a rock in a lake.

And watch the ripples . . .

[1]
[2]
[3]

ABOUT THE AUTHOR

David D. Sullivan, M A, M. Div, L P C, C A D C

David is a singer-songwriter who loves the outdoors, and has a passion for helping people move forward in life.

Made in the USA
Columbia, SC
27 January 2024